U0024010

「悅」讀美國史的
二十四堂課

涂成吉　著

自序

　　美國文化之多元與創意及美國人性格之生動及率真，讓美國史一直有著獨特的閱讀魅力。所以，寫一本好讀、看得到重點、深思有用的美國史，一直是自己暗自發願的心事。

　　待切實執筆，或許用力太過，文意不是深奧就流於冗贅；思過後，易以經典文獻下筆引路，不但主題濃縮明確，且其文辭優美、意義深遠，只要加以歷史上的分析解說，自能「好讀，見重點，富啟發」，達到讀者「悅讀」目的；所謂綱舉則目張，寫作順勢如破竹，終得順利完成一本不同一般的好讀美國史。

　　書中所挑選的二十四篇經典佳作，按歷史階段排列，代表筆者認定美國歷史生活的二十四件轉捩點：自獨立革命、立憲建國、內戰、經濟大恐慌、冷戰、黑人民權、越戰、水門事件、特赦尼克森、九一一事件至歐巴馬當選，選萃關鍵大事與代表人物，從中體會美國人民於國家重大危機中，從承受、感動到面對過程中，呈現一個民族及偉大國家的茁壯與經驗。此外，民主國家的成熟也不一定是建立在光鮮成功的結局，失敗與過失也一樣可以鍛造榮耀，如二十世紀初美國進步主義的「耙糞」（台灣稱之「爆料」）運動、高爾在「二〇〇〇年的敗選感言」與柯林頓在「緋聞案」的向全國致歉，同樣可以看到一個偉大國家面對錯誤與失敗時，採取的是勇於改革而不是硬拗的另面反思。

　　讀史乃收鑑往知來之效，美國最偉大的文明奉獻就是成功地化民主成政治制度之可行，進而證實是目前人類最理想的生活選擇，從「生命、財產與追求幸福」之基本人權，「民有、民治、

民享」的政府概念，再到「言論、宗教與免於恐懼及貧乏」之人
類四大自由號召，以至經濟大恐慌後，強調以照顧弱勢為旨之
「社會福利國」施政；而其間遭遇的內、外挑戰如政黨惡鬥、族
群對立、經濟不景氣乃至二十一世紀民主最大之敵人──當權者
之權力貪腐，美國人民堅持民主、自由與司法獨立的理想，特別
是極富震撼之「美國控告尼克森案」，見證「天子犯法與庶民同
罪」的法治精神，都很值得當今我們發省、借鏡。

　　所謂「國者，人之積也。」，美國人民強悍但善良，理想卻
也知道變通，自大但能反省，保守卻喜於創意，崇尚個人作風卻
又有極濃厚之愛國主義；美國人穩健中又求新求變的文化行為，
縱令驚濤駭浪中，得保國家不斷的穩定前行。因此，「美國民族
文學──超越主義」及「威廉詹姆士之實用主義」兩篇文獻是最
能自內在層面，探測說明美國民族性組成乃兼顧理性和感性的人
格內涵及混合理想與實用的行為特質，綜合而言，就是所謂的中
道路線。

　　待歐巴馬完成他的宣誓大典，本書也到最後段落，自「是！
我們做得到」至「負責任的新時代」，短短一年時間，歐巴馬完
成了他傳奇的夢想之路，身為美國史上第一位黑人總統，歐巴
馬昭示一段苦難歷史的終結，和一個新的國家團結時代，金恩的
美國夢終於實現。至於，美國女性的美國夢，何時展開新頁？在
美國保守氣圍下，美國女權運動是穩定中求成長，自一八四八年
史丹頓女士發表「男性摧毀力」爭取女性投票權起，至一九八四
年費拉洛「副總統提名演說」成為第一位女性副總統提名人。
二十四年後，二○○八年大選，當民主黨希拉蕊可能完成更大夢
想──總統候選人時，共和黨也提名阿拉斯加州州長莎拉裴林作

競選搭檔，以示這個保守的老大黨也有進步思想的時候，我們絕
對相信美國第一位女性的總統必然在本世紀出現，讓婦女終底完
成她們的美國夢。

　　本書編寫是以達成讀者徹底感受美國歷史的發展過程為宗
旨，因此，為配合美國歷史經典文獻的清晰閱讀，寫作安排層
次上，分成（一）前言部分：是作者就主題的整體分析與評論；
（二）歷史背景部分：整理關鍵性事件，就文獻之源由背景，行
深入淺出的解說；（三）文憲介紹：對所節錄原文及中譯，作重
點的提示與解說；另外，本書開頭之最動人的佳句部分，不但是
長篇文獻一語中的的濃縮，讀者不妨記憶下來，絕對是加強英文
說、寫上的有力語彙。

　　最後，謹以本書獻給我的女、兒——敏、騰，謝謝他們在我
一年多時間，每日作書時候與我相伴，事實上我也想為他們寫一
本好看、有益的書，敏在八月的基測放榜，考上中山女高，此書
正巧作為父親最佳的賀禮吧！

民國九十八年二月於林口醒吾學院

目次

第一篇　美國獨立宣言
～大國誕生人權立國

湯瑪斯‧傑佛遜

▶▶▶最動人的佳句！**The most touching words**！

All men are created equal ,with certain unalienable rights: Life, Liberty and the pursuit of Happiness.

～Thomas Jefferson

人生而平等，賦予以下不可剝奪的權利：生命、財產與追求幸福的權利。

～湯瑪斯‧傑佛遜

前言

　　一四九二年，美洲新大陸的發現，其實是一個意外的地理寶藏，而這一意外與我們中國竟有直接的關係。因此，在討論美國的獨立誕生之前，我們需先瞭解當時的歷史背景：十字軍東征後，歐人開始仰慕中國之貨物，在競相往東航行的東、西通商航道中，義大利人哥倫布之新貿易路線是獨樹一幟，他不信「世界是平的」，打算自歐洲往西航行，橫渡大西洋，登陸東土，以交易中國之寶貨。哥倫布豈知歐、亞大陸間，美洲橫互其中，意外當上東西文化交流的使者；錯把斯湖當西湖的他，更豈知他予世人之寶物──美洲，更百萬倍於絲、茶；一五〇六年哥倫布

11

至死都堅持他所發現的是印度，非新大陸。這一歷史的任性，使得今天美洲大陸上的原住民，依然張冠李戴地被稱為印度人（Indians，通譯印第安人）。也因為他的發現，第一個在這塊土地上孕化出的民族——美國人，終於在二八四年後，一七七六年，宣告美利堅合眾國成立，其「獨立宣言」高舉人權作最高之立國原則，馬克思亦謂是「人類第一部人權宣言」，召示「人生而平等，享有不可剝奪的自由、財產與追求幸福的天賦權利。」，正式帶領人類進入以民為主的生活制度。

歷史背景

絲路。十字軍東征（1096～1291）打開東西貿易窗口，歐洲人終於見識到東方精品，比如，中國瓷器在藝術上之精美，這對不懂上釉技術只能燒陶的歐洲人簡直嘆為觀止，遂以中國——china稱呼瓷器之名；至於絲綢之光滑柔韌，西人更乾脆把當時的東西貿易陸路就以絲路（silkroad）稱呼，這條走「絲」之路，充分表明西人對絲綢之渴望。除了瓷器與絲所生對東方文化的羨慕，茶與香料之重要性，則顯現在西人日常生活之所需，由於西人嗜食肉類，茶則有助消化功用，西人對茶之仰賴，可見所愛紅茶原來是茶葉不耐長途海運，受潮發酵所致，雖已變質，西人依然甘之如飴。至於香料，則不但是有助食物美味用，還可充文化未開之歐人作擦拭身體，去除異味的法寶。從此，駱駝商賈競相東行於絲路之上，中國成為西方商人可以取得暴利的市場。

地球是圓的：大膽西行。早期的東西貿易路線，不論是歐洲出發，經中亞，翻越蔥嶺，經新疆、內蒙接河西走廊進入中國的絲綢之路，或經中亞由紅海出印度洋抵印度或穿越麻六甲到中國

的海線，都被義大利商賈壟斷控制，這對積極尋找財富，極欲伸張王權的國家如西班牙、葡萄牙自然不滿。義國商人老神在在之另一重大原因就是歐洲當時仍處神權時代，篤信天圓地方，去東方只能東行，除此別無他法。舊思想的突破直到十四世紀文藝復興運動，我思故我在，開啟人本思想，追求知識，蔚為風尚。法國大思想家蒙田甚至高呼「無知是罪」，所有事物除懷疑以外皆可懷疑。因此，當人們每晚看到月亮是圓的或船隻行進時桅杆的遠近變化，會懷疑海平面並不是平的，如果地球是圓的，自然可以打破義人對東西貿易路線壟斷。義大利人哥倫布首先將大膽西行構想向葡萄牙國王推銷碰壁後，卻獲得西班牙女王依莎貝拉的贊助。一四九二年八月三日，在船員的恐懼與懷疑中，哥倫布帶領三艘船向西航行，經過七十日，就在船員決定要脅叛亂，打算放棄的最後一刻，十月十二日，歌倫布發現了陸地，由於當地人皮膚黝黑，哥倫布以為來到印度。雖然哥倫布號稱到了東方，但隨著見聞對照與探勘，越來越多的人發現這片土地並非歌倫布口中的印度，一五○○年佛羅倫斯人亞美利哥（V. Amerigo）冒險繞航新大陸，沿途手繪第一張的美洲地圖，歐人視之，就將這塊新土以其名取亞美利加──America紀念，美洲遂正式浮現地表。

　　大國誕生：新民族的形成。常人有興趣美國者，除前述──**美國是如何發現？**最好奇的問題，莫過──**美國為何脫離其母國獨立？又為何能在不到兩百年時間，發展成為世界首強？美國的價值核心──美國夢是什麼？**我想這幾個問題，正好構成主題「**大國誕生：新民族的形成**」一個精簡的內容架構。

　　當舊大陸的歐洲王室政權知道哥倫布所發現的是片新土後，繼西班牙、葡萄牙佔有中南美洲後；至於地理、氣候條件甚差的

北美洲（這也說明為何古印第安人三大文明：瑪雅、阿茲提克及印加帝國都發生在中南美），至少就有荷蘭、瑞典、法國、英國在這塊無主之地上宣示主權，但為何是英國人取得最後殖民的勝利，根本原因就是大英帝國不光是在北美插旗宣示，重要是英人有完整的移民政策，進行有效的佔領，勇敢接受這片最大人類自然實驗場的物競天擇，汰弱留強，為美國留下強種先人。

一五八八年英國女王伊莉莎白擊敗西班牙無敵艦隊，稱霸大西洋，一六〇八年英國在北美詹姆士城建立第一個殖民地，因紀念女王伊莉莎白，稱之維吉尼亞，但是這批移民只想找尋黃金，不事耕作，宛若烏合之眾，人生地不熟下，隨之而來的饑饉、印地安人騷擾與疾病，自死傷慘重。真正站穩移民腳步則待一六二〇年，一批搭著「五月花號」的清教徒在今天的麻塞諸塞州的普里茅斯港登陸，這批移民由於反抗英國國教大受迫害，仍不改其志；他們強悍、有紀律及理想的人格特質，是克服惡劣自然環境的最有效抗體，更重要是他們在這片新大陸上所追求的是實現夢想中的信仰自由而非黃金，歷史上，美國人習以這一批人視為其移民祖先。清教徒後，後續移民如桂格教派或歐洲平民，傾向上是渴望定居，追求新生活者，性格上本就具備理想、自信及堅毅的基因，再經過自然天擇的熔爐、孕化與快速的本土化後，一個新興民族──美國人就此形成。

從沒民意的稅到不自由毋寧死。美國最早移民另一個共同特質就是，他們都是平民，在沒有階級，人人平等下，『美國夢』（American Dream）成為他們之間的核心價值，個人有選擇的自由，民主成為他們的生活制度，美國人民相信靠自己的努力，不是家族血統，就有實現自己夢想的可能，何況在全然的荒野環

境中，貴族頭銜是保不住命。英國母國在這一百五十六年的殖民中，似乎完全漠視與無知他這批海外子民，不論思想、觀念與生活方式，早已漸行漸遠。

　　英國與殖民地正式衝突，要到一七五四年與法國在爭奪北美與印度戰爭結束後開始，英國為彌補戰爭損失，進行一系列對殖民地人民徵稅如印花稅、糖稅到茶葉稅，初起，殖民地人都偏向於行政救濟的社會抗爭，並無脫離母國號召，只希望英國能依國會基於民意方式來徵稅，但美洲殖民地卻沒有代表在英國國會，因此這些稅被殖民地人民稱之「沒有民意的稅」「Tax without Representation」。這種民怨直到波士頓茶葉黨事件後開始變質成暴力行動，閱讀美國歷史者會發現一個有趣的巧合，美洲的發現因為茶，美國的獨立革命也導火於茶，一七七四年波士頓市民假扮印第安人憤將英國東印度公司船上的茶葉倒進大海，英國改採武力流血鎮壓後，十三州代表緊急聚會召開第一次大陸會議上，維吉尼亞州代表派翠克亨利喊出：「不自由，毋寧死，我是美國人。」，開始喚起民族共識，本土意識論述更關鍵的強化來自佩恩（Thomas Paine）所撰寫的一本小冊『常識』（Common Sense），要求美國人民以常識判斷「以美國之廣大竟要聽命幾千里外狹小的英國統治」之荒謬，他們是一個不同的民族——**美國人**，已經有不同的生活選擇——**主權在民**，鼓吹與堅信「美國獨立可以有更好的前途發展。」，社會的抗爭才轉向政治革命，美國人民終被說服願為獨立而戰。

文獻介紹

美國獨立宣言節錄

湯瑪斯・傑佛遜

　　美國獨立宣言是近代歐美史上重要的篇章，也是人類發展動人心弦的一頁，在當時東、西方皆崇尚君權神授的專制時代，這一初生之國卻震撼的表示「人生而平等，享有不可奪走的自由、財產與追求幸福的天賦權利。」，「統治者乃基於受治者的同意，違背者，人民有權加以推翻。」信仰，開啟了人類歷史從君權過渡到民權的第一頁，使主權在民從理想口號成為事實。馬克思謂：美國獨立宣言乃人類史上的第一個人權宣言。十三年後，法國大革命繼起，終於推翻君主專制，民主、自由與平等成為人類的普世價值。

　　由湯瑪斯傑佛遜執筆之美國獨立宣言，文分三部分：第一部分說明其政治哲學核心，是擷取節當時歐洲兩大政治哲學家：洛克『主權在民』及盧騷『天賦人權』的思想融合；第二部分，則巨列了英王喬治三世如何侵犯了殖民地人民幸福、人權的暴政措施；第三部分，則宣佈美利堅十三州脫離英國，宣告獨立。

The Declaration of Independence

Thomas Jefferson

When in the course of human events, it becomes necessary for one people to dissolve the political bands which have connected them with another, a decent respect to the opinions of mankind requires that they should declare the causes which impel them to the separation.

We hold these truths to be self-evident, that all men are created equal, that they are endowed by their Creator with certain unalienable rights, that among these are Life, Liberty and the pursuit of Happiness. To secure these rights, Governments are instituted among Men, deriving their just powers from the consent of the governed. That whenever any Form of Government becomes destructive of these ends, it is the Right of the People to abolish it, and to institute new Government, lay its foundation on such principles and organizing its powers in such form, as to them shall seem most likely to effect their Safety and Happiness. Prudence, indeed, will indicate that

在人類事件的過程裏，當一個民族必需解除與連結他們的另一民族的政治關係約束時，基於對人民意見的莊嚴尊重，他們必須宣告迫使這項分離決定的原因。

因此，我們認為以下的事實是不證自明的：人生而平等，人被造物主賦予以下不可剝奪的權利：生命、財產與追求幸福的權利。為保障這些權利，政府是人民所建立，政府的合法權力源自人民的同意。任何時候，任何形式的政府只要違害這些目標，人民就有權廢除這個政府，並建立新政府，並根據前提的原則作為建立政府及權力分配的基礎，達到有效保護人民的安全及幸福。的確為慎重起見，經長時間所建立的政府不應只是輕微和短暫的

Governments long established should not be changed for light and transient causes; and accordingly all experience has shown that mankind are more disposed to suffer, while evils are sufferable, than to right themselves by abolishing the forms to which they are accustomed. But when a long train of abuses and usurpations evinces a design to reduce them under absolute Despotism, it is their right, it is their duty, to throw such Government, and to provide new Guards for their security. The history of the present King of Great Britain is a history of repeated injuries and usurpations, all having in direct object the establishment of an absolute Tyranny over the states.

To prove this, let Facts be submitted to a candid world:

He has refused his Assent to Laws, the most wholesome and necessary for the public good.

He has dissolved Representative House repeatedly,…

He has endeavored to prevent the population of these States…

原因而加廢除，過去的經驗證明，只要還能忍受的苦難，人民都會盡可能忍耐，而無意以自身的權益來廢除他們久已習慣的政府。但是當證明政府一連串的濫權和剝奪，企圖把人民置於絕對的暴政之下，人民就有權利也有義務推翻政府，提供新的權利保障。現今大英帝國君王的歷史，就是一連串傷害和剝奪的歷史，他所有直接的目標，就是施行暴政於十三州。

為證明所言屬實，我們向世人提出以下事實：

他拒絕批准對人民利益最完善及必需的法律。

他一再的解散各州的議會……

他不斷壓制各州增加人口……

He has obstructed the Administration of Justice,…

He has combined with others to subject us a jurisdiction, giving his Assent to their acts of pretended legislation:

For cutting off our Trade with all parts of the world:

For imposing taxes on us without our consent:

For depriving us in many cases, of the benefits of Trial by Jury

He is at this time transporting large armies of foreign mercenaries to complete the works of death, desolation, and tyranny…

He has constrained our fellow Citizens taken Captive on the high Seas to become the executioners of their friends and brethren…

In every stage of these Oppressions We have petitioned for Redress in the most humble terms : our repeated Petitions have been answered by repeated injury. A Prince, whose character is thus marked by every act which may define a Tyrant, is unfit to be the ruler of a free people.

他阻撓司法的執行……

為了將我們制於壓迫之下，他聯合並授權一些人偽造法律，以達下列目的：

切斷我們與世界各地的貿易；

未經我們同意而向我們徵稅；

在法律案件中，剝奪我們陪審團審判的權益；

他此刻正調動大批的外國傭兵來完成殺害、蹂躪及暴政的工作；

他在公海上俘虜我們的同胞，並強迫他們成為屠殺朋友與弟兄的劊子手；

在每一階段的英國壓迫中，我們已經以最卑微的言詞，請

We, therefore, the Representatives of the United States of America, in General Congress, Assembled, solemnly publish and declare that they are Absolved from all Allegiance to the British Crowns and that all political connection between them and the State of Great Britain.

願以求救濟,然而我們一再的請願,得到的回應,卻是一再的傷害。當一個君王所有行為,已足以定義為暴君,並具有這樣性格,那他也不適任作為自由人民的統治者。

因此,我們,在美利堅合眾國大陸會議集會的代表,莊嚴地宣佈十三州人民完全解除對大英帝王的效忠及一切與大英帝國之間政治關係的中止。

第二篇　制憲會議閉幕演講文
～民主政府之聖經

班傑明‧富蘭克林

▶ 最動人的佳句！**The most touching words**！

Within these walls they were born, and here they shall die.
　　　　　　　　　　　　　　　　　　～Benjamin Franklin

這些批評既生於會議廳內，就讓他們也長眠於內。
　　　　　　　　　　　　　　　　　　～班傑明‧富蘭克林

前言

　　獨立宣言規劃下的國家理想藍圖，是以人民為頭家，政府施政必以民意為依歸。但如何落實理想，建制一個實際的民主政府，確是歷史首遭。作法上，美國建國先賢（founding fathers）是根據洛克的社會契約論，決心白紙黑字立下一部人民的權利契約書，亦就是憲法，其中清楚規範著政府的組成與限制及人權的保障；因此，制憲會議就是實踐這民主工程最關鍵的一個環節。

　　美國一七八七年的制憲會議其實是漢彌頓與麥狄遜等人一個精心的佈局，這實歸咎於一七八一年美國第一部憲法『邦聯條款』（Article of Confederation），把戰後的十三州弄得分崩離析，不符發展需要；為國家長久計，乃假修改『邦聯條款』之名，召集各州代表後，卻行制定新憲之實。會議於一七八七年五

月十四日在費城召開，十二州參加，實際與會代表計五十五名，採閉門秘密商議方式，內容不得對外公佈，九月十七日完成憲法原文，僅七條，文字簡明，極富包容、彈性，能與社會脈絡保持同步，歷久彌新；其中諸多理念如分權與制衡、定期選舉、司法獨立和人權條款，已彷彿如「聖經」般被日後民主國家所效法。然與會期間，各方幾度爭論，會議頻頻瀕臨絕裂，謹賴國之大老富蘭克林屢屢以雋永語慧，團結各方，才不致破局，尤其是討論結束後，面對各州議會是否批准，新憲前景未卜之刻，富蘭克林的閉會演說更是簡明有力，較日後的聯邦主義人士的理性說文，更見憂國憂民的豐富感情之心。

歷史背景

邦聯時代。一七七六年，獨立革命戰爭爆發，十三州紛紛以獨立響應。一七八一年，大陸會議通過『邦聯條款』，這是美國第一本憲法，「邦聯」也成了美國最早的國體，直到華盛頓一七八九年當選首任總統，計行之九年。由於美國是先有州，再有國，在十三個州（國家）不願放棄本身主權，如外交、軍隊、貿易、貨幣的主權下，因此邦聯政府的權力極度限縮，一切決策是以國會為中心的合議制進行，沒有實權的行政首長，也不能徵稅、沒有自主軍隊及管理州際貿易的權力，任何重要事務又必須十三州同意，邦聯政府宛如論壇（Forum），這般政府安排，一七八三年戰爭結束後，國家根本無法應付馬上面臨的重建與發展的考驗，秩序問題快速顯現，各州在戰時債務的無力償還下，只有加重徵稅，各州又有各自的貨幣、關稅，造成貿易的混亂。一七八六年終於導致麻州農民謝斯（Daniel Shays）的叛亂，有如星火燎原的擴大至全國，邦聯政府

卻束手無策，這才驚醒到美國再不改良一個有力的中央政府，十三州將分崩離析，國家也要蕩然無存。

　　制憲大會。最用心於廢止這部積弱不振的『邦聯條款』就是漢彌頓，醉心於一個強而有力的中央集權政府，他贏得了日後有「憲法之父」稱謂的麥狄遜加入，初起，改革邦聯的建議雖頗具聲勢，但仍不敵十三州人民「國家愈小，個人自由愈保」根深柢固的概念，咸信州還是最能保障人權的政治單位。漢彌頓的計畫直到華盛頓的支持，才獲得重大突破；華盛頓原本對「制憲」興趣不大，但謝斯的叛亂改變了他的想法，願意擔任制憲大會的主席，聰明透頂的漢彌頓知道如果堂而皇之昭告要制訂一部新憲，排山倒海而來的爭議，別說不想來的，即使想來的也不敢參加，絕對是胎死腹中。因此，最好辦法就是心照不宣的以「修憲」之名，向十三州發出邀請，果然取得十二州（羅德島自始至終反對）蒞會，實際出席有五十五名代表與會；由於假「修憲」之名行「制憲」之實，因此會議全程保密，免橫生枝節，會議長達四個月，爭議不斷，幸賴華盛頓的臨危不亂及大老富蘭克林的語重心長，一七八七年九月終於完成新憲，共三十九名代表簽字。

　　民主政府之聖經。一七八七年的制憲會議，會中建國先賢之據理力爭，或是以該州的地方利益為出發點，或是以國家的團結發展為重，但出自這五十五位先賢智慧的人類第一部民主國家的成文憲法，經他們討論所生的諸多理念，歷經時間的考驗，已為世界所有民主國家立憲時必然的參照、複製，英國政治家格雷史東甚至讚揚一七八七年美國憲法的出世，是「當世人類腦力所構思出最完美的作品。」，這些重要的設計，讓民主的制度從理想

變成可行，使民主真正的變成人類最好的生活選擇，當今各國憲法普遍採用於美國憲法的基本價值有：

(一) **聯邦制度**：美國立憲第一個挑戰，就是需要一個強有力政府，這意味州必須放棄既有的部分利權，但美國民眾仍受孟德斯鳩「政府變大則人權相對變小」思想影響，這一部份賴麥狄遜理論：大的共和國反有利人權的保障，因為一個多元的社會，將使各種力量相互競爭而抵銷，難以一枝獨秀，則獨裁不出，因此承諾「最好的政府就是管的最少的政府」，撫平州權擁護者的疑懼，首創聯邦政府制，成了太弱的邦聯與太強的中央集權政府間最好的妥協。

(二) **三權分立，相互制衡**：政府架構，分成立法、司法、行政三大部門，每一部門首長選舉方式也不同，以示互不隸屬，譬如：總統以全國，參議員以州，眾議員則以單一選區作選舉單位，大法官則是總統提名但需參議院同意。為防止一權獨大，制度設計彼此相互牽制，總統雖掌握內政、外交及人事大權，但國會有預算及彈劾，大法官雖受總統提名及國會組織預算牽制，但卻具備終身職位保障與憲法解釋的終審權。

(三) **代議制共和**：固然直接民主是民意之最高表現，但條件上以小國寡民，如城邦國家為可行，此外，直接民主易流於民粹，決策品質易失之專業，因此最好的方式就是尋求有賢能之人管理政府，控制方法則是定期的選舉制度。總統四年一任改選，宛若定期的「政變」，並以兩任為限，國會則不予限制，大法官則是只要行為良好，享終生保障制。

(四) **司法獨立**：美國首創三權分立——行政、立法、司法各自獨立、相互自衡，作現代民主政府運作之架構。但衡量各國三

權分立的鼎足之勢，司法卻常是最弱的一角，原因不外大法官之提名掌握在行政總統之手，而法院之組織預算又操之立法國會，加以司法採被動「不告不理」精神，這使司法權因而弱化。美國先賢知曉民主倘無司法之捍衛，必因行政、立法濫權而毀壞，因而一八〇三年Marbury v. Madison案，立下「司法審查」（judicial review）慣例，任何國家爭議以高院之判決為最終之意見。美國高院自此常在關鍵的時機，扮演了解決國事紛爭及推進社會進步之關鍵力量，如黑人民權、言論自由、墮胎甚至兩千年大選選票之判定，呈現令權力者敬畏，不敢忽視的民主力量。

(五) **人權條款**：美國憲法出世，最受人爭議者就是不見人權的部分，麥迪遜立刻從善如流，補列十條修正案，總成【人權法案】（Bill of Rights），以保障人類最基本權利，如：言論、新聞、宗教、居所、人身及民、刑事中被告的權利：被告有保持緘默權、被告必須有辯護律師與陪審團的設立、有利証人的召喚，一罪不二判與程序合法等。這些人權條款，自此成為各國憲法中不可缺少的篇章。

依規定，新憲需全國四分之三州批准，方得生效，一八七八年新罕布什夏州成為第十州通過之，該憲法正式成為美國之根本大法；一百三十年來，該憲法也不過增加了十七條修正案，有效維持美國社會穩定與國家發展，守護民主制度於不墜。今日，不論中、外國家每見總統就任宣誓，唸道「余誓必遵守憲法且捍衛憲法」時，其莊嚴與慎重，令人不禁感念百餘年前，富蘭克林、華盛頓、漢彌頓、麥迪遜一群人在會議中，為國為民之長遠幸福與願景設想時，動人及睿智表現。

制憲會議閉幕演講文

班傑明·富蘭克林

美國聯邦政府慣例在所發行紙幣上，印上總統肖像加以區別面額，如一元紙幣上是喬治華盛頓，二元的傑佛遜，五元是林肯，二十元是傑克遜等，五十元是格蘭特。但有惟二的例外，一位是十元幣上的漢彌頓，另一位就是百元幣上的富蘭克林，漢彌頓在筆者眼中，可謂是美國建國之父中，論才智言是最高明者，作總統實綽綽有餘，但一生漢彌頓作不到總統，也是輸在太聰明，個性恃才傲物，鋒芒太露；相對地，富蘭克林性格上，確是完全相反的「非典型」政治人物——淡泊權力，宛若一位慈祥的長者，一生勤勉、儉樸與實事求是，對人生抱持樂觀態度，遇國家關鍵時刻，總是語帶機鋒、幽默，以雋永語句化解緊張，愛國之心無人懷疑，是美國先賢之中最受人景仰與信任者，以中國人之三不朽「立功、立德、立言」，富蘭克林當之無愧。其家喻戶曉名言有：「時間就是金錢。Remember, that time is money.」、「誠實是最好的政策。Honesty is the best policy.」、「人生最確定的事，就是死亡與繳稅。In this world nothing can be said to be certain ,except death and taxes.」、「從來沒有好的戰爭與不好的和平。There was never a good war, or a bad peace.」，都是極具富蘭克林風格，既常識又帶說服力的話語。

Speech in the Convention
At the Conclusion of Its Deliberations

Benjamin Franklin

Mr. President,

I confessed, that I do not approve of this Constitution at present; but, Sir, I am not sure I shall never approve it; for I have experienced may instances of being obliged, by better information or fuller consideration, to change my opinions even on important subjects. It is therefore that, the older I grow, the more apt I am to doubt my own judgment of others. Most men, indeed, as well as most sects in religion, think themselves in possession of all truth, and that whenever others differ from them, it is so far error. Steele, a protestant, tell the pope that the only difference between our tow churches in….doctrine, is , the Romish Church is infallible, and the Church of England is never in the wrong. …….it so naturally as a certain French Lady , who , in a little

主席先生：

我坦承此時此刻我也並不贊同這部憲法，但各位先進，未來，我則不確定我會依然反對。因為我有過很多經驗，尤其是重大事務上，經過更充分資訊或更周全的考慮後，常使我必須改變原來的決定。因此，我越成長，我越會質疑自己是否過早對他人的論斷。也確實，大部份的人就像是宗教各派別一樣，總認為只有自己掌握的是真理，抵觸他們，就是錯誤。史提爾是一位新教徒，曾告訴教宗：新、舊兩教教義上惟一的不同，就是天主教總是錯的，英國國教就是不會錯的。這好比一法國女士與其姐妹鬥嘴，總愛說：反正我就是對的。

dispute with her sister, said, "But I meet with nobody but myself that is always right. "

In these sentiments, Sir, I agree to this Constitution, with all its faults,- because I think a general government necessary for us, and there is no form of government but what may be a blessing to the people, if well administered; and I believe, father, this is likely to be well administered for a couple of years, and can only end in despotism… I doubt, too , whether any other convention we can obtain, may be able to make a better Constitution; for, when you assemble a number of men, to have the advantage of their joint wisdom, you inevitably assemble with those men all their prejudices, their passions, their error of opinions, their local interests, and their selfish views. From such an assembly can a perfect production be expected? It astonishes me, sir, to find this system to perfection as it does; and I think it will astonish our enemies, who are waiting with confidence to hear that our councils are confounded like those of the builders of Babel…

在這種感情的氛圍下，我接納這部憲法，概括承受她所有的缺點；因為我們需要一個廣大的政府，我也不在意這一個政府的形式，因為只要能有效運作，就是人民的福氣，而且我也相信她能在未來數年順利施行並終止專制。同時我也懷疑我們是否還能再召開一次這樣的制憲會談，討論出比現在還好的結果，因為當你聚合了一群人時，固然享有集合眾人之智慧的優點，但同時也涵納了偏見、激情、民意的誤導、地方利益和私人觀點。就此而言，我們能期待自這樣的會談中，產生完美的結果嗎？各位，如果在這樣的情形制度下，能夠修訂出一部憲法是完美無瑕，不但震驚於我，也會驚嚇到那些信心滿滿，正期望我們各說各話，雜

The opinions I have had of its errors…I have never whispered a syllable of them abroad. Within these walls they were born, and here they shall die. Much of the strength and efficiency of any government, in procuring and securing happiness to the people, depends on opinion, on the general opinion of the goodness of that government. I hope , therefore, for our own sakes, as a part of the people, and for the sake of our posterity, that we shall act heartily and unanimously in recommending this Constitution.

亂無章，醜態畢露的敵人。

　　我也有對這部憲法缺失的批評言論，但我卻絕不會對外聲張。這些批評既生於會議廳內，就讓他們也長埋於內。任何政府追求、保障人民幸福的力量與效率，都得依賴輿論的支持，尤其倚重對政府善意的普遍民意。因此，看在人民一部分的我們與後世子孫的份上，我希望我們同心一致的推薦並擁戴這一部新憲法。

第三篇　總統就職演講詞
～從政黨惡鬥到理性問政

湯瑪斯‧傑佛遜

▶▶ 最動人的佳句！**The most touching words**！

We are all Republicans, we are all Federalists.

　　　　　　　　　　　　　　　　～Thomas Jefferson

我們都是共和黨，我們都是聯邦黨。

　　　　　　　　　　　　　　　　～湯瑪斯‧傑佛遜

前言

　　二○○○～二○○八年，台灣兩度政黨輪替，在這一段民主化過程，台灣陷入前所未有之「政黨惡鬥」，其危害之深，不單國政空轉廢弛，理性問政變成夢想；朝野兩黨「只問藍綠，不問是非」，政治人物的作秀、叫囂與為反對而反對，更讓人看盡民主政治的庸俗化，不禁懷疑政黨政治真可代表民主政治？

　　同樣的場景現象──「政黨惡鬥」正是美國民主初祚的實驗歷程裏，首先遭遇的嚴屬考驗。由於第一任總統喬治華盛頓不論人品、威望，足堪全民總統，兩任八年（1789～1797），政黨惡鬥算是勉強壓抑下來；然一旦卸任，兩黨（聯邦黨與反聯邦黨亦稱傑佛遜民主共和黨）黨爭復起，鬥爭之烈與妒恨之深（竟至執政黨副總統槍殺了反對黨主席）簡直難以想像，幾動搖初期國本。

　　一八○一年大選，美國民主先賢傑佛遜在激烈勝出後，卻以大智慧、謙卑勿喜的低姿態，用詞之情切道出「我們都是聯邦黨，我們都是共和黨」，展現民主包容與和解之可貴精神；在最短的時間內化解仇恨，轉化出成熟理性的美國兩黨共識之政治傳統，使政黨成為協助民主國家政府運作更臻完善之必備條件。這也是筆者特別挑選此文，不只供我國內政治人物警惕，益望我國人借他山之石，不減台灣民主繼續深化的信心。

歷史背景

　　政黨是必要之惡（*necessary evil*）？一七七六年美國獨立宣言中闡揚了**主權在民**的政府政治思想；一七八七年通過史上首部成文憲法，首創現代**共和代議制**政府，但細觀在這政治實驗中，美國憲政上是完全沒有設想讓政黨在政府中有任何角色的的扮演。然自古以來，結黨結派乃人物天性，美國自建國始，黨派之爭即興，國父喬治華盛頓任滿的臨別演講中，即痛心告誡：「政黨是亂政之源，政黨長此以往，黨見日深，嫉視日甚，是政府最大的敵人。」；華盛頓且**以火（fire）比喻政黨，大家需慎防變成烈焰（flame），因為其非取暖之用，而是吞噬民主政治。**以當時確實情況言，雖不能說華盛頓的憂慮是錯的，即使至今，政黨仍有如華盛頓所列：「干擾議會、削弱行政，挑撥人民對立、猜忌……」，甚至權力腐化或利益分贓的詬病；即聖人孔夫子亦曰：君子之交淡如水，故「群而不黨」；但就現代言，民主政治之健全已是極度依賴政黨功能上的歸納民意、整合政見、推出適當候選人或是政黨在國會的居間協調使政府施政成為可能，特別是反對黨的監督、政黨輪替已經是民主政治的常軌，可見當今民主政治實在就是政黨政治。

美國政黨之來由。美國獨立革命時就有愛國黨（Patriots）與保皇黨（Royals）之爭，結果支持英國的保皇黨敗下陣來，北逃英屬加拿大庇護，即至今，加拿大仍列大英國協之內。待革命建國，首任華盛頓政府成立，黨派繼起，分別由財政部長漢彌頓領導之聯邦黨（Federalists）與國務卿傑佛遜率領的反聯邦黨亦稱傑佛遜民主共和黨（anti-Federalists / Jeffersonian Republicans），日後並分別演化成為美國今天的共和黨與民主黨。兩黨在國家政見上是南轅北轍，聯邦黨主中央集權，支持設立國家銀行及保護性關稅，反聯邦黨則贊成地方（州）分權；聯邦黨主要是工商、富人集團，支持反聯邦黨份子則屬農、工、移民的中下階層；外交上，聯邦黨是親英，反聯邦黨親法。華盛頓在位八年，兩黨明爭暗鬥，表面和平已難維持，一旦華盛頓決定不三度連任，兩黨更是覬覦大位。

美國政黨惡鬥：一七九六與一八○○年兩次大選教訓。一七九六年大選，聯邦黨由現任副總統亞當斯代表參選，反聯邦黨則由黨魁傑佛遜親自領兵，由於是首度黨對黨之民主選舉，雙方是無所不用其極，前言談到美國憲法是完全沒有設想到政黨角色的存在，最明顯例子就在總統選舉的選票設計規定上，按憲法原始規範是選舉人在一張白紙上分別書寫下兩人的姓名，再計票，最多得票者任總統，次多者為副總統，這是完全忽略政黨角色的設計，使得一七九六年大選，兩黨鬥爭後果愈加激烈，計票結果：聯邦黨亞當斯第一高票，反聯邦黨傑佛遜次之，敵對政黨的兩人分任總統、副總統，有如水火一室，簡直難以想像施政成為可行。

未來四年，兩黨惡鬥更是不念國家利益，勝選至上。亞當斯挾執政黨之在位優勢，竟通過「外僑與叛亂法」，立法打壓向來

投票支持反聯邦黨的外來移民，規定進入美國後要有更長的居留時間，才能投票；對批評政府的媒體，則以判亂罪處刑；傑佛遜乃道出新聞自由之名言：「如果要我選擇一個國家是有政府卻沒有媒體，則我寧可選擇有媒體而沒有政府」，由此而來。為對抗聯邦黨政府保護北方工商資本家之高關稅，反聯邦黨傑佛遜也不甘示弱提出「無效原則」，就是任何聯邦的法律，州有權加以否決，進而鼓動南方各州脫離聯邦獨立。

　　一八○○年大選中，兩黨有了四年前的前車之鑑，雖特別提出同黨的副總統搭擋人選，解決了名單上任意書寫兩人的難題，計票結果，反聯邦黨的傑佛遜與布爾最多票，因政黨壁壘分明，兩人自然也是票數相同，惟白紙上並無列明誰是正誰是副（僅管大家心知肚明，傑佛遜是總統，布爾副總統），聯邦黨趁機再起爭議；照憲法規定當票數相同，總統當選人難產時是交由眾議院決定，這時聯邦黨又是眾議院之多數黨，為報復落選，聯邦黨竟打算將傑佛遜與布爾正副總統對調，來個乾坤大移，而後經過三十個小時的國會討論與投票，傑佛遜方得確定當選美國第三任總統，但政黨之罔顧民意與國家利益，直將國政視同兒戲，足讓世人匪夷所思。傑佛遜就任後，政黨惡鬥仍方興未艾，副總統布爾與聯邦黨領導人漢彌頓生怨，竟相約決鬥，槍擊反對黨黨魁漢彌頓致死，更是莫此為甚，讓人懷疑這個標榜民意的民主政府，在政黨的介入下能存在多久。一八○一年三月四日，傑佛遜發表的首任就職演講詞，就是在以上時空背景下的有感而發。

文獻介紹

總統就職演講詞節錄

湯瑪斯‧傑佛遜

　　湯瑪斯‧傑佛遜是獨立宣言的執筆人，也是美國所有建國先賢中鼓吹民主信仰之中最具辯才者。一八○○年的第四次總統大選是美國史上第一次由政黨正式運作下的選舉，那一次政黨激烈的惡鬥，湯瑪斯‧傑佛遜是民主共和黨的代表候選人，擊敗了聯邦黨的美國第二任總統亞當斯，完成美國史上第一次的政黨輪替的和平轉移。傑佛遜在這篇演講詞中充滿著弭平選舉仇恨與同心合作的誠懇言詞，政黨誠然因競爭而有激烈惡鬥，但選後，則因回復理性與容忍的問政，開始日後美國兩黨政治之運作習慣，而成為美國政治傳統中之經典。他在一八○一年三月四日發表的首任就職演講詞，堪稱是民主哲學的經典不朽之作。

First Inaugural Address, 1801

Thomas Jefferson

During the contest of opinion through which we have passed ; but this being now decided by the voice of the nation , according to the rules of the Constitution, all will arrange themselves under the will of the law, and unite in common efforts of for the common good. All, too , will bear in mind this sacred principle ,that though the will of the majority is in all cases to prevail, that will be to rightful must be reasonable; that the minority possess their equal rights, and to violate would be oppression.

Let us, then, fellow citizens, unite with one heart and one mind. Let us restore to harmony and affection without which liberty and even life itself are but dreary things. And let us reflect that , having banished from our land that religious intolerance under which mankind so long bled and suffered, we have gained little if we countenance a political

我們剛經歷了一場人民意見的競爭,但現在這已由全國民意予以決定,也公告了結果。依據憲法規範,每一個人在法律的意志之下,將自我接受調整,團結一致為公共的利益努力。我們都知道,雖然,少數服從多數是在所有情況中奉行不渝的神聖法則,但它的正當及合理性必須是少數也能擁有他們平等的權利,如果加以違反,就是壓迫。

因此,我親愛的人民,讓我們團結在一條心與一個意志。也讓我們回復和諧與愛,因為沒有他們,自由與生命的本身,不過是陰沉憂鬱之物。我們更要深思當我們驅離讓人類受盡殺戮與流血的宗教迫害於這塊土地之後,如果我們再暗自包容鼓勵獨裁,邪

intolerance as despotic, as wicked, and bloody persecutions.

But every difference of opinions is not a difference of principle. We have called by different names brethren of the same principle. We are all Republicans, we are all Federalists. If there be any among us who would wish to dissolve this Union or to change its republican form, let them stand undisturbed as monuments of the safety with which error of opinion may be tolerated where reason is left free to combat it.

Let us, then, with courage and confidence pursue our attachment to union and representative government. Kindly separated by nature and a wide ocean from the havoc of one quarter of the globe; possessing a chosen country, with room enough for our descendants to the thousandth and thousandth generation – with all these blessings, what more is necessary to make us a happy and a prosperous people? Still one thing more, fellow citizens- a wise and frugal government , which shall restrain men from injuring one another,……

惡與政治血腥的迫害，那我們終將一無所得。

　　但是每次意見的不同，不代表就是原則的不同；我們對信仰同一原則的弟兄們，也常冠以不同的稱呼。我們都是聯邦黨，我們都是共和黨。我們之中如果有人想解散聯邦或改變共和政體，就讓他安然地不受侵犯，只要理性能自由地去抗衡，就算是錯誤的言論也可以被容忍的。

　　讓我們用勇氣與信心，執著地追求團結與維持代議制政府。感恩於自然與大洋讓我們免於舊大陸的大災禍，並擁有上帝挑選的子民及足可為我們萬世子孫的生活空間，然而在這一切得天獨厚的恩典中，如果還需一樣事情，才能使我們成為快樂與富裕的人民的

About to enter, fellow citizens, on the exercise of duties, I ask so much confidence only as may give firmness and effect to the legal administration of your affairs. I shall often go wrong through defect) of judgment. When right , I shall often be thought wrong by those whose positions will not continue a view of the whole ground. I ask your indulgence for my own errors , which will never be intentional …and my future solicitude will be to retain the good opinion of those who have bestowed it in advance , to conciliate that of others by doing them all the good in my power. And may that Infinite Power which rules the destinies of the universe lead our councils to what is best and give them a favorable issue for your peace and prosperity.

話，那就是一個能防止人群彼此傷害的智慧且清廉之政府。

　　我親愛的人民在我即將執行總統職責之時，我希望你們予我信心，讓我堅定有效的依法施政。我必定會因判斷的缺失而犯錯，或常常即使我是對的，但有些人因為偏執的觀點仍視我為錯誤。我希望在我犯錯時能得到你們的寬容，因為我絕非故意如此。我未來的關注是給予我支持之意見，我會保留在心；至於其他意見者，我將就我職權，一切以他們最大利益之作為來安撫。最後希望全能的上帝保佑我們未來所作每一個有關人民和平與繁榮的決策都是最好的，並且都能達到最理想期望的結果。

第四篇　蓋茨堡演講詞
～族群融合之國力重生

亞伯拉罕‧林肯

▶▶▶ 最動人的佳句！**The most touching words**！

And that government of the people, by the people , for the people, shall not perish from the earth.

～Abraham Lincoln

「為民所有，為民所治，為民所享」之政府永不消失於世。

～亞伯拉罕‧林肯

前言

　　繼政黨惡鬥之後，第二個嚴厲考驗這個年輕國家的命運，就是黑奴制度的存廢爭議，進而引生之內戰。但正本清源，美國走到內戰這一地步，實來自南北人民地域差別下，所生族群間的猜忌與對立的惡果。華盛頓在他一七九七年卸任告別演說中，即已預告：

　　「威脅未來團結有很多因素，最可怕將是以地域差別為根據所建立的各種黨派，彼此歪曲地域不同的觀點和目標。這種歪曲所生之怨恨與不滿，使那些本應親如兄弟之人變得互不相容。」

　　自殖民時代起，南方務農，北方重工商的經濟差異，南方人民就一直感受是北方廉價原料的供應者，卻得承受北方工業資

本家與金融銀行家商品與貸款的經濟剝削，這種因發展走向不同而生之族群互信不足，使美國南方根本無法以立國理想之人權或文明的常識看待奴隸制度（當時歐洲已拋棄奴隸制度，廢奴正當性已不具多少爭辯的空間），認為北方基於道德及立國理想「人生而自由平等」的解奴動作，不過是消滅南方的陰謀，最終演變至南北戰爭。四年的南北內戰，造成美國共六十萬人民死亡，即使將美國在第一次世界大戰死亡十五萬人，二次大戰達二十五萬人，越戰五萬人，全部加總仍不如這場內戰；代價之大，是美國歷史上最產慘痛之悲劇，連林肯也難免這場南北人民仇恨對立下的犧牲者。

內戰之後，美國舉國團結，全力拼經濟，南方因工業現代化，南北發展逐漸平衡，自然也消弭地域主義的仇恨，矢志建立「為民所有，為民所治，為民所享」國家，使國力重生，全力邁向強國大道。

歷史背景

獨特之美國奴制：奴隸制度自古皆有，但美國之黑奴制度卻有著極不尋常之處：第一、不同於一般因戰俘或債務成奴，美國奴隸身份竟以膚色決定；第二、在一個標榜自由人權社會制度的矛盾下，它迫使南方必須用盡一切合理藉口，包括：智力、體能到聖經故事與極端種族理論為蓄奴制渡開脫，證明黑人是「低劣」、「有罪」的人種及天生奴隸；其所造成之歧視刻板印象，至今仍存在極多數美國人心；第三、羅馬帝國時期，曾為奴隸的人與其後代，並沒有像美國黑奴即使成為自由人後，仍有抹不掉的歧視與恥辱的烙印。因此自奴隸到解奴，再自隔離歧視到黑人

民權運動，黑人行為是動見觀瞻，成為美國內部一個長久的社會議題。

美國黑奴與南北內戰。歷史上，黑奴最早進入美國可溯自一六一九年，一艘荷蘭船運了二十名黑人抵達北美；十八世紀，當南方農作採行單一作物如煙草及棉花之大量種植的莊園經濟後，由於黑人在體質上最能適應南方高溫多濕氣候與抵抗熱病，黑奴人數才開始大量輸入美國南方；而單一作物的大規模種植，易竭盡地力，南方急需西進另闢新土，新土闢，則奴制立，循環交錯，南方經濟開始與黑奴制度結為密不可分的一體，尾大不掉，奴隸問題也變得益加複雜。

黑人儘管也是最早的美國人（雖屬非志願性的移民），當革命之檄文「獨立宣言」義正詞嚴「人生而平等，享有不可剝奪之自由、財產與追求幸福的天賦權利。」時，黑奴制度卻諷刺的正大行其道於斯土，事實上，當時執筆之傑佛遜甚至華盛頓本身即為大奴隸主；一七八七年憲法上的「3/5條款」（Three Fifths clause），明定黑人只等於3/5個人，黑奴只是「會說話的牲口」，美國夢不是他們所能擁有的。早期美國人道主義者，尚能在良心驅使下將黑奴送返非洲，建立國家，譬如賴比瑞亞（Liberia，意即自由，其國旗亦仿美國星條旗製作，惟只有一星）；但隨著美國由於不斷向西擴張領土，新增立的州可否施行奴制？成了重大爭議，南北政治人物竟達成「1820年妥協案」，相約在美國領土畫下一道36度30分緯度線，該線以北禁止奴隸制度，以南可以，一國兩制，美國形同實裂。這一個恐怖平衡的攤牌時刻，終於在一九五七年到來。而壓垮這一平衡的最後一根稻草，竟來自最高法院，迥異憲政傳統上，對重大政治性爭議題目，高院一貫採迴避態度，最

高法院於當年「史考特案」竟判決「1820年妥協案」乃違憲之舉，「奴隸是財產，主人可任意帶領到全國各地」，言下之意奴隸制度，可隨意由奴隸主散佈美國疆域之上，南方取得大勝。由於美國任何政治的爭議，最高法院的判決就是終審，就當時看，改變黑奴現狀只有付諸一戰。

一八六〇年大選，共和黨候選人林肯甫當選，南方各州紛紛宣佈脫離聯邦獨立，推戴維斯總統，另組美利堅同盟國（CSA），隔年，內戰爆發。林肯雖反對奴隸，主張一個國家不可能是一半自由，一半奴隸，但值得澄清是：林肯在解除奴隸政策上，並不激進的要求立刻解放奴隸；為維持南方的經濟與尊嚴，林肯溫和允許維持現有的奴隸制度但不得再擴大，對現有的奴主，應採勸說或賠償的方式，要求其釋放奴隸。內戰一起，基於戰略的考量，林肯為免刺激其他同情奴隸制度州的脫離聯邦，他也是以「捍衛聯邦完整」（defend the union）之憲法名義而戰，並非抬出解放奴隸的師出大名；直待一八六三年在戰事取得突破，決定南北勝負的蓋茨堡一役後，林肯才名正言順，定調南北內戰是解除奴隸為人類平等與人權價值而戰。

開戰時刻。北軍不論在人數、裝備、糧草都是壓倒性的勝過只有棉花的南方，加上擁有海軍的北軍一開始就進行海上封鎖，使南方棉花無法輸出，換取武器。林肯與北軍將領自信滿滿，可以速戰速決，但這場戰爭卻遠超預期的打了整整四年，主因就是領導南方將領李將軍（Robert Lee）的用兵如神，以寡擊眾，化被動為主動，使東戰場一直僵持在維吉尼亞州，北軍難越雷池，林肯也懊惱無法覓得足以抗衡之強領，這窘境直到在西戰場作戰傑出的葛蘭特（U. Grant）將軍出現才情況轉好，自嘆不如李將

軍的足智多謀，北軍葛蘭特採取堅壁清野戰略，所過之地，盡加燒毀，北軍終於攻進南方，亞特蘭大受害至深，經不起長期消耗下，南軍終於不支投降，但這般南方灰燼的戰略，著實傷害了南人情感，林肯的被刺，無疑是最高的付出代價。美國也直到南北戰爭之後，人民以往都是說United States are....方改成United States is...，聯邦政府才真正具有駕馭全國的威信，人民結為一體。

文獻介紹

蓋茨堡演講詞

亞伯拉罕・林肯

　　壯烈的蓋茨堡戰役於一八六三年七月在這個賓州小鎮的街上及其周圍地區短兵相接，激戰三天之久，造成雙方五萬人員的傷亡，也是南北內戰的轉捩點，奠定北軍內戰勝利的基礎。國會因此決定將這片美國戰士最大犧牲的戰場建為國家公墓。一八六三年十一月十九日，林肯這篇講詞也正是為該墓地揭幕禮而作，最初並不為人們注目，大家矚目期待者乃哈佛大學校長艾佛特的演說，洋洋灑灑，講了兩小時，待林肯上台，則只說了二百七十個字之後，艾佛特相形大為失色。林肯一生幾乎沒有受過正式教育，全靠自學與苦讀學習英文語法，卻能言簡意賅與真切感人的道出呼喚人心勇往開拓新世紀的有力話語。林肯的蓋茨堡演講詞是美國人認定最雄辯動人的一篇演說，美國民主理想奮鬥目的就是建立一個「民有，民治，民享」政府，這六個字改造了這個國家與整個世界。

The Gettysburg Address

Abraham Lincoln

Four score and seven years ago our fathers brought forth on this continent a new nation, conceived in liberty, and dedicated to the proposition that all men are created equal.

Now we are engaged in a great civil war testing whether that nation or any nation so conceived and so dedicated, can long endure. We are met on a great battle-field of that war. We have come to dedicated a portion of that field as a final resting place for those who here gave their lives that that nation might live. It is altogether fitting and proper that we should do this.

But, in a large sense, we can not dedicate –we can not consecrate –we can not hallow-this ground. The brave men, living and dead, who struggled here, have consecrate it, far above our poor power to add or detract .The world will little note, nor long remember what we say here,

八十七年前，我們的祖先在這塊大陸上，建立一個新國家，她孕育於自由，致力於一個理念——人生而平等。

現在我們所從事的這場偉大內戰，正考驗著這個或任何致力於自由，人生而平等的國家能否長存。我們現在聚首於這一個偉大的戰場上，我們計畫獻出這戰場的一部分作為那群犧牲了生命卻保全了這個國家的人最後安息之地；這樣的安排是完全適當與合理的。

但在更合理的意識下，我們根本也沒有將這塊土地獻出、加以神聖或神化的能力。因為，是這片戰場奮戰的人——不論是陣亡或存活者，老早將它神聖化了，遠非我們微薄的力量所能增

but it can never forget what they did here. It is for us the living, rather, to be dedicated here to the unfinished work which they who fought here have thus far so nobly advanced. It is rather for us to be here dedicated to the great task remaining before us -that we here highly resolved that these dead shall not have died in vain-that this nation, under God, shall have a new birth of freedom- and that government of the people, by the people , for the people , shall not perish from the earth.

減。未來的人也不會注意，甚至理會，我們在這說了些什麼，但他們絕對不會忘記這群人在這塊土地上的貢獻。所以對仍活在當下的我們，最應該做的就是致力這群烈士未完成的工作，為了不讓他們白白犧牲，我們所要完成他們遺留的偉大工作，就是上帝之下，讓這個國家將有重生的自由，建立一個「為民所有，為民所治，為民所享」政府，永遠不消失於世。

第五篇　美國超越主義文學
～人本理想與自然性靈的合諧

亨利・大衛・梭羅

▶▶▶ 最動人的佳句！**The most touching words**！

I never found the companion that was so companionable as
solitude. We are for the most part more lonely when we go abroad
among men than when we stay in our chambers.

～Henry D. Thoreau

我發現最好的伴侶竟是獨處。大多時間，我們發現側身人
群中，卻比獨處室內更寂寞。

～亨利・大衛・梭羅

前言

超越主義（transcendentalism）是十九世紀中期，一群東北部
文人所發起的美國文學本土化運動，探索反映美國人民追求個人
主義與崇尚自然簡樸的精神生活，故有美國國家文學之稱。事實
上，百餘年來，超越主義的文學作品，常以電影、電視方式，不
時與大家接觸，但「超越主義」一詞，卻為大眾所陌生，譬如，
在電視頻道常見由Daniel Day Louis主演之電影《大地英豪》或霍
桑小說作品《紅字》及大家耳熟能詳之《白鯨記》、傑克倫敦之
《野性的呼喚》或馬克吐溫的《湯姆歷險記》等都是美國國家文

學──超越主義發軔作品，將美國人民獨立自主精神與這片千萬年來一樣自由與自然的土地、山川環境結合，刻劃出美國人民追求個人幸福，止於至善，簡單、充實的生活態度表露無遺。

文獻選材上特別以梭羅《湖濱散記》中〈獨處〉一篇作為賞析的代表作品，全書記錄梭羅在華爾騰湖畔兩年返璞歸真的獨居日子及如何融會自然的生活意境，展現梭羅享受獨處、沉思及與自然神交為師友的日子，充分展現「極簡」及「環保」概念的生活風，更是啟發現代「樂活、慢活」之生活美學先驅者。

歷史背景

美國超越主義文學。1802年，英國文學批評家希尼史密斯（Sydney Smith），針對美國文學實力，作了一番尖酸卻不失真實嘲諷：「在本世紀，誰讀過一本美國人寫的書？誰看過美國人寫的歌劇？誰曾觀賞過美國人所作一幅畫或一件雕刻？」這一俐落話語雖深刻道出美國當時文學成就上的自卑貧乏，但也激起1850年代美國國家文學解放運動，造就美國本土文學理論──超越主義的誕生和美國文學史上最人文薈萃的豐富一頁。

超越主義的出現，實踐了美國人文學立國之夢，美國之所以偉大或說美國的實力，即其追求個人主義的獨特文化；也是這股人本特質才能不斷吸引世界抱持理想與真誠之人，不畏艱困移居到這片新世界，不但完成個人夢想，且共同為人類理想而奮鬥。超越主義的文學核心正是：個人主義與自然，再結合「天人通靈」的神秘思想。這些美國獨特人文、自然素材的運用，體現出美國人理想與道德的優越性，的確使美國本土作家成功脫離了舊大陸的文學遺緒與框架束縛。

人本與自然合一。美國超越主義學者除擷取歐洲浪漫主義中個人思想、理性本善精神外，創作上，更將此一心靈訴求，結合了天地自然。超越主義中，最知名也是該學說領導人當屬艾默生，艾默生曾為新教牧師，1832年後專心於寫作演說，致力宣揚個人解放，與自然通靈（communion with the natural world），為美國十九世紀最重要及傑出的知識領袖，平時，他臥居麻州康考特（Concord）家中，當代知識份子爭相出入，在「談笑有鴻儒，往來無白丁」中，超越主義思想於焉成形。一八四二年的演說中，艾默生為超越主義思想的界說：「超越主義者主張心靈聯想主義，相信奇蹟、啟發與極度喜悅。對前人舊俗，我們常不假思索的採信，怯於自我實現。超越主義者是決不流於世俗，只作自己。」

至於超越主義中神秘部分的自然與人類的互動關係中，艾默生相信，當個人清明的內在心性置身於自然世界，赤足林木田野，隨風雨脈動呼吸，最能明心見性。這種揉和歐洲浪漫思想及美國自然的思想主張，實質上與中國道家哲學天人合一及禪宗『直指心性，立地成佛』觀點，頗有異曲同工之處。在《自然》（Nature）一文中，艾氏篤信「自然是人類五官的延伸。」，尤其當個人與自然合一之時，則可達到人類最大精神力量，也就是所謂「超靈」（oversoul）艾默生對個人精神力量的樂觀、信任，喚起了美國文學自信，可以一如科學上的成就，同樣創造出偉大的文藝作品。

超越主義這種文學的「頓悟」，務實面上，也是針對美國文學沒有豐富背景，遺產貧乏的解套，其主張只要經由自覺，同樣可以有偉大的文學創作，不一定需植基於過去的文化累積，畢竟偉大的作品來自個人心靈的解放發揮，而非過往傳統的率由舊

章，因此超越主義雖有速食文化之嫌，但卻也為美國獨立文學創作之路，找到最適時的理論出口。

就大部份超越主義作家作品觀察，都是對個人精神及大地自然光明面的推揚；人性本善所以個人的判斷總是理性、成功、美滿，往往是以喜劇結局。但超越主義作家中，也不乏對人性力量做反面思考解釋，形成一股主流。突出者如《白鯨記》，作者梅爾維爾藉書中船長艾巴的報復白鯨，結局竟以身殉，暗喻個人自我實現的堅持，不只是個人的解放，也會是自我毀滅。此外，霍桑著作《紅字》則嘲諷清教徒思想對個人尊嚴、自主的摧殘，令人感到個人地位在世俗環境中的渺小，人為的力量是無法抗拒命運的安排。霍桑生於清教徒思想最濃之地麻州賽倫，霍桑以其冷漠筆調，傳達書中女主角海思特因未婚生子被佩上紅字，一如古人刺面，所受教義禁錮與壓抑下的堅毅與無助，有如海思特所謂「黑暗的必然性」，這種喀爾文主義宿命思想在《紅字》中，很自然地表示出來。

十九世紀中葉超越主義闡揚個人解放，理性至上的人本思想，不但更符合求新求變，強調個人創造力的工商社會，同時，美國在資本主義放任自由化所致的社會負面效果，也刺激超越主義作家的理想與道德心，投身參與一系列美國當時的社會改革運動如：勞工待遇、都市貧民窟、女權、禁酒、黑奴解放、獄政等，使美國在追求精神與理想下，懂得反省，改革與進步，至二十世紀成為世界首強，則又不得不歸根於此一學說的助益。

如果說教育是一個人的涵養，那麼文學則可謂是一國之內涵。如今，民主制度與個人自由，尊重自然與崇尚極簡，成為當代普世及主流價值之時，更加叫人敬佩艾默生、梭羅等文學前輩的先知與智慧，而作品《湖濱散記》、《白鯨記》、《草葉集》

也是永不感覺與時代褪色脫節的著作，讓每一代讀者品讀時候，都有貼切的感受與這世界還能更好的改革信念，其中魅力所在也許就是人性之目標就在不停的探索，止於至善吧！

文獻介紹

湖濱散記

亨利‧大衛‧梭羅

【獨處　節錄】

超越主義另一具代表性領導人物則是亨利‧大衛‧梭羅（Henry David Thoreau），身為艾默生摯友，梭羅則更激進於主張懷疑、突破社會上一切既定現象、制度，梭羅以為最好的政府不是管得最少的政府，而是什麼都不該管的。因此他質疑一個贊成奴隸的政府合法性，也因為拒繳人頭稅而下獄，其著「人民抵制政府」，主張一個違反個人道德施政的政府，人民有理反對，並是最早提出以消極反抗或不遵守手段因應惡法者。此一論點深深影響日後印度甘地及黑人民權領袖金恩博士所採用的非暴力運動（nonviolence）。

梭羅一如艾默生也表達了對自然尊重與溝通的興趣，梭羅提出在快速變遷社會中，個人最佳適應之道就是讓身體、物質上的需求愈簡單愈好，推行獨處、沉思、極簡的生活實驗，為此，梭羅隱居康考特林間Walden湖畔兩年與自然為伍，並在獨居中完成其代表作《湖濱散記》。

Walden

"I went to the woods because I wished to live deliberately ,…
I wanted to live deep and suck out all the marrow of life, to live so
sturdily and Spartanlike as to put to rout out all that was not life……
Simplify, Simplify."

Solitude

This is a delicious evening, when the whole body is one sense,
and imbibes delight through every pore. I go and come with a strange
liberty in Nature, a part of herself. I have my horizon bounded by
woods all to myself. I have, as it were, my own sun and moon and stars
,and a little world all to myself. At night there was never a traveler
passed my house, or knocked at my door , more than if I were the first
or last man ; …

　　我走進森林，是因為我希望能從容不迫地生活，我希望活出
生命的真髓，物質只需滿足生活最基本所需，……總之，極簡，
極簡。

　　這是一個秀色可餐的傍晚，全身融貫化成一感，喜悅得以無
入而不自得。我有一種優遊在大自然來去中，奇妙的自在；我與
自然已結合一體。我以林木為界，隔出了自身的地平線，在這個
小天地裏，我有自己的日、月、星辰。在夜晚，我的居所從不見
旅人路過，更別說光臨，彷彿我是這化外之地的第一也是最後
一人。

Yet I experience sometimes that the most sweet and tender, the most innocent and encouraging society may be found in any natural object. There can be no very black melancholy to him who lives in the midst of Nature and has his senses still. While I enjoy the friendship of seasons I trust that nothing can make life a burden to me. ...it seems as if I were more favored by the gods...I have never felt lonesome, or in the least oppressed by a sense of solitude.

I find it wholesome to be alone the greater part of the time. To be in company, even with the best, is soon wearisome and dissipating. I love to be alone. I never found the company that was so companionable as solitude. We are for the most part more lonely when we go abroad among men than when we stay in our chambers.

Society is commonly is too cheap. We meet at the meals ... at socials ... We have had to agree on a certain set of rules ,called etiquette and politeness, to make this frequent meeting tolerable, ...; we live thick and are in each other's way, and stumble over one

然而我卻經驗了最美妙、最溫柔的時光,只要是自然之物,就能在其中發現最純真與興奮的聚合,任何活在自然中的人,暗沉的憂鬱或麻木不仁是不可能發生在他身上。當我在享受季節的友善,沒有任何事可讓我感覺生命會是一項負擔,似乎我得到更多神的眷顧,我從不感到寂寞,甚至感受不到一點單獨之苦。

我發現獨處是生活時光中最美好與完整的時刻。就算與最宜同好相伴,很快即感消磨與浪擲。我喜歡單獨,我發現最好的伴侶竟是獨處。大多時間,我們發現側身人群中,卻比獨處室內更寂寞。

社會普遍是膚淺的。我們不斷在飲食、社交場合中相聚,我們只好訂下一些禮儀或禮貌的規範,好弄得這些經常的聚會可以

another, and I think that we thus lose some respect for one another.

The indescribable innocence and beneficence of Nature- of sun and wind and rain, of summer and winter- such health, such cheer, they afford forever! And such sympathy have they ever with our race, that all Nature would be affected, and the sun's brightness fade, and the winds would sigh humanely, and the clouds rain tears, and the woods shed their leaves and put on mourning in midsummer, if any man should ever have a just cause grieve. Shall I not have intelligence with the earth? Am I not partly leaves and vegetable mould myself ?

讓大家忍受。我們生活充滿擁擠、妨礙與阻塞，結果反而失去了彼此的尊重。

太陽、風、雨，夏天、冬天構成的自然，有著無以言表的純真與仁慈，使健康和欣喜永遠不竭。自然也會表達對人類的同情，陽光有暗淡，風有人性般的哀號，雲會淚如雨下，有如人因事感傷時。人與天地間豈無知與無情？我本身難道不是草木一部分？

第六篇　美國實用主義

～有效務實的人生哲學

威廉‧詹姆斯

▶▶▶最動人的佳句！**The most touching words**！

The pragmatist clings to facts and concreteness, observes truth at its work in particular cases.

～William James

實用主義者執著於事實與具體性，認定真理是根據它在特定的事件中，有效與否為準。

～威廉‧詹姆斯

前言

接觸美國人經驗者，發現他們在待人處事的應對上，常予人直接、坦白與實事求是的印象，面對困難與挑戰，他們習慣直搗問題的核心，不喜空談大道理，解決之道是「只要有效（works），就是對的」作風，很令人印象深刻；這般務實不務虛的性格與美國「實用主義（pragmatism）」哲學有著絕對關係，可以說「實用主義」哲學正是反映美國人生活與個性上最道地的人生觀。

實用主義是十九世紀末與二十世紀之交興起於美國的一種哲學運動。最早提出實用主義是皮耳士（Charles Sanders Peirce），

他於一八七八年提出了pragmatism一詞，到了一九○四年，威廉詹姆斯出版了"A New Name for Some Old Ways of Thinking"一書，實用主義的理論才有系統化的論述，將實用主義帶進道德哲學及宗教哲學的領域中，成為美國人性格與處事之核心內涵，而世人也多由他的著作認識實用主義。而到了杜威，他最具代表性的口號「Learn by Doing」，將實用主義之積極態度，追求有效的核心價值進一步應用到許多學術領域的方面。至於，實用主義最有名的國外信徒，當屬八○年代，帶領中國改革開放的鄧小平，他的「不管黑貓、白貓，能抓老鼠的就是好貓。」與「真理必須通過事實的檢驗」名言，一語道破「實用主義」的中心主旨。

歷史背景

實用主義的形成。詹姆斯開宗明義說明實用主義不過是一個科學的方法（method），目的就是解決形而上（metaphysics）的清談爭論，建立了一套探究邏輯和工具主義的真理理論，「有用就是真理，而有用者就是能有好的結果（consequences）。」

任何思想的形成基本都是人類與其環境互動及需求下的刺激產物。一六○八年，北美新大陸第一個殖民地──詹姆士鎮（James town）設立後，美國移民祖先在一切百廢待舉的自然洪荒原始環境中，憑藉著個人主義與有效生存的拓荒精神，基本上就是實用主義的先驅。一八六四年內戰結束，解決南北族群衝突，迄十九世紀末，美國展開產業革命，是全力拼經濟的時代，在這個時候一個有效、實際與經事致用的思想是更符合工商社會的環境需要，鋪設了實用主義哲學萌芽的溫床。

之外，十九世紀後期出現的達爾文進化論，對當時實用主義是個重要的影響，實用主義的真實理論，深受達爾文進化論的影響。詹姆斯言：「思想信仰在生活中的真實性必須是內在個體與外在的現實相容才算真實。信仰是隨不安的環境而動，真實的信仰要能安然引導我們於環境之中，因此，生存不但是智能的考驗，也是生態的適應，不切實際的信仰自不具真理價值。」實用主義之「有效」與達爾文「適者生存」的進化論，兩者的關係由此可見。

詹姆斯生平與思想：詹姆斯生於1842年，自幼家庭富裕，受到了特殊的家庭教育。他的父親亨利詹姆斯也是一個哲學家。因為長期隨著家人旅居歐洲，使他養成開放與包容的學術態度。詹姆斯的興趣廣泛，在早期，詹姆斯不顧父親反對矢志習畫，之後周遊考古，再進入哈佛大學研究醫學；稍後，研究心理學，《心理學原理》一書，成為美國心理學界之聖經。最後，轉向哲學，當"A New Name for Some Old Ways of Thinking, in December 1904"出版的時候，他已經是年過六旬的人了。

威廉詹姆斯，雖被尊稱是美國心理學之父，但最為人稱道之成就卻是在「實用主義」的闡揚立說。詹姆斯的實用主義哲學以真理論為中心。詹姆斯的實用主義主要分真理論和方法論兩大部分，所謂方法無非就是達到真理的方法。詹姆斯認為哲學並不是主觀的抽象意識，實用主義是一個工具性哲學，是幫助人們在特殊情況下，清楚自己的想法與需要的工具，而考驗這些不論是宗教的或科學、道德事務想法的真實與否，是依據其實際的後果；詹姆斯強調行為的效果，是根本否認理性作用。其次，既然真理就是「有效」，宗教哲學亦不例外於詹姆斯實用主義的應用，當

宗教信念和行為也能夠帶來益處的時候，它們就是真理。詹姆斯認為，宗教的真理性並不在於它是否反映了客觀的存在，也不在於它的邏輯結構，而在於它「有用」。在日常生活中，經常有這樣一種現象，即人們有時需要宗教，所以從「真理是有用的」這個結論可以直接得出「宗教是有用的，因而也是真理」的結論，**直率的說：「別管它是真是假，反正只要有用，你就可以信它；你認為沒有用，就別相信它。」把宗教問題從「真實性」的問題轉向「有用性」，是實用主義之所以「實用」以解決哲學爭議的**最佳例子，它使宗教理論避開了千年來一直無奈與困擾宗教家的科學問題。

最後針對詹姆斯關於經驗與現實世界本質的觀點：詹姆斯時常把思想看做是「意識的主觀精神狀態」。依據這樣的觀點，意識是一種能夠感知外部物質世界的一種獨特的現象；所謂意識只是一種主觀的精神狀態，他與客觀的物質世界的關係不是相互依存，而是各自獨立的。**思想和物質都是要在經驗中連結起來，經驗是思想和物質相通的橋樑。簡言之，物質世界就是依據自然科學的原則而被我們描述的經驗世界；精神世界就是依據心理學的原則而被我們描述的經驗世界。兩者在本質上都是一樣的，都是「經驗」的一部份。但彼此之間是互相獨立的。**在他的晚年，詹姆斯認為現實世界的終極本質是和經驗本身完全一致的。他認為，一般的常識所認為的現實與「實在」之間的區別完全是經驗範圍內的區別。詹姆斯舉例道：我們說「海市蜃樓的經驗是一種幻象」，並不是說否認我們自己有「海市蜃樓」的經驗，或否認它的存在。我們所否認的只是按照我們所說的那一種「真實的存在」的標準去衡量的經驗。實際上，詹姆斯認為，整個世界既包

含著可靠的現實，也包含著海市蜃樓式的幻象。「經驗」成為包羅萬象的範疇，把一切物質的、精神的、幻想的、可靠的現象通通都包羅進去了。

文獻介紹

一些思考舊法的新名稱第二講

威廉・詹姆斯

〈何謂實用主義？〉（節錄）

　　美國「超越主義」，傳達美國人理想與至善的內在精神面；「實用主義」則代表美國人應對的外在方法，強調經世致用，有效解決，務實決不務虛的處事之道。歷史大師杭亭頓說：「美國人是理想（utopia）與現實的混合。」，這兩面性格的交替，清楚說明美國民族兼顧理性和感性的人格內涵及理想與實用的行為特質，綜合而言，就是中道路線。因此，本文特別選錄了威廉詹姆士《一些思考舊法的新名稱》中之第二講〈何謂實用主義？〉，詹姆斯開宗明義表達「實用主義」乃不耐於哲學「形而上」無盡的爭論，而提出只要實際的結果有效，且不與其他經驗衝突，就是真理的檢驗方法。如此坦白直接的態度，無怪乎，美國人常受欠深度，不重視想法，只要辦法的速食文化批評，不過就事實來看，美國人不過是實事求是的民族，無興趣於哲學常流於清談、口水戰的部分罷了！

A New Name for Some Old Ways of Thinking
Lecture II
What Pragmatism Means ?

William James

The pragmatic method is primarily a method of settling metaphysical disputes that otherwise might be interminable. The pragmatic method is to try to interpret each notion by tracing its respective practical consequences. If no practical difference whatever can be traced, then the alternatives mean practically the same thing, and all dispute is idle.

A glance at the history of the idea will show you still better what pragmatism means. The term is derived from the same Greek word pragma, meaning action, from which our words 'practice' and 'practical' come.

It was first introduced into philosophy by Mr. Charles Peirce in 1878. ... after pointing out that our beliefs are really rules for action, said

　　實用主義主要是解決哲學形而上爭議的方法，不然這類爭議將沒有結束的一天。實用主義的方法是要極力追溯實際的後果，再依此解釋每一概念。沒有實際的結果可溯，則所有的討論方案，事實上都意謂相同，也難怪各說各話，爭議永無止息。

　　稍微過目一下思想史，會有助你更加了解實用主義的意義。實用主義一詞是由希臘文衍生而來，其原來的意思是行動，而實踐與實際的兩個字就是從行動一字衍生出來。

　　最早提出實用主義是皮耳士，他於一八七八年提出了實用主義一詞。皮耳士指出我們的信仰其實是行動的準則，經由行動再發展出思想的意義。要清楚了解一項事物之意涵，我們只需去考

that, to develop a thought's meaning, … To attain perfect clearness in our thoughts of an object, then, we need only consider what conceivable effects of a practical kind the object may involve . It is astonishing to see how many philosophical disputes collapse into insignificance the moment you subject them to this simple test of tracing a concrete consequence. The whole function of philosophy ought to be to find out what definite difference it will make, ….

There is absolutely nothing new in the pragmatic method. Socrates was an adept at it. Aristotle used it methodically. Locke, Berkeley, and Hume made momentous contributions to truth by its means. But these forerunners of pragmatism used it in fragments: they were preluders only. I believe in that destiny, and I hope I may end by inspiring you with my belief.

Pragmatism represents a perfectly familiar attitude in philosophy, …It means as against dogma, artificiality, and the pretence of finality in truth…It is a method only. Science and metaphysics would come much nearer together, would in fact work absolutely hand in hand. …

量該事物所實際帶來的後果即可。……這方法讓我極為驚異相當多的哲學爭議只要套用此一實際後果的簡單測驗後,一切的爭論就迎刃而解。哲學之用本應就是發現它所製造的差異……

實用主義並非新鮮之物。蘇格拉底已是這方面的能手。亞理斯多德也方法性的使用這一觀念。洛克、伯克萊與休姆也在實用主義的真理作了很多貢獻。但他們只能說是片斷使用實用主義的前提者。我相信這一命運的繼承,而希望我是以信仰啟發你們,畫下最末句點者。

實用主義代表著哲學上一個熟悉的態度;它反對教條、虛空與假冒宿命的真理。它不過是一個方法,藉此方法使科學和形而

Metaphysics has usually followed a very primitive kind of quest. … But if you follow the pragmatic method, you must bring out of each word its practical cash-value, set it at work within the stream of your experience. Theories thus become instruments, not answers to enigmas, in which we can rest. Pragmatism unstiffens all our theories, …. it harmonises with many ancient philosophic tendencies in emphasising practical aspects …. But as the sciences have developed farther, the notion has gained ground that most, perhaps all, of our laws are only approximations. ... no theory is absolutely a transcript of reality, but that any one of them may from some point of view be useful. … ideas become true just in so far as they help us to get into satisfactory relation with other parts of our experience.

…the scope of pragmatism – first, a method; and second, a genetic theory of what is meant by truth. …Rationalism is comfortable only in the presence of abstractions. This pragmatist talk about truths in the plural, about their utility and satisfactoriness, about the success with

上學更緊密實際的攜手工作。形而上學通常遵循一個原始方式的探索，但是按照實用主義的方法，你必須析離出每一個字的實際「面值」，並在你的經驗之中運作。理論只是工具，並非謎底答案。實用主義鬆綁所有理論的束縛，強調實際面，以調和古老的哲學趨向。但是當科學越加前進時，大多數之（也許全部）法則也只能達到接近的程度，沒有理論是可以呈現事實的全貌，部分的理論只能說從某些觀點言是有用的。思想有用是因為它能幫助我們與自身其他的經驗達到滿足的關係。

實用主義的領域包括方法論與真理論。理性主義只有在抽象呈現時，才能感到自在。實用主義是以複數（可數是表示具體之

which they 'work,' etc.,

The pragmatist clings to facts and concreteness, observes truth at its work in particular cases. It brings old and new harmoniously together. It converts a static relation of 'correspondence' between our minds and reality, into that of a rich and active commerce between particular thoughts of ours, and the great universe of other experiences in which they play their parts and have their uses.

If theological ideas prove to have a value for concrete life, they will be true, for pragmatism, in the sense of being good for so much.… I am well aware how odd it must seem to some of you to hear me say that an idea is 'true' so long as to believe it is profitable to our lives. For how much more they are true, will depend entirely on their relations to the other truths that also have to be acknowledged. My belief in the Absolute, based on the good it does me, must run the gauntlet of all my other beliefs. Nevertheless, it clashes with other truths of mine whose benefits I hate to give up …. it entangles me in metaphysical

事，而非抽象觀念）表達真理，重視的是實用、滿足與有效的層面。

　　實用主義者執著於事實與具體性，觀察真理是以在特定事件中它有效與否為準。實用主義將新舊調和；它將我們的觀念與事實的靜態聯繫關係轉變成一種使我們想法與其他廣大經驗豐富與動態的交流。

　　就實用主義言，如果神學思想證明對人們具體生活有價值，亦就是具備好的意義，那他們就有真理。我瞭解你們會感到奇怪，當聽到我說：只要相信一個思想對生命有益，這個思想就是真理。至於有多少的真理性，那就看他們與其他也被認知是真理

paradoxes that are unacceptable, etc.,... without adding the trouble of carrying these intellectual inconsistencies, I personally just give up the Absolute; or else as a professional philosopher, I try to justify them by some other principle.

In short, ... Rationalism sticks to logic .... Empiricism sticks to the external senses. Pragmatism is willing to take anything, to follow either logic or the senses and mystical experiences if they have practical consequences. ...But you see already how democratic she is. Her manners are as various and flexible, her resources as rich and endless.

事物之間的關係而定;我對神的信仰是基於信奉於我有益,但也要去面對我對其他信仰的考驗。一旦它與我堅持的其他信念衝突時,而將我捲入不可接受形而上的矛盾時,我也許會不想再增加意識不合的麻煩,而放棄個人對神的信仰;或許我也會像一個哲學教授想盡辦法尋求其他原則加以合理化。

簡而言之,理性主義堅守邏輯;經驗主義則固執於外部感應。實用主義則願意接納邏輯、感應或神秘經驗,只要他們能有實際的後果。你已經看到實用主義的包容性與它的風格多樣與彈性;它的資產豐富與無盡。

第七篇　男性摧毀力

～節制與平衡的美國女權運動

伊麗莎白・史丹頓

▶▶▶ 最動人的佳句！**The most touching words**！

We ask woman's enfranchisement, as the first step toward the recognition of that essential element in government that can only secure the health, strength, and prosperity of the nation.

～Elizabeth Cady Stanton

我們要求女子投票權是要政府認識到這是它基本要素的第一步，如此方能確保國家的健全、實力與繁榮。

～伊麗莎白・史丹頓

前言

美國今日動輒可見女性獨立與自主氣勢，譬如美國洋基超級球星A-Rod之緋聞，依法保障，如果離婚，其妻子辛蒂可要求A-Rod交付近半之上億財產，充當贍養費；再者，電視名劇「慾望城市」中，幾位熟女之大膽開放，不時令人臉紅的限制級對話；而差點成為美國第一位女性總統候選人希拉蕊的強勢風采，更是不讓鬚眉，可見美國女性已非男人附屬。但是如果我們仔細回顧歷史，美國女性確是直到二十紀或說八十八年前才得擁有投票權，而美國一切女權與女性價值的快速推進，皆開端於爭取投票資格的成功。此段經過是美國歷史文化上相當重要的一頁篇章。

　　美國最重要女權領導人當屬伊麗莎白‧凱第‧史丹頓，一八四八年，史丹頓於紐約州塞內卡瀑布市（Seneca Falls, New York）召開「女權運動大會」，史丹頓仿照獨立宣言，宣讀「所有的男人與女人皆生來平等」，其中最重要的決議就是女性也得擁有投票權，使美國的女權運動開始組織性的發展。史丹頓女士經過近半世紀的奮鬥，直到一九二〇年，美國通過憲法第十九條修正案，才賦予了美國成人女子投票權，雖然，史丹頓女士於一九〇二年先行過世，美國女性權利也因此飛快進展，進入兩性平等的時代。

歷史背景

　　隱性的族群。二十世紀前，美國女性可說是完全男性的附屬品，女性在社會地位上可說是隱性到幾乎是隱形了。女人一旦結婚，所有財產就歸丈夫所有，男子也有權所有女性的勞務所得；即使離異，丈夫仍得握有一切財產及子女所有權，美國保守傳統觀念堅信女性生理與心理之柔弱，不該與男性競爭公共職業，社會、宗教（清教徒）認為女性的一生職場就在家庭，最偉大的志業就是養兒育女，相夫教子，不需拋頭露面。因此，所謂的生命、財產與自由的基本人權中，女人一直到二十紀之前都是不得享有財產權，民主社會中美國女性連最基本的投票參政權也沒有，自然政客也無需在乎女人的想法及權利。

　　出生於一八一五年紐約的伊麗莎白‧凱第‧史丹頓就是在這樣的背景下，矢志獻身女性平權運動。史丹頓自幼即接觸解奴運動，並經由同情一個種族被壓迫的啟發，進而延伸到關懷美國女性的不平待遇；加上她父親任職法官機緣下，史丹頓博覽法律書籍，更讓她看清女性社會法律的弱勢，立志投入女性民權之爭取。

　　史丹頓為表示女性平權的決心，也自本身的婚姻大事作起，在婚禮的誓詞中，她主動刪去了婚後一切「從夫」的字眼，但真正促使史丹頓女士進入女權運動之刺激者，乃一八四〇年隨夫婿赴倫敦參加世界反奴大會時，竟遭主辦單位拒絕進入會場，上台公開發言，原因竟是於社會體制不合，女性不宜拋頭露面，這才使史丹頓女士自覺到女性與黑奴原來是一樣的弱勢，無絲毫之優越，惟一差異是黑奴尚有改變之機遇，女性的命運已是既定成俗，不會因黑人民權的改善而連帶受惠。

　　一八四八年，史丹頓女士乃於美國紐約州塞內卡瀑布市召開女權大會，美國女權才開始有了組織性運動之發展，史丹頓女士寫下「情緒宣言」，史丹頓女士除以「男女皆生而平等」補充獨立宣言並痛陳：

　　「世界迄今仍不見一真正偉大與道德的民族之誕生，就是因為生命的泉水自源頭起就貶抑女性。」

　　史丹頓女士在會中主張了最具遠見但也爭議最大的決議就是女子投票權之通過。雖然一八四八年，就歐洲仍在君主專制下的女性而言，此一目標未免太不實際，就美國女子言也認為不具優先，但事後證明美國女權的前進，還是當女性有了決定性的選票，男性政客才非得在乎。

　　史丹頓的最重要的人生際遇當屬結識了蘇珊安東尼，她也成了日後美國女權運動最具動力的推手。畢竟史丹頓是七個子女的母親，居家顧子，使她無法四處奔走，大大限制了她的行動，但一八五一年當史丹頓與蘇珊安東尼結為夥伴後，史丹頓轉而努力著述，再交由蘇珊安東尼代言，安用她極富魅力的語調與活力，恢復女人自信，並讓男人自覺認識到女性獨特、珍貴的人格特值。

　　美國人權遞演上，我們發現女權與黑人權利的發展有著某種同步的糾結。獨立宣言中，大家投注關切的是黑人不在天賦人權保障之列，不平憲法中將黑人只視同五分之三個人對待，但這一切的剝奪到了一八六三年至六五年美國先後連續通過保障黑人投票權的第十三、十四、十五條修正案中，對女性權利卻支字未提，佔美國一半人口的女性方警覺她們在民權上，實較黑人不如。內戰結束後，史丹頓決心與黑人民權全面脫鉤，發起第十六條婦女投票修正案運動。一八六九年，史丹頓與蘇珊安東尼進一步組成「全國女子投票權協會」，擴大女子權利至同工同酬、離婚法、教育改革及廢除一切歧視女性的法律。二十世紀早期，許多國家已開始給予婦女投票權，特別是在第一次世界大戰結束前後，這與女人在戰爭中表現甚至較男性更任勞任怨的貢獻有關；此外，威爾遜總統十四點和平計畫中對國際殖民地命運所採取的「民族自決」觀點，相對於在國內佔半數人口的女人，美國再也難以「寧與外人，不與家奴」地拒絕給予女性投票權，一九二〇年，美國通過憲法第十九條修正案，終底達成美國成人女子的投票權。

　　女權運動但難有女性主義。究其實，史丹頓女士所爭取者不過是女性最基本權利者，居家顧子還是她的重心，她對女性的優勢——純真、人品、道德、感性的特質推銷，基本上，也符合當時男性主流社會所能接受的範疇認定，其所爭取者不過是拿回該有之基本公平的民權，能不分種族、性別、膚色與大家站在同一起跑點上。這與現代女性主義者企圖在兩性之間創造女性優越的主導權是完全有別，糾纏美國憲法修正案通過時間長達十年之久的平等權利法案（ERA），最後仍無功而退，其中即牽涉到美國

社會的禁忌議題——墮胎，性自主，脫離傳統家庭，女人比男人更好的主張，使女性主義的見地仍難容美國主流社會，甚至美國多數女性也不見贊成，再度證明美國保守強大的社會氛圍力，女性權力的擴大較之黑人更見艱難。顯例可證，則是二〇〇八年美國民主黨希拉蕊與歐巴瑪之初選競爭，在愛阿華州初選上，當希拉蕊展現強勢性格，咄咄逼人時，選民反而厭惡，但當她流淚表現敗選委曲時，卻又贏回選民同情支持，這說明了美國人民對女性的框架仍在溫柔婉約；至於國事大任，美國選民最後還是選擇了歐巴瑪，這說明黑人權利總優先於女人一步呢？還是美國人心理上對黑人的歷史虧欠實在太大？我們只能說歷史要前進的一小步，往往是需要人類想法的一大步邁進吧！

男性摧毀力

伊麗莎白・史丹頓

　　一八六八年，伊麗莎白・凱第・史丹頓女士在華府所召開之女人投票權大會上，發表了這篇挑戰男性傳統優越論的有力演講。史丹頓女士從歷史經驗證明，「雄性元素意謂摧毀、嚴厲、自私、激化、好戰、暴力、征服、佔有，孕育於爭議、混亂、病症與死亡。這血腥與殘酷的紀錄不斷揭露在歷史的篇章。」，史丹頓質疑百年來女性基本民權之忽略除環境與社會傳統的認定外，重要的因素是女人也甘於容忍此一根深蒂固男尊女卑價值，因此，「革命必先革心」，她開始以說理的文辭極力論述女性比男性具有更優質的品性與道德，男性統治下的暴庚與毀滅，就是因為沒有女性的政治意見的參與，而史丹頓女士提出的解決之道就是停止貶抑女性的價值，加入女性建設力的觀點、意見、品德、動機、偏好，去調合男性的摧毀力，達到史丹頓女士希望男女平等參政，建設正常文明國家理想，繼黑白種族問題告一段落後，史丹頓女士補上了美國民權最大一塊缺漏的拼圖。

The Destructive Male

Elizabeth Cady Stanton

I urge a sixteenth amendment, because 'manhood suffrage, or a man's government, is civil, religious, and social disorganization. The male element is a destructive force, stern, selfish, aggrandizing, loving war, violence, conquest, acquisition, breeding in discord, disorder, disease, and death. See what a record of blood and cruelty the pages of history reveal! Through what slavery, slaughter, and sacrifice, through what inquisitions and imprisonments, pains and persecutions, black codes and gloomy creeds, the soul of humanity has struggled for the centuries, while mercy has veiled her face and all hearts have been dead alike to love and hope!

The male element has held high carnival thus far; it has fairly run riot from the beginning, overpowering the feminine element everywhere, crushing out all the diviner qualities in human nature

我催促著第十六條修正案的成立，因為成年男人投票權或一個完全男性意志的政府是民眾、宗教與社會的失序解體。雄性元素其意謂是摧毀力、嚴厲、自私、激化、好戰、暴力、征服、佔有，成長於爭議、混亂、病症與死亡。這血腥與殘酷的紀錄不斷揭露在歷史的篇章。經過奴隸、屠殺與犧牲，經過折磨與監禁，痛苦與迫害，歧視的法律與教條，人性的靈魂已奮鬥數世紀之久，期間憐憫遮蓋了她的臉龐，所有心靈也隨著希望與愛消逝。

自前世紀起，男性成員舉行嘉年華會，有如他們自始就好行動盪，在任何領域都壓制著女性份子，破壞一切人性中更神聖的特質。社會不過是男性主體本身的反射，女性的想法無足輕重；

71

within the last century. Society is but the reflection of man himself, untempered by woman's thought; the hard iron rule we feel alike in the church, the state, and the home. No one need wonder at the disorganization, at the fragmentary condition of everything, when we remember that man, who represents but half a complete being, with but half an idea on every subject, has undertaken the absolute control of all sublunary matters.

People object to the demands of those, because they say 'the right of suffrage will make the women masculine. That is just the difficulty in which we are involved today. The strong, natural characteristics of womanhood are repressed and ignored in dependence, for so long as man feeds woman she will try to please the giver and adapt herself to his condition. To keep a foothold in society, woman must be as near like man as possible, reflect his ideas, opinions, virtues, motives, prejudices, and vices. She must respect his statutes, though they strip her of every inalienable right, and conflict with that higher law written

宗教、國家與家庭上,女性有如在鐵腕的統制之下。當我們想到只代表一半人口與任何事務也只代表一半意見的男人卻得獨享所有事務的絕對控制,就不足為怪萬物失序或破裂的狀況了。

所有反對女性投票權的理由不外是予女人投票權將使女人變得雄赳赳男子氣概。這正是我們今天運動的困難所在。女人原本堅強、自然的個性正在依賴中被壓抑與忽略,因為只要女人繼續被男人豢養她就必須討好與順從男人的條件。女人要在社會上立足,就必得盡可能苟同於男性,反應出男性的觀點、意見、品德、動機、偏好與負面性。女人必須尊重男性的地位,儘管男性剝奪了女人之天賦權利並反抗上帝之手所寫下女性靈魂的法則。

by the finger of God on her own soul.

She must look at everything from its dollar-and-cent point of view, or she is a mere romancer. To mourn over the miseries of others, the poverty of the poor, their hardships in jails, prisons, asylums, the horrors of war, cruelty, and brutality in every form, all this would be mere sentimentalizing. To protest against the intrigue, bribery, and corruption of public life,… would be arrant nonsense.

In this way man has been molding woman to his ideas by direct and positive influences,… And now man himself stands appalled at the results of his own excesses, and mourns in bitterness that falsehood, selfishness, and violence are the law of life. The need of this hour is not territory, gold mines, railroads, or specie payments but a new evangel of womanhood, to exalt purity, virtue, morality, true religion, to lift man up into the higher realms of thought and action.

We ask woman's enfranchisement, as the first step toward the recognition of that essential element in government that can only

女人一定是用斤斤計較觀點看待事情，或說女人不過就是浪漫工具。女人於他人苦難、貧窮、監獄困苦、救濟院、戰爭的恐怖、殘酷與暴行之任何形式的哀傷不過是感情用事；至於去反抗陰謀、賄賂，公共貪污就太無聊。

男人就是這般以他直接的積極影響力，根據他的意志去塑造女性。而現在男人總算驚懼於他們偏差的後果且苦惱於虛偽、自私與暴力變成了人生的法則。因此，此刻需要的不是土地、金礦、鐵路或是硬貨幣支付，而是女性的福音去讚美純真、人品、道德、宗教，將男性提升至更高的思想與行為層次。

我們要求女子投票權是使政府認識到這是它基本成份的第一

secure the health, strength, and prosperity of the nation. Whatever is done to lift woman to her true position will help to usher in a new day of peace and perfection for the race.

In speaking of the masculine element, I do not wish to be understood to say that all men are hard, selfish, and brutal,....; but I refer to those characteristics, that distinguish what is called the stronger sex. For example, the love of acquisition and conquest, the very pioneers of civilization, when expended on the earth, the sea, the elements, the riches and forces of nature, are powers of destruction when used to subjugate one man to another or to sacrifice nations to ambition.

Here that great conservator of woman's love, if permitted to assert itself, as it naturally would in freedom against oppression, violence, and war, would hold all these destructive forces in check, for woman knows the cost of life better than man does, and not with her consent would one drop of blood ever be shed, one life sacrificed in vain.

步，如此方能確保國家的健全、實力與繁榮。只有完成女性真實地位的一切提升，方有和平新生活與族群完美的到來。

至於談到所謂雄性元素，我不希望被誤解所有男性都是強硬、自私與殘酷，我談論這些特質主要是區隔出何謂強勢性別。譬如，佔有與征服的喜好，文明的開拓，海洋與土地的擴張，財富與力量的性質，都是毀滅性的力量，因為他們都是用來壓迫一個人屈服於另一個人，或是將國家犧牲在野心之下。

然而女性愛的偉大蓄積，可牽制所有毀滅性的力量，如同她以自由對抗壓迫、戰爭與暴力的天性一樣，因為女人較男人更清楚生命的代價，沒有她們的同意，絕不會流一滴血，或允許一個

With violence and disturbance in the natural world, we see a constant effort to maintain an equilibrium of forces. Nature, like a loving mother, is ever trying to keep land and sea, mountain and valley, each in its place, to hush the angry winds and waves, balance the extremes of heat and cold, of rain and drought, that peace, harmony, and beauty may reign supreme. There is a striking analogy between matter and mind, and the present disorganization of society warns us that in the dethronement of woman we have let loose the elements of violence and ruin that she only has the power to curb. If the civilization of the age calls for an extension of the suffrage, surely a government of the most virtuous educated men and women would better represent the whole and protect the interests of all than could the representation of either sex alone.

生命無謂的犧牲。

　　暴力與混亂充斥之自然世界，讓我們看到一穩定維持各方力量平衡的努力。自然有如慈愛母親，不停使海、陸與天地、山谷，安於其位；平息暴風與海浪，均衡酷暑與寒冬及乾涸與水患，讓安寧、和諧與美好駕馭自然。同樣一個想法與事實上之強烈類比，警告我們排除女性只會使我們放縱暴力與破壞，也只有女人可以阻止現行社會解體。如果時代的文明要求我們擴大予女性投票權，自然一個由最富道德教養的男女共組的政府是絕對比任何單一性別代表的政府更能代表與保護全民的利益。

第八篇　耙糞者

～爆料揭弊媒體治國

泰迪‧羅斯福

▶▶▶ 最動人的佳句！**The most touching words**！

The men with the muck-rakes are often indispensable to the well-being of society; but only if they know when to stop raking the muck, ...

～Theodore ("Teddy") Roosevelt

耙糞之人對社會的福祉是不可或缺的；但這存乎他們知道何時適可而止……

～泰迪‧羅斯福

前言

　　美國二十世紀初，由於資本主義過度放任，政、商貪腐盛行，國家發展陷入失衡，民氣可用之下，惟賴美國新聞界的「耙糞」（muckraking）運動，不斷的揭發，制止了腐敗的蔓延滋生，促進了社會的進步體質。

　　二〇〇〇年起，台灣社會也掀起「耙糞」現象，稱之「爆料文化」，一群所謂名嘴在傳媒揭弊、爆料，導致一連串政、商貪腐行為無所遁形。這群第四權媒體下的「第五縱隊」，雖然有時無的放矢，常未審先判，指揮辦案，引來爆料正當性之非議。還

有進而衍生以窺伺名人為業之「狗仔隊」，更是嚴重侵犯隱私，甚至釀成無法挽回之悲劇，如英國王妃戴安娜因躲避狗仔，車禍中香消玉殞。但我們知道司法常是遲到的正義，往往只能作事後的補救，相較揭發政府貪腐之耙糞，確使許多來自公權力本身掩護、策動之貪腐犯罪，由於揭發見光，及早胎死腹中。

　　證本溯源，這種媒體自由下衍生之耙糞或狗仔現象，大行於美國二十紀初之進步主義運動，而老羅斯福正是這一運動的有力支持者，鼓勵耙糞者揭出社會種種觸目驚心的黑暗，不但毫無所謂動搖國本，顛覆社會安定之虞，相反地，促使美國進行自我反省、改革，前衛地立法於環境保護、勞工權利保障、食品衛生規範，重新煥發活力，使美國社會更加穩定和健康發展。

歷史背景

　　進步主義運動。十九世紀末二十世紀初，經過南北戰爭後的美國經濟迅速發展，社會空前富裕，進入資本家「鍍金時代」，急劇的工業化和城市化，也產生了種種社會問題。其中最嚴重普遍的是政商貪污、腐敗，造成了巨大的社會危機。

　　進步主義運動就是反應這一段二十世紀初美國歷史上，一股社會公平的改革運動和思潮。進步主義努力改革者，乃過度放任美國資本主義，所生之政、商貪婪和腐敗的盛行，包括政府、企業、社會正義，以至婦女、道德等各方面的失衡惡化。而運動開端，始自美國新聞界開始的「耙糞」（muckraking）運動，有力制止了腐敗的蔓延滋生，促進了公共社會的改良，他們披露政治腐敗並打擊公共資源的壟斷事業，像水利、鐵路和瓦斯等，他們的揭弊、貢獻無所不包，從人民生活最基本之食品、藥物、衛

生及工作環境的立法保障，至一九一三年美國第十六條憲法修正案，授予聯邦政府依人民、公司之收入多寡，徵收所得稅，以達社會賦稅之公平，同年，第十七條憲法修正案，規定直接選舉參議員與初選的舉辦及一九二〇年美國第十九條憲法修正案，婦女聯邦選舉投票權的批准。這一段時間，真正是媒體治國，大大彌補了受企業資本家包圍而無力改革的政府公權力貫徹，得以保持美國國力的更新，一面仍維持了資本主義的活力創新，但也引進入社會主義照顧弱勢的公平正義精神。

　　老羅斯福與耙糞運動。從廣義上看，進步主義運動就是美國自十九世紀末以來，城市平民對政府與工商生產者勾結、壟斷下所生弊端，不滿的揭發醜聞和城市改革運動，而「揭發黑幕者」的「耙糞者」一詞，即是專門用來指老羅斯福時代的那些新聞記者和小說家。因為政府本身已深陷資本家的包圍與勾串，只有仰賴媒體的耙糞者為進步主義之先鋒，加以制衡，使執政者引以為誡。

　　在這場進步主義運動中，總統老羅斯福扮演了重要角色，耙糞運動即啟源於他和一位紐約記者談話，羅斯福總統坦言：為了通過某些利國利民的條款，有時他不得不與參議院和眾議院做某種交易。羅斯福總統說出為了得到一名參議員的支持，他不得不任命這位參議員情婦的弟弟當某市地方檢察官。該記者當即如實報導，尖銳地指出這實際是一種賄賂，引起軒然大波。不久，羅斯福總統在記者招待會上不滿地將這些專門揭弊的記者稱之為「耙糞者」。而長於政治精算，觀測風勢的老羅斯福，也趁民氣可用，搭上這股風潮，成為最支持這項社會改革運動的總統，開啟所謂「公平政策」（Fair Deal），他要求國會立法，對托拉斯的經營活動給予合理的

限制，使國會於一九〇六年通過了《赫本法案》（Hepburn Act），授權州際貿易委員會設置鐵路運費上限。同年，他還促使國會通過《食品和藥物純淨法案》和《肉類產品監督法案》，對養畜和肉類加工企業進行稽查和實施強制衛生標準。老羅斯福是第一位對環境保護有長遠考量的總統，及早認知到「我們的發展與永久財富與資源保護有密切的關係。」，一九〇五年，他敦促國會成立美國林業服務局，管理國有森林和土地。老羅斯福設立的國家公園和自然保護區面積比其所有前任所設總和還多，舉世聞名的大峽谷國家公園就是其中之一。

　　老羅斯福是美國最早具社會主義理想的進步改革總統，在一九一二年，還成立美國第一個進步主義的進步黨，它也是美國近代史上最成功的第三政黨，受到人民的愛戴，成為拉許摩爾山上與華盛頓、傑佛遜與林肯並列，成為美國四位最偉大的總統之一。

文獻介紹

耙糞者

泰迪‧羅斯福

　　一九〇六年四月，老羅斯福在這篇文章中，為美國進步改革運動，吹起揭發貪腐的攻擊號角，老羅斯福引用宗教小說家布尼安「朝聖者前行」中的主角人物——手拿耙具，目不旁視，只知道低頭朝下，掃出滿目穢物的「耙糞者」，比擬那些專門揭貪露腐的新聞記者。雖然，這是一群烏鴉，但直言不怕當道的勇氣，反而得到人民的肯定，成為一種受人讚許的尊稱。由於他們仗義直言和追求社會公正的理想性格，把社會中的陰暗現象，毫不留情地暴露在陽光之下，促使公民社會猛醒，動員民眾保護自身與社會公益，通過各種立法，有力遏制了腐敗的滋生，迅速緩解了已成劍拔弩張之勢的社會勞資矛盾。

　　然文中，老羅斯福也言明，社會之公平也不是拉下一方，使另一方得到提升，以安撫工商資本家，他並非「反商」，他追求者乃「公平政策」（Fair Deal）之施政。

The Man with the Muck-rake
14 April 1906

Theodore ("Teddy") Roosevelt

Over a century ago Washington laid the corner-stone of the Capitol in what was then little more than a tract of wooded wilderness here beside the Potomac. We now find it necessary to provide great additional buildings for the business of the government. We now administer the affairs of a nation in which the extraordinary growth of population has been outstripped by the growth of wealth and the growth in complex interests.

The material problems that face us to-day are not such as they were in Washington's time, but the underlying facts of human nature are the same now as they were then. Under altered external form we war with the same tendencies toward evil that were evident in Washington's time.

一個世紀前，在波多馬克河邊的一片荒蕪林地，華盛頓為國會大廈的開工，立下基石。時至今日，我們發現必須提供更多額外的建物，才能滿足政府不斷擴大增長的業務。目前，我們所管理的國家業務，不論財富與利益的複雜提升，已超越了人口數量的非凡成長。

今天，我們所面對的物質問題已大不同華盛頓時期，但人性的根本事實卻一如已往，只不過外在形式的改變。一如華盛頓時代，我們還是有著與邪惡戰鬥的同樣趨勢。

It is about some of these that I wish to say a word to-day. In Bunyan's "Pilgrim's Progress" you may recall the description of the Man with the Muck-rake, the man who could look no way but downward, with the muck-rake in his hand; who was offered a celestial crown for his muck-rake, ... continued to rake to himself the filth of the floor.

In "Pilgrim's Progress" the Man with the Muck-rake is set forth as the example whose vision is fixed on carnal instead of on spiritual things. Yet he also typifies the man who in this life consistently refuses to see aught that is lofty, and fixes his eyes with solemn intentness only on that which is vile and debasing. Now, it is very necessary that we should not flinch from seeing what is vile and debasing. There is filth on the floor and it must be scraped up with the muck-rake; and there are times and places where this service is the most needed of all the services that can be performed. But the man who never thinks or speaks or writes, save of his feats with the muck-rake, speedily becomes, not

　　因為以上的事實，我希望今天表達一點看法。在布尼安「朝聖者的前行」裏，你也許會回想起那一位手拿耙具的人，因他清理髒穢的工作，有如受晃天上王冠，他總是低頭察看地上，不斷朝自己，耙出地上的垃圾。

　　在「朝聖者的前行」裏，這位耙糞者被設定成的榜樣是眼光總是固定在世俗而非精神的事物。這位耙糞者也被形塑成是一貫拒絕注目生活中高尚的事情，卻慎重其事的只察看墮落與卑鄙的發生。現在，我們實在有必要不能再輕忽、看待墮落與卑鄙的發生。對地上的穢物，一定要耙出清除。有太多的時機與地點，需要這最迫切實施的服務。這位不思、不言、不作，除了以他手中

a help to society, not an incitement to good, but one of the most potent forces for evil.

There are, in the body politic, economic and social, many and grave evils, and there is urgent necessity for the sternest war upon them. There should be relentless exposure of and attack upon every evil man whether politician or business man, every evil practice, whether in politics, in business, or in social life. I hail as a benefactor every writer or speaker, every man who, on the platform, or in book, magazine, or newspaper, with merciless severity makes such attack, provided always that he in his turn remembers that the attack is of use only if it is absolutely truthful. The liar is no whit better than the thief, and if his mendacity takes the form of slander, he may be worse than most thieves.

耙具，摘奸發伏，已經迅速變成，既不是社會的助力，亦非善良的誘發，卻絕對是抗拒邪惡最有能耐的勢力。

有太多邪惡的人與事存在我們政治、經濟與社會體制內，實有最嚴厲的必要對此惡行宣戰。對這些不論是政治或商業的邪惡之徒及其政、商與社會之邪惡行為，應該要有無情的揭發。身為受益人，我大聲讚許不論是演說的人或作家，及任何在講台、書本、雜誌及報紙上，發於聲或出於筆，給予最嚴厲批評之人，只要他們能深記在作此攻訐時，決對是基於事實。需知道，說謊者同惡於盜賊，然而如果他採取的是惡意詆毀謊言的方式，則其惡更甚於盜賊。

Any excess is almost sure to invite a reaction; and, unfortunately, the reaction, instead of taking the form of punishment of those guilty of the excess, is very apt to take the form either of punishment of the unoffending or of giving immunity, to offenders. The effort to make financial or political profit out of the destruction of character can only result in public calamity. Gross and reckless assaults on character, whether on the stump or in newspaper, magazine, or book, create a morbid and vicious public sentiment, and at the same time act as a profound deterrent to able men of normal sensitiveness and tend to prevent them from entering the public service at any price.

…...let me say again that my plea is, not for immunity to but for the most unsparing exposure of the politician who betrays his trust, of the big business man who makes or spends his fortune in illegitimate or corrupt ways. There should be a resolute effort to hunt every such man out of the position he has disgraced. Expose the crime, and hunt down the criminal; but remember that even in the case of crime, if it

任何事只要過份，自然招致報應；然不幸的是，這個報應常常是行過份之罪過者沒受到處罰，反而常是無過者受罰，要不就是讓過失者豁免。以摧毀人格取得金錢與政治利益之努力，終將招致大眾的痛苦。利用演說、書籍、雜誌上，進行粗鄙與無情攻訐品德，不只會創造惡質的民眾情緒，同時也會對有正常情感及能力人士造成深遠的嚇阻，使他們在無論任何代價下，都不願從政為民公僕。

讓我再次重申我的訴求不是給予免除，而是毫不保留的揭發那些出賣自己信仰的政客，以及用非法貪污方式取用他們財富的奸商巨賈。對這些污蔑他們應有立場者，應該要有堅決獵補，無一倖免的行動努力。盡力曝露其罪行，罪犯繩之以法，但應記

is attacked in sensational, lurid, and untruthful fashion, the attack may do more damage to the public mind than the crime itself. It is because I feel that there should be no rest in the endless war against the forces of evil that I ask that the war be conducted with sanity as well as with resolution.

The men with the muck-rakes are often indispensable to the well-being of society; but only if they know when to stop raking the muck, and to look upward to the celestial crown above them, to the crown of worthy endeavor.

To assail the great and admitted evils of our political and industrial life with such crude and sweeping generalizations as to include decent men in the general condemnation means the searing of the public conscience. There results a general attitude either of cynical belief in and indifference to public corruption or else of a distrustful inability to discriminate between the good and the bad. Either attitude is fraught with untold damage to the country as a whole. The fool who has not

取的是,就算是犯罪的案例,如果攻擊流於情緒、悚懼、不實煽動,這一民眾心理之傷害將更甚於犯罪者本身。因為我相信對邪惡勢力的戰爭是永無止盡的,所以這場戰鬥必須是在清白與決心的條件下進行。

所以耙糞之人對社會的福祉是不可或缺的;但這存乎他們知道何時適可而止,並尊重他們頂上那頂上天賜晃,有所為而為的王冠。

在我們政治與工商生活中,抨擊巨大與被承認的邪惡,常是既殘酷又全面性的掃蕩,以致正直之士都受波及,這意謂著公共良知的麻痺。如此一來,對公共貪腐所產生的全面態度,不是憤世嫉俗,就是全然冷漠,不然也是懷疑且無能於分辯是非;不論

sense to discriminate between what is good and what is bad is as dangerous as the man who does discriminate and yet chooses the bad.

Hysterical sensationalism is the very poorest weapon wherewith to fight for lasting righteousness. The men who with stern sobriety and truth assail the many evils of our time, whether in the public press or in magazines, or in books, are the leaders and allies of all engaged in the work for social and political betterment. But if they give good reason for distrust of what they say, if they chill the ardor of those who demand truth as a primary virtue, they thereby betray the good cause, and play into the hands of the very men against whom they are nominally at war.

This truth should be kept constantly in mind by every free people desiring to preserve the sanity and poise …... Yet, on the other hand, it is vital not to permit this spirit to sanity and self-command to degenerate into mere mental stagnation. Bad though a state of hysterical excitement is, and evil though the results are which come from the violent oscillations such

是那一種態度，對國家整體的傷害，都是不可言喻的。而分不出善與惡之愚民與雖能分辯卻選擇惡行者，是一樣的危險。

歇斯底里式的煽情主義，是保衛長久正義最貧弱的武器。在大眾媒體、報章、雜誌上，任何神智清明且懷抱真誠者，所針對公共人物的邪惡行為進行的揭發攻擊，正是所有致力希望於這個社會與政治更加美好而結合人群的領導者。但是他們一旦給人理由懷疑他們所言或是他們所行讓追求真理是美德的熱忱人群失望，他們不但背離了這個運動，也會被對手玩弄在股掌之上。

這個事實對任何要保持冷靜平衡自由人士，是要時時刻刻放在心上的。但是，另一方面而言，防止這顆清明冷靜的精神

excitement invariably produces, yet a sodden acquiescence in evil is even worse. …. So far as this movement of agitation throughout the country takes the form of a fierce discontent with evil, of a determination to punish the authors of evil, whether in industry or politics, the feeling is to be heartily welcomed as a sign of healthy life.

It is a prime necessity that if the present unrest is to result in permanent good the emotion shall be translated into action, and that the action shall be marked by honesty, sanity, and self-restraint. There is mighty little good in a mere spasm of reform. The reform that counts is that which comes through steady, continuous growth; violent emotionalism leads to exhaustion.

As a matter of personal conviction, I feel that we shall ultimately have to consider the adoption of some such scheme as that of a progressive tax on all fortunes,— the tax, of course, to be imposed by the National and not the State Government.

陷於只是心理的呆滯，也是很重要的。儘管有時歇斯底里的激動不見得好，而由此所生之暴力的動盪是不義的，然而對邪惡行為無動於衷的默許卻更是大惡。……到目前，這起鼓動的風潮已在全國，朝向工商或政治作奸犯科之人，進行嚴厲不滿與決心的懲罰，這種感覺被衷心地歡迎是健全生活的象徵。

如果現在的動盪最後能招致永遠的善果，這股情緒應該轉化成行動，並被標榜是清廉、健康與自制。改革如果只是即興的衝動，是達不到什麼太大成果的。改革必須依靠穩定、持續的壯大，爆起爆落的情緒主義，只會徒增虛耗。

作為個人堅信的事項，我認為我們最後應該考量採納一些計

Again, the National Government must in some form exercise supervision over corporations engaged in interstate business—and all large corporations are engaged in interstate business—whether by license or otherwise, so as to permit us to deal with the far-reaching evils of overcapitalization.

The first requisite in the public servants who are to deal in this shape with corporations, whether as legislators or as executives, is honesty. This honesty can be no respecter of persons. There can be no such thing as unilateral honesty. The danger is not really from corrupt corporations; it springs from the corruption itself, whether exercised for or against corporations.

The men of wealth who today are trying to prevent the regulation and control of their business in the interest of the public by the proper government authorities will not succeed, in my judgment, in checking the progress of the movement. But if they did succeed they would find that they had sown the wind and would surely reap

議，如根據累進稅率，對所有的財產徵稅，自然，這個徵稅權是屬聯邦政府而非州政府。

聯邦政府也應針對所有進行州際貿易之企業公司，實施某些型式的監管，不管是牌照等，以處理過度資本化的邪惡。

處理大型企業之政府公務人員不論是來自行政或立法部門的首要條件就是清廉。此一清廉者乃在不分地位，一視同仁。也沒有比一味堅持清廉再重要的條件了。其實，貪婪企業的危險並不來自貪瀆企業，而是貪瀆的本身，這無關對企業的好惡關係。

依我判斷，富有階級今天努力試圖規避法律與政府為大眾利益所進行的商業管制是不會成功阻撓這項運動的前進。即便他們

the whirlwind, for they would ultimately provoke the violent excesses which accompany a reform coming by convulsion instead of by steady and natural growth.

More important than aught else is the development of the broadest sympathy of man for man. The welfare of the wage-worker, the welfare of the tiller of the soil, upon these depend the welfare of the entire country; their good is not to be sought in pulling down others; but their good must be the prime object of all our statesmanship.

Materially we must strive to secure a broader economic opportunity for all men, so that each shall have a better chance to show the stuff of which he is made.

Spiritually and ethically we must strive to bring about clean living and right thinking. We appreciate also that the things of the soul are immeasurably more important.

The foundation-stone of national life is, and ever must be, the high individual character of the average citizen.

成功，也必承受報應之苦，因為他們必然挑起改革隨之而來的暴力動蕩，而不是穩健自然的成長。

更勝一切的是，人與人之間相互憐憫的廣大發展。薪資工人與自耕農民的福祉也是國家全面福祉之所依，他們福利的尋求，並不是以拉下他人的犧牲達到，而是必須成為國家公權力的目的。

實質上來說就是我們必須努力保障所有人經濟的機會，讓每一個人都有更好展示天生我才必有用的機會。

精神上與倫理言，我們必須努力帶來乾淨與正確的生活思考。我們感受到靈魂的重要是無與倫比。

畢竟，國家生命的基礎是建立一般民眾的高尚人格。

第九篇　總統就職演講詞

～邁向「為民所享」的福利國

富蘭克林‧羅斯福

▶▶▶ 最動人的佳句！ **The most touching words**！

The only thing we have to fear is fear itself.

～F. D. Roosevelt

我們惟一要恐懼的，就是恐懼的本身。

～富蘭克林‧羅斯福

前言

　　二〇〇八年，在金融海嘯狂襲下，全球陷入空前經濟衰退的失業潮，各國無不受這股景氣嚴冬的考驗與人民迫切的回春期待。在美國歷史上，也有一段自一九二九年至一九四一年長達十二年「經濟大恐慌」的日子，全球陷入史上最大的經濟不景氣，這時美國經濟的生產、消費幾近停止，四分之一的人口失業，股市、房地產全面泡沫，股民自殺不斷，華爾街周圍旅館，房客check in時，最常被問就是：「睡覺？還是要跳樓？」。一九三三年，羅斯福就是在這場全球經濟災難邁入最高峰的情形下就任，深具領導魅力（charisma）的羅斯福，不但能準確掌握民之所欲與苦民所苦的同理心；或許他也束手無策，但總能維持住樂觀和希望，鼓舞百姓渡過寒冬，信心中等待春天的燕子到來。

他一面以動人的談話為信心跌入谷底的美國百姓打氣，另方面，他推出「新政」，不停以政府積極行動全面介入市場生產與分配，有人說是社會主義的革命，也有人說是資本主義的改革，其實羅斯福政府已認識到全球經濟緊密依存下，美國政府有義務介入民主社會公平正義的維護與積極照顧弱勢族群，以達真正「為民所享」的境地，自此，羅斯福帶領美國放棄達爾文「適者生存」加資本主義「自由放任」割喉式的競爭生活，走進日後社會福利國之民主時代。

歷史背景

經濟大恐慌（1929～1941）是人類工業革命以來，史上空前及意外的經濟災難，某種程度它也預告了全球化經濟，愈趨密切互動之「蝴蝶效應」時代的到來。

一戰後，當歐洲國家因戰爭凋零，缺乏硬貨幣的消費能力時，最具市場與消費實力的美國，卻因凡爾賽和約與盟邦鬧翻，重新走回孤立主義，雪上加霜的築起高關稅壁壘，導致他國也實施報復或保護性的關稅，抵制美貨輸入，懵懂無知的美國人民卻依然大肆吸金，投資生產，終於在一九二九年十月二十九日，美國股市猛爆性崩盤，從352點一路下跌至一九三二年羅斯福當選前的41點，90%的市值蒸發，華爾街股民高達2萬7千人，前仆後繼跳樓自殺，失業率高達25%，美國工業生產額消失1/3，邁入空前的蕭條與絕望，並由美國蔓延至全世界。

該如何面對這史無前例的經濟災難，考驗著全世界的政治領袖，而身為全球經濟火車頭的美國，主政之胡佛總統仍固守美國資本主義放任式的自由經濟政策，堅持政府不應干預介入民生與

市場經濟，即使對佔據聚集白宮大道前，埋鍋造飯多時，戲稱是「胡佛村Hoover -ville」的抗議貧民，胡佛依然不為所動，時限一到，命當時的麥克阿瑟上校強制驅離。工程師出身的胡佛以冷漠的傳統經濟理論及冰冷的數據去面對大眾的絕望與無助，是只有專業，卻失去一個領導者的慈悲與同理心，尤其此番之不景氣不同以往是本國經濟循環供需失衡所致，胡佛不但誤判了時勢，也證明不是一位時勢需要的領袖。

　　新政。相對地，羅斯福完全是這場束手無策經濟浩劫下的訂製人物，他把一個偉大總統最典型的關鍵特質展示無遺，他也許知道經濟不可能馬上好，但是人民的希望不能走，信心更不能減，如何維持人民的樂觀與願景，他馬上提出「新政」穩定人心，第一個百日中，羅斯福以不斷的行動及國會的全面配合下廣推法案，並以他個人獨特「有如北辰」的政治魅力，成為大眾之精神領袖。羅斯福用人不以黨派為限，內閣重要官員甚多保守之共和黨人擔任，尤其喜用哈佛大學教授為其智囊（brain trust），這群自由派學者，個性強也勇於求新，腦力激盪下提出大膽實驗構想，的確轉移民眾目光，讓人民產生期待心理。但為他加分最多者則是其妻艾蓮娜，從原本靦腆低調，到克服恐懼積極參與公益，為新政敢言敢說，其美譽更勝羅斯福。

　　大政府與福利國時代。新政在美國史上，有人說是社會主義革命，實不如說是資本主義的改革，在世界愈來愈「平」的情況下，景氣在彼此互動愈加敏感的波動下，新政最大意義就是：政府角色扮演不可能再是美國立國時期所信奉之「最好的政府就是最不管事的政府」，一昧放任資本主義「適者生存」弱肉強食的經濟行為，新政必須擔當社會弱勢的保護者，在「救濟、恢復

景氣與改革」的三階段下，進行工作有：健全體質銀行合併的金融改革，建立銀行存款保障制度，保護小額存款人民；股市資訊透明化，防止內線交易，徵富人稅。促進勞資和諧，設立最低工資；最高工時，加強工會地位。保障農民上，限制耕地面積，提高價格。至於全面性的社會福利，建立僱主與所雇者共同分擔之全民退休保險制度等，這種改良資本主義，結合凱因斯與中間偏左的社會主義政策，都是日後開創福利國家仿傚的基本規模，真正落實為民所享之社會民主體制。

　　新政的推行也並非勢如破竹，期間不斷受到政策過左過右的社會批判與政府權力是否過大，弄得羅斯福有時父子騎驢，新政至一九三七年，最高法院判決農業調整法案違憲後，羅斯福企圖以增加大法官九人至十五人反擊，招惹民怨後，力道開始減緩，一九三九年，新政幾乎已全面停止，然而同時歐洲戰爭全面爆發，隨戰爭而來的經濟需求，美國得以全面就業生產，也結束了這場生計浩劫的大恐慌。

文獻介紹

總統就職演講詞

富蘭克林‧羅斯福

　　針對胡佛總統堅持政府不介入經濟自由運作的保守作為，「冷靜」的看待這場全球性的經濟浩劫，不但是政策上的誤判，就人民感受言也不符社會對他的期待。一九三三年，人民選擇了代表魄力與希望的羅斯福，就職演說中，羅斯福主要分兩大方向：首先，他要求美國人恢復舊日的核心價值觀──犧牲、紀律、倫理、團結，「惟一的恐懼，就是恐懼的本身」，並舉重若輕將美國今日之危難，歸之於不過是「物質部分」（material things），是一群金錢玩弄者（money changers）貪婪的以私利敗壞人性與金融失序所致。其次，要求行動，行動才能改變，改變也才有希望。他要求國會與美國人民給予政府大破大立的行動權限，一個「凱因斯式」的大政府的時代從此到來。固然羅斯福並沒有以新政改變整體的大環境，但他真實的顯現了一個領導人不只是政策的冷峻決定者，在多變複雜的時代他更代表著是溫暖民心希望的力量。

First Inaugural Address, 1933

Franklin Delano Roosevelt

I am certain that my fellow Americans expect that on my induction into the Presidency I will address them with a candor and a decision which the present situation of our nation impels. This is the time to speak the truth, the whole truth, frankly and boldly. Nor need we shrink from honestly facing conditions in our country today. So first of all let me assert my firm belief that the only thing we have to fear is fear itself...

In every dark hour of our national life a leadership of frankness and vigor has met with that understanding and support of the people themselves which is essential to victory. I am convinced that you will again give that support to leadership in these critical days. In such a spirit on my part and on yours we face our common difficulties. They concern, thank God, only material things. Values have shrunken

　　國家正值危難所迫的情勢裏，我瞭解美國人民期待我就職此刻，我會向你們道出一個坦白的決定。的確，此刻也是大膽說出真話，坦白全部真相的時候了。我們再也無法迴避，必須誠實面對國家正遭遇的困境。所以，首先，讓我向你們確立我堅定的信仰就是：我們惟一要恐懼的，就是恐懼的本身。

　　在全國黑暗的生活時刻中，一個明快、強而有力的領導必須伴隨人民的諒解與支持，這是勝利所必須的。我相信身處危機的時局，你們將不吝予我領導的支持，一致面對我們共同的難關。感謝上帝，這些難關僅限於物質方面。財產已縮水到令人驚訝的程度，賦稅增加，我們支付的能力下跌，政府收入銳減，貿易凍

to fantastic levels: taxes have risen, our ability to pay has fallen, government of all kinds is faced by serious curtailment of income, the means of exchange are frozen in the currents of trade, the withered leaves of industrial enterprise lie on every side, farmers find no markets for their produce, the savings of many years in thousands of families are gone…. Only a foolish optimist can deny the dark realities of the moment.

Primarily, this is because … Practices of the unscrupulous money changers. They know only the rules of a generation of self-seekers. They have no vision, and when there is no vision the people perish. The money changers have fled their high seats in the temple of our civilization. We may now restore that temple to the ancient truths. The measure of the restoration lies in the extent to which we apply social values more noble than mere monetary profit.

Happiness lies not in the mere possession of money, it lies in the joy of achievement, in the thrill of creative effort. The joy and moral

結，工業凋零，農民找不到產品銷路，數以千計家庭儲蓄化為烏有。只有傻瓜才會對現在的黑暗現實感覺樂觀。

基本上，今天的困境都歸咎一群金錢操弄者，沒有道德的所作所為。他們只知道自利的規則，毫無遠見，人類沒有遠見，則難以長久。現在金錢操弄者已經失去他們文明殿堂的位置；我們正好可讓這殿堂回到古老的真理。而這回復的措施在於我們應用更高貴的社會價值，而不只是金錢利益。

快樂不只在金錢的握有，而是在享受成就的喜悅與努力創造的快感。工作所生之喜悅及道德的激勵，決不可因瘋狂追求利益被遺忘。錯誤的認定物質財富就是成功的標準與錯誤的信仰公職

stimulation of work no longer must be forgotten in the mad chase of evanescent profits … Recognition of the falsity of material wealth as the standard of success goes hand in hand with the abandonment of the false belief that public office and high political position are to be values only by the standards of pride of place and personal profit….. Small wonder that confidence languishes, for it thrives only on honesty, on honor, on the sacredness of obligations, on faithful protection, on unselfish performance. Without them it cannot live.

Restoration calls, however, not for changes in ethics alone. This nation asks for action, and action now.

Hand in hand with this, we must frankly recognize the over-balance of population in our industrial centers and, by engaging on a national scale in a redistribution, …. The task can be helped by the efforts to raise the values of agricultural products …. It can be helped preventing the foreclosure of our small homes and our farms. It can be helped by the insistence that the Federal, State, and local

與政治地位就是個人利祿及地位尊嚴的價值……也難怪會剝落信心，信心是成長於誠實、榮譽、義務的犧牲、信仰的保護及無私的表現。不如此，信心就不存在。

然而，復原不能只靠需倫理價值的改變。這個國家要求行動，現在就要行動。

攜手同心行動時，我們必需承認國家人口與工業生產分佈的失衡，所以一個全國性重分配的努力是需要的。這工作可藉提高農產品價格……。藉禁止查封我們弱小的家庭或農場……它也可由聯邦、州與地方政府堅持減低它們的成本需求……它可經由國家的計畫與管控交通、通訊及其他具有公共性質的事業。我們有

governments act on the demand that their cost be drastically reduced. It can be helped by national planning for and supervision of all forms of transportation and of communications and other utilities which have a definitely public character. There are many ways in which it can be helped, but it can never be helped merely by talking about it. We must act, and act quickly.

The basic thought that guides these specific means of national recovery is not narrowly nationalistic. It is a recognition of the old and permanently important manifestation of the American spirit of the pioneer. It is the way to recovery. It is the immediate way. It is the strongest assurance that the recovery will endure.

Action in this image and to this end is feasible under the form of government which we have inherited from our ancestors. Our Constitution is so simple and practical that it is possible always to meet extraordinary needs by changes …. I shall ask the Congress for broad executive power to wage a war against the emergency as great as the power that would be

很多的方法來達到目標，但絕不是只靠說教就能有用；我們必須行動，馬上行動。

這些領導國家復原特殊手段的基礎構想，不能狹隘的以民族主義看待。它是我們美國古老卻永恆的拓荒精神的肯定展現。這就是復甦之道，也是復甦能夠延續下去的最大保證。

我們所承繼的政府形態使這項行動的外表或目的都是可行的。我們簡約與實用的憲法總能配合國家需要的改變。我將要求國會授與更寬廣的行政權限以應付當前如同外患侵略一樣的緊急狀態。

given to me if we were in fact invaded by a foreign foe.

We do not distrust the future of essential democracy. The people of the United States have not failed. In their need they have registered a mandate that they want direct, vigorous action. They have asked for discipline and direction under leadership. They have made me the present instrument of their wishes. In the spirit of the gift I will take it.

　　我們沒有放棄民主的未來。美國人民沒有失敗。他們已經表達了委命，就是他們要一個直接並有力的行動；他們要求一個有紀律的領導。他們現在也要求我承擔實踐這些希望的人。我以接受餽贈的精神，樂於承擔這份責任。

第十篇　四大自由
〜揮別孤立主義踏上世界舞台

富蘭克林・羅斯福

▶▶▶ 最動人的佳句！**The most touching words**！

In the future days, we look forward to a world founded upon four essential human freedoms: freedom of speech, freedom of every person to worship God, freedom from want , freedom from fear.

　　　　　　　　　　　　　　　　　 〜 Franklin D. Roosevelt

在未來的日子，我們期待的世界是建立於以下四大基本自由——意見的自由，信仰的自由，免於匱乏的自由，免於恐懼的自由。

　　　　　　　　　　　　　　　　　　　　 〜富蘭克林・羅斯福

前言

今日美國國力之強，人謂是自羅馬帝國以來之最，但美國現今一枝獨秀的強盛，卻只是近五十年之事。這是因為美國自華盛頓以來，立國傳統上，對外奉行「孤立主義」，採取外交鎖國方針；期間，威爾遜的理想性格雖突破禁忌，參加了一次大戰，戰後卻敗興而歸；待一九三九年歐戰再度爆發，「孤立主義」的傳統束縛及一戰的慘痛經驗，美國非得走到歐洲與亞洲深陷納粹、日本鐵蹄，大敵當前時刻，才警覺中立政策與歐洲的綏靖，

才是姑息敵人輕啟戰端的禍首。羅斯福深深同情在希特勒飛機轟
炸下，邱吉爾「血、汗、淚」掙扎下的英國，終將不保，美國再
不挺身而出，中國亦難維持。一九四一年一月乃發表人類之四大
自由：言論、宗教、免於匱乏、免於恐懼的自由；是自「獨立宣
言」揭櫫天賦人權之生命、財產、自由之後，再進一步的延伸；
美國立誓為保護人類之四大自由，願意作所有愛好民主國家抵抗
極權之「兵工廠」，無條件的提供軍火支援。美國「四大自由」
的宣佈，實視同向軸心國發出了哀的美敦書。十一個月後，日本
偷襲美國夏威夷珍珠港，美國正式向軸心國宣戰。

歷史背景

超強之路。美國立國僅花上一百七十年，就輕易完成霸業，
扮演領導世界首強，但事實上美國自開國起，外交上就有「孤
立」與「干預」的兩股主張力量，相互制衡，積極走上國際舞台
是經過極大曲折過程，並不是那般順利。

孤立主義，自立國始，就是美國外交政策的最高指導原則，
華盛頓一七九七年之臨別演講中，殷切告誡美國人民：

「歐洲有一套基本利益法則——野心、競爭、利益、反覆無
常，如果我們捲入歐洲事務與他們的政治興衰串聯一起，或與他
們友好而結盟，或與他們敵對生衝突，都是不明智的，我們最好
的政策姿態就是保持中立。」

「遠離與歐洲舊大陸的糾纏」的教訓至一八二三年，發展成
「門羅主義」，美國敬告擊敗拿破崙而復辟的歐洲王權國家，尤
其是西班牙，休想恢復其舊勢力於西半球之美洲國家，而美國也
承諾決不介入歐洲的事務。就現實言，美國開國先賢這時採取接

近於「鎖國」的外交政策，無非是考量國家初立，羽翼未豐，專心修於內政，遠離國外是非，才是正道；加以得天獨厚的地緣保護下，果然二十紀初美國就擠身國際強林之內。

國際主義。二十紀初，美國國際主義興起，這主要歸因於：美國本土的西向開拓已經結束，尋找「新疆界」的呼聲四起，學者呼籲土地的不斷拓展是美國的「安全閥」，這種擴張的理論又結合了人種（ethnical）清高的優越感，美國人是「上帝挑選的子民」（God chosen people）有責任讓這個世界跟她一樣好，這是美國的「清楚使命（manifest destiny）」，這些理論使美國發動了美西戰爭，將西班牙徹底趕出了美洲，攫取了古巴、波多黎各及遠在她所宣稱「西半球」勢力範圍之外的菲律賓，美國準備好走入國際叢林的競爭。第二個助長美國國際主義的力量來自美國本身的工商發展，南北內戰後，美國高度工業化與歐洲帝國主義國家一樣有著需要海外市場及原料取得的迫切，美國對戰敗的西班牙索取菲律賓即著眼於遠東及中國市場的瓜分。

威爾遜夢碎。隨著美國的強富，走出孤立主義也是順理成章遲早的事，但卻一波三折。一次大戰終於在歐洲帝國主義國家間在殖民市場利益恩怨及軍備競賽中爆發。美國因德國潛艇在公海的威脅行為，終於違背了華盛頓的告誡，決與英法結盟，美國的物資與人員參戰是協約國戰勝的關鍵。但戰後國際新秩序的安排，卻看出美國與歐洲老大哥全然不同的國際觀，美國總統威爾遜以道德及理想構圖而提出之「十四點和平計畫」，與歐洲講究權力分贓、國家利益的現實主義，可說是完全格格不入，譬如：第一點之廢止秘密外交，旋即被這群歐洲政客訕笑外交豈能公開，到了與本身利益切身相關之戰後殖民地處置問題，威爾遜

竟然將這些原是戰前英法之勢力範圍，交由當地人民以「民族自決」原則處理，更叫英法大嘆所為何來？而最能代表威爾遜理想個性就是國際聯盟的成立，希望藉著這個「超國家」組織的協調合作，消弭人類的衝突及誤解，亦被歐洲現實主義視為高調。在這場新舊世界首度在國際舞台的交手中，美國極端感受到國父華盛頓對歐洲政治「野心、競爭、利益、反覆無常」的特質描述，加上大戰的盟邦借貸，戰後變成呆帳，僅芬蘭償完債務，在精神、財物兩失下，美國決心否決凡爾賽條約，重回孤立的道路。

歐洲姑息主義。一戰後，美國孤立主義復活也刺激了歐洲姑息主義的發展，兩大氣息交會，自然助長侵略者氣焰，一九三八年，一再退讓的英、法在慕尼黑協定出賣捷克，希望以「綏靖」換取希特勒和平的施捨；一九三九年，歐戰再度爆發，大洋彼岸的美國國會深恐外交的越界，一再通過堅守光榮孤立的「中立法案」，不准美國賣武器予交戰國；卻大賣石油、鋼鐵戰爭物資予侵略亞洲的日本，羅斯福雖傾向干預主義，卻也無可奈何，直到一九四一年眼見納粹德國席捲歐洲，法國亦自食惡果，淪陷敵手，歐洲僅存孤懸外海的英國苦撐待變，亞洲戰場，中國也是奄奄一息，美國終明白歐洲不安全，自身亦難安定，如四大洲淪入獨裁統治，美國亦難獨存，美國民心方才思變，決心重回她已經無法脫離的世界事務及領導的命運。

四大自由節錄

富蘭克林・羅斯福

　　〈四大自由〉一文，無異是一篇羅斯福給二次大戰軸心國家的最後通牒，告訴美國人民為何而戰，師出有名之檄文，宣示美國不可能再坐視德國在歐洲如入無人之境的侵略。立國至此一百七十年的孤立外交，從此走入歷史，美國正式踏上國際舞台，承擔領導的重任。

　　如同美國獨立宣言，用「生命、財產與追求快樂」之天賦人權，號召殖民地人民革命時一般；羅斯福為維護世界民主自由的不致陷入法西斯獨裁者之手而滅絕，提出人類基本人權的四大自由保障：「言論、宗教、經濟上，免於匱乏及政治上，免於恐懼的自由」，美國為保護四大自由，應勇敢與極權對立，揮別孤立主義。「四大自由」可說是「獨立宣言」生命、財產與追求快樂及「蓋茨堡演講詞」中「民有，民治，民享」之後，更完整對民主與人權的理想定義與闡揚文獻。

The Four Freedoms

Franklin D. Roosevelt

When the World War broke out in 1914, it seem to contain only small threat of danger to our own American future. But, as time went on, the American people began to visualize what the downfall of democratic nations might mean to our own democracy.

We need not over-emphasize imperfections in the Peace of Versailles. We should remember the Peace of 1919 was far less unjust the kind than the kind of "pacification" which began even before Munich, and which is being carried on under the new order of tyranny that seeks to spread over every continent today.

Every realist knows that the democratic life is at this moment being directly assailed in every part of the world….During sixteen months this assault has blotted out the whole pattern of democratic life in an appalling number of independent nations. The assailments are

一九一四年爆發第一次世界大戰,初起,它似乎對美國的前途只有微乎其微危險的威脅,但是隨時間的前進,美國人民卻目睹民主國家的一一傾覆,所可能對我們的民主所生的意義。

我們無需再強調凡爾賽條約的缺失。我們應記取的是早在慕尼黑協定前,盛行歐洲之「綏靖政策」遠比這一九一九年之和平協定更加不義;而此一姑息主義在新侵略者暴政的命令下,企圖向其他各大洲擴張。

所有務實者都知道此刻民主制度正在世界每一地區受到直接的攻擊。十六個月的時間,這項攻擊已摧毀驚人數量的獨立國家與她們的民主生活。這項侵害攻擊現仍進行於不論大小的其他國家。身

sill on the march threatening other nations, great and small. As your President, I find it necessary to report that the future and the safety of our country and of our democracy are overwhelmingly involved in events far beyond our borders.

Armed defense of democratic existence is now being gallantly waged in four continents. If that defense fails, all the population and all the resources of Europe, Asia, Africa and Australasia will be dominated by the conquers.

No realistic American can expect from a dictator's peace internationally generosity, or return of true independence, or world disarmament, or freedom of expression , or freedom of religion.. Such a peace would bring no security for us or for our neighbors.

I have recently pointed out how quickly the tempo of modern warfare could bring into our very midst the physical attack which we must expect if the dictator nations win the war.

為你們的總統，我認為有必要向你們報告我們國家自身安全及民主之前途與我們國界之外的這些事件有著全面密不可分之關係。

武力保衛民主的生存現正如火如荼的進行在四大洲。如果保衛行動失敗，歐、亞、非、大洋四大洲的人口、資源都將被侵略者所掌握。

只要是務實的美國人當毫不期望來自獨裁者所施捨之國際和平、真正的回復獨立、世界裁軍、言論自由、宗教自由。這樣的和平不可能為我們或我們的鄰邦帶來安全。

最近我已經指出現代戰爭的武力攻擊節奏是如何頃刻間即可兵臨我們的境內，我們不得不如此預料，如果獨裁者一旦贏得戰爭。

Our most useful and immediate role is to act as an arsenal for them as well as for ourselves. They do not need manpower. They do need billions of dollars worth of the weapons of defense. The time is near when they will not be able to pay for them all in ready cash. We cannot tell them that they must surrender, merely because of inability to pay for the weapons which we know they must have.

Let us say to the democracies : "We Americans are vitally concerned in your defense of freedom. We are putting forth our energies, our resources and our organizing powers to give you the strength to regain and maintain a free world. We shall send you in ever increasing numbers, ships, planes, tanks, guns. This is our purpose and pledge," In fulfillment of this purpose, we will not be intimidated by the threats of dictators.

In the future days, which we seek to make secure, we look forward to a world founded upon four essential human freedoms.

我們現在最有效與立即的角色就是扮演民主國家的兵工廠。他們不缺人力,他們需要的是價值數以十億美元計的防衛武器。如此緊急是因為他們現在已經沒有能力付出現款來購買這些武器。我們豈能要他們投降,只因為他們無力現金支付他們必須擁有的武器。

讓我們對愛好民主的國家說:我們重大關切你們對自由的捍衛。我們將獻出我們的資源、精力及組織性的力量,保障與維持一個自由的世界。我們將持續運送你們更多的船艦、飛機、坦克、槍炮。這是我們的目的與保證,為實踐此目標,我們絕不接受獨裁者之恐嚇。

The first is freedom of speech and expression-everywhere in the world.

The second is freedom of every person to worship God in his own way-everywhere in the world.

The third is freedom from want- secure to every nation a healthy peace time life for its inhabitants- everywhere in the world.

The fourth is freedom from fear- no nation will be in a position to commit an act physical aggression against any neighbor-anywhere in the world.

在我們所致力尋求之未來的日子，我們期待未來的世界是建築於以下四大基本自由。

第一大自由是在世界任何地區的人民都有意見與表達的自由。

第二大自由是在世界任何地區的人民都有按照他自己的方式，信仰宗教的自由。

第三大自由是在世界任何地區的人民都有免於匱乏的自由，每一國家都能為其居民保有健全和平的生活。

第四大自由是在世界任何地區的人民都有免於恐懼的自由，沒有國家對其鄰邦採取侵略行為。

第十一篇　長電報
～美國「圍堵」大戰略之催生

喬治・肯楠

▶▶▶ 最動人的佳句！**The most touching words**！

United States policy toward the Soviet Union must be that of long-term, patient but firm and vigilant containment of Russian expansive tendencies.

～George Kennan

面對蘇聯的擴張傾向，美國政策必須是長期、耐心卻堅定及警戒的加以圍堵。

～喬治・肯楠

前言

　　一九四五年四月，盟軍攻克柏林，希特勒以自殺結束歐洲戰事，八月，亞洲戰場也由美國在日本投下原子彈終結，眼看二次大戰結束，英、法、德國力耗竭，在倉皇辭廟下，他們戰前殖民勢力範圍所形成之權力真空，正被蘇聯一一赤化填補——東歐落入鐵幕，亞、非、中東與南歐都有共產勢力的橫行。美國對戰後的世局既無法自外，但面對全新洗牌後的國際新局、如何維護自由世界的完整與抗衡蘇聯這個有著滲透力十足的意識形態對手，卻顯得既徬徨且無助，這個缺乏戰略方向的困惑直到喬治肯楠於一九四六年向白宮領導人發出〈長電報〉一文，才算結束。

一九四七年，肯楠以X為筆名，將〈長電報〉取名〈蘇聯行為之根源〉，發表於《外交事務》季刊，方公諸於世。就肯楠的觀點，二次大戰後的局勢，是美國承接領導自由世界的歷史機會，而〈長電報〉一文被公認是在冷戰方興，分析蘇聯行為及反共主張中最精闢暨影響力的文章，未來四十餘年冷戰外交中，美國捍衛自由世界之大戰略──圍堵政策，從此孕育而生。

歷史背景

冷戰。美國退出結束一次大戰的凡爾賽和平協定之後，歐洲又走回強權政治的老路，英法戰勝國對戰敗德國無止盡的索賠，終於使希特勒之納粹黨在大選中利用民族主義號召，取得政權，重整軍備，發動二戰，美國只好匆匆結束「光榮孤立」，被迫再度參戰，至一九四五年結束戰爭。

二戰後的國際體系是空前獨特的，首先，二次大戰是被原子彈結束，原子彈的出現使戰爭不再是權利分配或回復和平最有效之手段，因為他它可能是以人類的毀滅性收場；其次，自一八一五年以來的國際政治所強調的國家基於生存利益下而不斷進行利益交換以維持權力平衡的多國或多邊外交，變成自由與共產意識形態誓不兩立，雙方的競爭是毫無妥協；因此，雖然國際體系是兩大集團針鋒相對，但在核子相互毀滅的後果下，卻呈現不能付諸熱戰，只能「冷戰」的僵持、吊詭型態。面對蘇聯這個陌生的對手及無限上綱的人類毀滅代價，一九四六年喬治肯楠的〈長電報〉一文，即為美國尋求冷戰因應之道而作，不但為美國找到領導世界的對症良藥，最後也成就了自由世界的勝出。

圍堵。肯楠以歷史的演進及親身在共產蘇聯的實地觀察，獨

到的解析俄國人「仇外」與「不安全感」的歷史本質，並有效結合共產主義的擴張使命，形容蘇聯之國家行為有如「**一條涓涓不息的河流，向其目的地穩定行進，直到填滿這個權力的盆地內每一個角落及縫隙，因此，美國必須以耐心、決心，設立一長期的政策加以圍堵。**」，圍堵政策從此成為自杜魯門迄雷根時代，美國應付冷戰時代（1945～1989）之最高外交指導原則。考慮到核子戰爭的毀滅性後果，圍堵既能展示美國反共擴張的嚇阻決心，但也有克制玉石俱焚的理性與耐性，當全球歷經韓戰、柏林圍牆、古巴飛彈危機、台海危機等瀕臨核子戰爭邊緣時，美、蘇都能在最後一刻勒馬懸崖，不致冒進，使人類免於毀滅之浩劫。圍堵政策以拖待變所造成的長期對峙，終於使共產世界因經濟的耗盡而無以為繼，應驗了肯楠最終所預計之「**大量增加蘇聯執行擴張政策的耗損代價，也只有以這樣方式，才可以促成蘇聯擴張行為招致崩潰的後果。**」，一九八九年象徵共產長城的柏林圍牆倒塌，東歐與蘇聯以和平的方式放棄共產主義，結束了這一段人類最極端生活制度選擇的瘋狂鬥爭。

文獻介紹

長電報節錄

喬治・肯楠

　　喬治肯楠是資深美國駐蘇聯外交官，俄語流利，通曉俄史的他，曾經長期觀察蘇聯內戰的發展影響，列寧革命成功後，他親睹了蘇聯集體化農場和共產恐怖統治。一九四四～四六年間，喬治肯楠任美國大使館館長並擔任駐蘇大使哈里曼顧問。有見二次大戰，原子彈在日本所展示的滅絕力，美、蘇陷入「相互保證毀滅」（Mutual Assured Destruction, MAD）的兩難，一九四六年，堅決反共的肯楠，針對蘇聯無止無盡的擴張行為，進行歷史與民族心理面的分析，終於發表了這篇決定美國日後四十餘年冷戰的大戰略──「圍堵」政策。

　　「圍堵」戰略避免了美蘇熱戰，創造日後的冷戰體系，使美蘇呈現長期的僵持對峙，所有的發展一如肯楠的預料，蘇聯終於因國力不支而崩潰，一九八九年，隨著象徵共產集團的柏林圍牆倒塌，早期被人們視為洪水猛獸之共產主義，不過半世紀，就被棄入歷史之灰燼。

Long Telegram

George Kennan

The political personality of Soviet power as we know it today is the product of ideology and circumstances. There can be few tasks of psychological analysis to trace the interaction of these two forces and the relative role of each in the determination of official conduct.

Stalin ,and those whom he led in the struggle.. were not the men to tolerate rival political forces in the sphere of power. Their sense of insecurity was too great. From the Russian-Asiatic world out of which they had emerged they carried with them a skepticism as to the possibility of permanent and peaceful coexistence of rival forces. They insisted on the submission or destruction of all competing power.

For ideology, as we have seen, taught them that the outside world was hostile and that it was their duty eventually to overthrow the political forces beyond their borders. In 1924 Stalin specifically defend the

今天就我們所知，蘇聯權力人格是意識及環境兩大力量下的產物。目前，研究決定這兩種行為力量彼此互動及角色的心理分析，實不多見。

史達林與其徒眾是決無法容忍其權力範圍內有任何政治反對者。他們有極大的不安全感。在他們所處的歐亞大陸上，他們根本懷疑能與鄰國有永遠和平共存的可能；他們堅持只有屈服或摧毀一切敵對競爭的勢力。

這種思想意識教育他們對外界必須維持敵意，他們最終的任務就是推翻一切國界外的反對勢力。一九二四年，史達林特別支持贊同「壓迫之來源」的理論，說明只要資本主義存在於世，就

retention of the "organs of suppression", meaning, "as long as there is a capitalistic encirclement there will be danger of intervention ….. Now the maintenance of this pattern of Soviet power , namely, the pursuit of unlimited authority domestically, accompanied by the cultivation of the semi-myth of implacable foreign hostility, has gone so far shape the actual machinery of Soviet power today. The "organs of suppression", in which the Soviet leaders had sought security from rival forces, became the masters of those whom they were designed to serve.

It must be inevitably assumed in Moscow that the aims of the capitalist world are antagonistic to the Soviet regime…..And from it flow many of the phenomena which we find disturbing in the Kremlin's conduct of foreign policy: the secretiveness, the lack of frankness, the wary duplicity, and the basic unfriendliness of purpose. There can be variations of degree and of emphasis. ….when that happens there will be always Americans leap forward with cheerful announcement that "the Russians changed." But we should not be misled by tactical maneuvers.

隨時存在侵犯的危險。現在蘇聯維持這一權力模式，對內，無止盡追求威權；對外，幾近神話似的仇外，構成了今天蘇聯權力的結構。「壓迫之來源」教育蘇聯領導人安全的來源是得自敵人的鬥爭，已經變成他們所服膺之金科玉律。

莫斯科不可避免地假設：資本主義世界就是要危害蘇聯政權。依照此觀點，流露出各種蘇聯外交行為現象：神秘、欺騙、模稜兩可與目的上敵意。但是他們也會採取各種不同程度的變通與優先強調，每當這種情況發生時，總有人會跳躍歡呼：蘇聯改變了！但我們決不能被他們戰術性的轉變所誤導。

Thus the Kremlin has no compunction about retreating in the face of superior barrier. Its political action is a fluid stream which moves constantly, wherever it is permitted to move, toward a given goal. Its main concern is to make sure that it has filled every nook and cranny available in the basin of world power. The main thing is that there always be pressure, unceasing constant pressure, toward the desired goal.

In these circumstances it is clear that the main element of any United States policy toward the Soviet Union must be that of long-term, patient but firm and vigilant containment of Russian expansive tendencies.

It would be an exaggeration to say that American behavior could bring about the early fall of Soviet power. But the United States has to increase enormously the strains under which Soviet policy must operate, to force upon the Kremlin a far greater degree of moderation and circumspection, and in this way promote tendencies which must eventually find their outlet in either the breakup or the gradual mellowing of Soviet power.

因此，當蘇聯在遇到巨大障礙，彈性採取撤退行動時，是毫不受立場良心譴責的。其政治行為有如一條涓涓不息的河流，盡其可行地向其目的地穩定行進，且不斷的給予目標壓力，直到確定填滿這個權力盆地內每一個角落及縫隙。

在此情形下，美國面對蘇聯擴張的傾向，必須有一套具備長期、耐心卻堅定及警戒元素的圍堵性政策。

如果說這樣的行動就可以很快迫使蘇聯垮台是誇張了些。但美國必須大量增加蘇聯執行擴張政策的耗損代價，強迫蘇聯行為採取更大幅度的溫和與慎重考慮，也只有以這樣方式，才可以促成蘇聯擴張行為不是招致崩潰的後果就是漸趨溫和成熟的可能。

第十二篇　麥帥國會告別文

～一位反共老兵的告白

道格拉斯・麥克阿瑟

▶▶ 最動人的佳句！**The most touching words**！

The old soldiers never die; they just fade away.

～Douglas MacArthur

老兵不死，只是逐漸凋零。

～道格拉斯・麥克阿瑟

前言

　　一九五○年，美、蘇冷戰方酣，六月二十五日，第一場熱戰終於在亞洲朝鮮半島爆發，原本是考驗美國貫徹「圍堵」政策決心，美、蘇對決的預期戲碼，然而隨著戰爭的進行，焦點卻意外搶戲至美國國內杜魯門總統與聯軍統帥麥克阿瑟將相失和插曲。

　　杜魯門與麥克阿瑟之間對「圍堵」政策的看法是有別的。杜魯門外交上是傾向「重歐輕亞」，亞洲仍非美國的優先利益，因此，他企求的是一場「有限戰爭」，堅決反對台灣軍力介入這場戰事，避免擴大戰事，只希望回復朝鮮半島的原狀。麥帥則以除惡務盡的態度，主張一場「全面戰爭」，出兵中國，他尤期待借重蔣介石領導下台灣五十萬精良大軍的參戰，徹底剷除亞洲共產勢力。麥帥的激進戰爭訴求，終於迫使杜魯門一九五一年四月

十一日，以三軍統帥的身份，將麥帥免職。麥帥雖失去了戰場，成了一孤獨的老兵，但其所展現的軍人忠誠與愛國風骨，卻贏得了美國人民對他的無比尊敬。

持平而論，杜、麥的爭議，純粹是政治家與軍事家本位思考的堅持。杜魯門著眼於民主陣營中堅之歐洲復興，才進行馬歇爾計畫不久，亞洲之日本實力也尚需時間恢復，韓國在地緣的次要性下，韓戰自需加以「冷」處理；麥帥則是以軍人「勝利是沒有代替品」的信念，加以軍事天才的自信，期望配合台灣軍隊一舉改變整個亞洲的政治地理，雖過於簡單、冒進，但他所提之太平洋安全的島鏈戰略，卻是日後美國所奉行不悖保衛亞洲的最高指導戰略，台灣也因此改變原先要被美國拋棄命運，成為麥帥口中之亞洲永不沉沒之航空母艦，重回民主陣營，再現生機。台北之麥帥公路即為感念麥帥對保衛台灣的貢獻而建，相較台北另條羅斯福（簽訂雅爾達密約出賣中國）公路，麥帥公路似更具懷念與意義！

歷史背景

韓戰。一九四九年十二月，國民政府敗退來台，一九五〇年一月中，美國務卿艾契遜就迫不及待的落井下石，在全國記者俱樂部發表「週邊戰略」，聲明「美國在亞洲防衛佈局，台灣與韓國不在美國西太平洋防線之內。」，等於向共產侵略勢力獻上台灣與南韓，北韓首領金日成果然在美國官方政策的誘導與毛澤東「禮讓」下，搶先出兵，六月二十五日，韓戰爆發。南韓在李承晚領導下，全國形同一盤散沙，政治爭鬥不斷，國力虛弱，二十八日，漢城淪陷，北韓軍隊勢如破竹，攻勢凌厲，不到兩個

月即佔領絕大部分南韓領土，李承晚政府被逼至南部釜山角落，奄奄一息。六月二十七日，杜魯門下令美軍參加朝鮮作戰，七月七日，美國透過聯合國安理會決議組織「聯軍」，參加朝鮮戰爭，命麥克阿瑟任聯軍統帥。在南韓軍隊潰不成軍，臨危受命，所能掌握的兵力有限，這位有「美國戰神」稱號者，帶兵作戰向以創新、冒險著稱，「出奇制勝」一向是麥帥拳拳服膺的戰術，麥帥制定了一項空前大膽的奇襲計劃，九月，美國海軍陸戰隊登陸南韓北部仁川港口，挺進漢城，攔腰砍斷入侵南韓的部隊，南北夾擊，全盤殲滅北韓軍，有人認為仁川登陸是有史以來最漂亮的兩棲作戰之一，也可能是軍事史上最後一次大規模登陸戰，媲美二戰盟軍登陸德國諾曼第。

　　仁川登陸迅速扭轉戰局，勝利的歡樂和過度的信心使麥帥失去了理智的判斷，他在漢城主持李承晚復行視事典禮時，決定衝破三十八度線向北進攻，直達中韓邊界的鴨綠江，要求杜魯門應允台灣軍隊參與戰事，於大陸東南沿海用兵牽制，首尾呼應。杜魯門無法制止他，只能告訴他：聯軍部隊不可使用於中韓邊界，僅能派南韓軍隊前往，至於國府蔣介石的部隊更不可能使用，予中共、蘇聯介入口實，導致第三次世界大戰。麥克阿瑟依然故我堅持己見，杜、麥失和上演，隔空放話，不時交火。一九五〇年十月十五日，杜魯門決絳尊親赴威克（Wake）島與麥克阿瑟相會，杜慎重否決麥帥一再提出之允諾國府軍隊參戰的提議，但同時杜、麥雙方卻一致預料中共不會參與韓戰，麥帥甚至發下豪語，即使失算，只要中共膽敢渡（鴨綠）江，美軍將寫下「世界軍史上的最大殺戮」。十一月二十四日時，麥克阿瑟發動「聖誕節攻勢」，還對美兵保證：大家可以回家過聖誕節。詎料，三天

之後，十一月二十七日，中共彭德懷率領三十萬「抗美援朝」志願軍，如潮水般地南下與美軍兵戎相見。中國抗美援朝的志願軍先頭部隊第四十軍於十月十九日晚上秘密跨過鴨綠江，十月二十五日，中國人民志願軍以夜戰和人海戰術痛擊進入北韓境內的聯軍，造成聯軍大撤退。聯軍在冰天雪地被包圍、被打死以及丟棄無數精良武器和裝備的鏡頭，成了麥帥和美軍最難堪、最屈辱的歷史畫面。

　　「將在外，君命有所不受」一向是麥帥剛愎自用的態度，過去羅斯福容忍他，杜魯門也一再向他讓步。但年已七十的麥帥堅持要把戰火帶至中國東北，建議調派台灣蔣介石部隊前往東北作戰，甚至要求動用原子彈轟炸東北；全面違背杜魯門縮小戰場、勿擾東北的命令，公開抨擊白宮和國防部。終於杜魯門毅然於一九五一年四月十一日，以「未能全力支持美國和聯合國的政策」為由撤了他的職，由李奇威接任，當麥克阿瑟知道這件事時，只悄悄的跟妻子說：「珍，我們終於可以回家了。」。儘管杜魯門顧全大局的政治家理性是符合局面的需要，但麥克阿瑟牛仔式黑白分明感性的訴求卻更貼切人心，麥克阿瑟回到美國後，在華盛頓受到了萬人空巷的英雄式歡迎，許多大城市都爆發了支持麥克阿瑟，反對杜魯門的遊行示威活動，杜魯門支持率下降到了26%，四個州的議會通過了決議，要求杜魯門總統收回成命。一九五一年四月十九日，麥克阿瑟在國會大廈發表了題為《老兵不死》的著名演講，流露出一位老兵言者諄諄的衷心告白，成就冷戰時代，最動人及振奮人心的一篇反共經典文獻。

　　台灣之命運，也因韓戰與麥帥而改變。從白皮書原先設下之「塵埃落定」，打算任國府自生自滅；韓戰使美國對台政策

丕變，轉而採行「台海中立化」，派遣第七艦隊進入台灣海峽，保衛台灣免於中共侵犯。麥克阿瑟在國會發表《老兵不死》全篇演說最高潮的一句，獲得全場如雷與最持久的掌聲，就在麥帥堅定呼籲「**無論如何，台灣絕對不可淪入共產黨統治。**」，麥帥指出保衛亞洲太平洋的島鏈戰略中，台灣是最重要的灘頭堡，台灣失守，菲律賓不保，東亞的日本、韓國亦將孤立。從此，美國修正「重歐輕亞」的方針，而調整至「兩洋並重」，開始重建亞洲戰略，進行集體安全的圍堵聯盟。韓戰加麥克阿瑟使亞洲生機再起，台灣在美蘇冷戰中也搖身一變為亞洲反共堅定島鏈的一環，才有一九五四年華府與台北「中美共同防禦條約」簽署，兩國再度回復二次大戰時軍事同盟之休戚與共；一掃自一九四九年以來美國對華「塵埃落定」的外交低潮狀態，而代以一個嶄新及密切的軍事同盟關係架構，開啟兩國緊密與友好的階段。

文獻介紹

麥帥國會告別文

道格拉斯·麥克阿瑟

　　第二次世界大戰中最著名的照片之一，就是麥克阿瑟男性十足的打扮──嘴叼玉米芯煙斗，身著咔嘰布軍服，頭戴一頂戰鬥軟帽，眼戴乙副黑色AO墨鏡，重返菲律賓時，灘頭涉水的帥氣前行。麥帥是一個非凡的軍事天才，思維敏捷、膽略過人、統兵有方、意志堅強，常在逆境中創造順境，並能運用其對語言與文字的掌握，適時發出振奮士氣的豪語，巴丹島之役，撤離菲島後，自澳洲向菲律賓人民廣播：I Shall Return（我必重返。）本文中之In war there is no substitute for victory.（戰爭中勝利是沒有代品。）The old soldiers never die; they just fade away.（老兵不死，只是逐漸凋零。），都已成為動容感人的膾炙佳言，而這篇國會告別文，堪稱是美國軍人中，極少數既富戰略思維亦兼具文采內涵之全能佳作。

Farewell Address to Congress

Douglas MacArthur

Mr. President, Mr. Speaker, and Distinguished Members of the Congress:

I stand on this rostrum with a sense of deep humility and great pride -- humility in the wake of those great American architects of our history who have stood here before me; pride in the reflection that this forum of legislative debate represents human liberty. I do not stand here as advocate for any partisan cause, ... solely expressing the considered viewpoint of a fellow American.

I address you with neither rancor nor bitterness in the fading twilight of life, with but one purpose in mind: to serve my country. While Asia is commonly referred to as the Gateway to Europe, it is no less true that Europe is the Gateway to Asia, and the broad influence of the one cannot fail to have its impact upon the other. There are

主席、議長與敬愛的國會議員們：

懷抱著深沉的謙卑與偉大的驕傲，我站上國會的講壇——謙卑是面對著美國歷史上偉大的建國之父，我也能跟隨他們的腳步至此，驕傲的是國會論壇的辯論代表著人類自由的省思。我並不是以任何黨派運動的擁護者而來，不過是想表達一位美國百姓的思考觀點。

在我生命已近垂暮之年，我不懷怨恨亦無苦水向你們訴說，我心中惟一目的無非——報效國家。當亞洲常被喻為是歐洲大門之時，更真實的是歐洲也是亞洲的大門；兩洲彼此予對方都有廣大的影響與衝擊力量。某些人聲稱我們的力量不足保衛兩大洋防線，所以不可分散我們的努力。對此言論，我實在想不到有比失

those who claim our strength is inadequate to protect on both fronts, that we cannot divide our effort. I can think of no greater expression of defeatism. ……You can not appease or otherwise surrender to communism in Asia without simultaneously undermining our efforts to halt its advance in Europe.

The Pacific was a potential area of advance for any predatory force intent upon striking at the bordering land areas. Our strategic frontier then shifted to embrace the entire Pacific Ocean…… Indeed, it acts as a protective shield for all of the Americas and all free lands of the Pacific Ocean area. We control it to the shores of Asia by a chain of islands extending in an arc from the Aleutians to the Mariannas held by us and our free allies. From this island chain we can dominate with sea and air power every Asiatic port from Vladivostok to Singapore and prevent any hostile movement into the Pacific.

Under such conditions, the Pacific no longer represents menacing avenues of approach for a prospective invader. It assumes, instead, the

敗主義更貼切形容的字眼了。你不可能在亞洲向共產主義姑息或投降之同時，卻能無損我們在歐洲阻擋共產侵犯的努力。

對企圖攻擊大洋周邊地區的侵略勢力，太平洋長期就是他們潛在進犯區域。因此我們將戰略前緣擴大至擁抱整個太平洋，為美國與太平洋地區的自由國家形成了一個保護盾牌。由我們與自由盟邦所掌握並沿著大洋的亞洲海岸線所建立的弧形島鏈──自阿留申群島延伸以至馬里亞納群島，從此一島鏈，自海參威以至新加坡，我們以海、空武力主宰著每一亞洲海岸線的港口，並嚇阻任何敵意勢力進犯亞洲。

在這樣的情況下，太平洋不再代表未來侵略者前進威脅的暢通

friendly aspect of a peaceful lake. The holding of this littoral defense line in the western Pacific is entirely dependent upon holding all segments thereof; for any major breach of that line by an unfriendly power would render vulnerable to determined attack every other major segment.

For that reason, I have strongly recommended in the past, as a matter of military urgency, that under no circumstances must Formosa fall under Communist control. Such an eventuality would at once threaten the freedom of the Philippines and the loss of Japan and might well force our western frontier back to the coast of California, Oregon and Washington.

I have from the beginning believed that the Chinese Communists' support of the North Koreans was the dominant one. Their interests are, at present, parallel with those of the Soviet. But I believe that the aggressiveness recently displayed not only in Korea but also in Indo-China and Tibet and pointing potentially toward the South reflects predominantly the same lust for the expansion of power.

大路。相反的是，她將成為友善的和平湖水，有效控制這條西太平洋的防衛沿線，需完全依賴所有部分的掌控；因為任何防線上重要據點被敵對勢力切斷，都將使其他據點面對決定性攻擊時變得脆弱。

為此，我過去即以軍務上的緊迫，強烈建議無論如何台灣絕對不可淪陷共產黨統治。這樣的結局後果必將立即性威脅到菲律賓的自由與日本的失守，甚至使我們西太平洋的防衛線退防至加州、奧勒岡州與華盛頓州的海岸線。

我自始堅信中國共產黨就是北韓侵略者的幕後操控者，他們目前與蘇聯也是利益同路人。我確信最近以來，侵略勢力不只出現在北韓，他們在中南半島、西藏甚至潛在性的向南推進，支配

On Formosa, the government of the Republic of China has had the opportunity to refute by action much of the malicious gossip which so undermined the strength of its leadership on the Chinese mainland. The Formosan people are receiving a just and enlightened administration with majority representation on the organs of government, and politically, economically, and socially they appear to be advancing along sound and constructive lines.

With this brief insight into the surrounding areas, I now turn to the Korean conflict. ….Apart from the military need, as I saw It, to neutralize the sanctuary protection given the enemy north of the Yalu, I felt that military necessity in the conduct of the war made necessary: removal of restrictions on the forces of the Republic of China on Formosa, with logistical support to contribute to their effective operations against the common enemy.

性顯露了擴張貪婪的力量。

有關台灣，中華民國政府已用行動反駁導致他們失去大陸的許多惡意醜化。台灣人民目前正接受一個公正、開明並具多數代表的政府治理。政治上，經濟上與社會上，他們似乎都是朝向健全與建設性的路線邁進。

經由簡要的透視週邊的地帶後，我現在將轉入韓戰的衝突……，除了軍事上需要外，如我所見，要徹底阻斷北鴨綠江地區（中國所屬地區）提供北韓敵人庇護所，我以為在進行這場戰爭中，一項軍事的必要決定：就是去除一切對中華民國台灣的軍事限制，並提供他們針對共同敵人，一切有效軍事行動的後勤援助。

Efforts have been made to distort my position. It has been said, in effect, that I was a warmonger. I know war as few other men now living know it, ….But once war is forced upon us, there is no other alternative than to apply every available means to bring it to a swift end.

War's very object is victory, not prolonged indecision.

In war there is no substitute for victory.

There are some who, for varying reasons, would appease Red China. They are blind to history's clear lesson, for history teaches with unmistakable emphasis that appeasement but begets new and bloodier war. Like blackmail, it lays the basis for new and successively greater demands until, as in blackmail, violence becomes the only other alternative.

The tragedy of Korea is further heightened by the fact that its military action is confined to its territorial limits…. Of the nations of the world, Korea alone, up to now, is the sole one which has risked its

一些人不斷努力扭曲我的立場，並將我談論成是戰爭販子。我對戰爭的清楚一如現在僅存少數人一樣的了解。但是戰爭一旦逼迫降臨，除運用一切可得手段將其迅速殲滅，也沒有其他選擇。

戰爭的非常目的就是勝利，不是拖延的猶豫不決。

在戰爭中，勝利是沒有代替品。

也有一些人以不同理由欲姑息共產中國。他們無視盲目於歷史明白的教訓，歷史已準確的教導：姑息只會帶來更加血腥與新的戰爭。如同勒索，姑息討好只會為更多接二連三新的勒索埋下基礎，直到有天，暴力變成唯一的選擇。

韓國悲劇的增加，是因為它的軍事行動被局限在韓國領土上。

all against communism. ... They have chosen to risk death rather than slavery. Their last words to me were: "Don't scuttle the Pacific!"

I am closing my 52 years of military service. When I joined the Army, even before the turn of the century, it was the fulfillment of all of my boyish hopes and dreams. The world has turned over many times since I took the oath on the plain at West Point, and the hopes and dreams have long since vanished, but I still remember the refrain of one of the most popular barrack ballads of that day which proclaimed most proudly that " old soldiers never die; they just fade away."

And like the old soldier of that ballad, I now close my military career and just fade away, an old soldier who tried to do his duty as God gave him the light to see that duty.

Good Bye.

目前為止世界上，韓國是惟一冒死賭上所有一切對抗共產之國家。他們寧死也不願被奴役。他們最後給我的話是：「別搞沉了太平洋！」

我即將結束我五十二年的軍旅生涯。在本世紀前，當我加入陸軍時，它是我兒時一切希望與夢想的實現。自我在西點宣誓入伍，世界已幾經翻覆，而那些希望與夢想也消磨殆盡，但我仍記著當日最流行的一首軍歌中重複詞句，充滿自豪地宣示「老兵不死，只是逐漸凋零」。

有如軍歌中的那名老兵，我將就此結束我的軍旅生涯與凋零，一位努力盡職，受上帝賜予光明見識到他責任的老兵。

再會。

第十三篇　總統就職演講詞

～開創求新、變革的六〇年代

約翰‧甘迺迪

▶ 最動人的佳句！**The most touching words**！

Ask not what your country can do for you, ask what you can do for your country.

～John F. Kennedy

別問國家能為你作什麼，而是你能為國家作什麼。

～約翰‧甘迺迪

前言

　　經過五〇年代沉悶、緊繃的杜魯門與艾森豪兩任總統領導，一九六〇年，美國內政、外交進入了最複雜及挑戰的時刻，美國人民卻不苟俗於世，突破年齡與宗教禁忌，大膽接受以「求新、求變」為號召的約翰甘迺迪帶領他們走進驚濤駭浪的六〇年代，也的確在短短不到三年任期中，內、外世局是驚心動魄，國內，越戰、民權與青年反文化運動的風起雲湧，自由主義者認為是思想與民智的解放，保守者則以為是傳統與秩序的崩解；對外，美蘇對峙已臻最白熱化時刻，豬灣事件、柏林圍牆、「驚爆十三天」的古巴飛彈危機接踵而來，頻頻逼進核戰邊緣，但這位初生之犢的美國年輕總統屢屢以其過人的膽識、自信及冷靜，帶領世

局及美國避開全球核子毀滅災難，希望以新思維、反省與理性的
精神，來化解人類的各式紛爭。

甘迺迪這位英年早逝的美國第三十四任總統，在美國人心
目中一直有著不可割捨的迷戀。集年輕、英俊外表及一流口才的
優厚條件，是甘迺迪家族神話創造的不斷來源，甘迺迪也是美國
歷屆總統中最富「話題魅力」者，及至最後以被刺結束多彩的一
生，真相至今仍眾說紛紜，也許這種隕歿方式，只會讓後人對他
有著更無止無盡的懷念吧！

歷史背景

反共與恐共的五○年代。整個五○年代，共產與自由陣營不
斷的叫陣，杜魯門除繼續「圍堵」共產蘇聯有如「穩定流水」與
無孔不入般的赤化外，繼任的艾森豪更加碼到「核子報復」，短
短十年的明爭暗鬥，美國歷經了韓戰、柏林危機、蘇伊士運河危
機、匈牙利革命、兩次台海危機，中南半島戰事，國際世局每一
刻都籠罩在一觸即發的核子大戰中。此時美國，國外在反共，同
時，國內在恐共；「麥卡錫主義」從國務院、大學校園到好萊塢
到處橫行，只要一旦冠上共產黨或同路人的大帽子，只能「莫須
有」俯首認罪。滿佈緊繃與隨時絕望、乏味的五○年代，經過剛
毅卻沉悶的杜魯門與溫和卻老病纏身的艾森豪兩任總統，美國人
民對六○年代的到來，自然有著希望不一樣的領導盼望，清新、
活力的甘迺迪正是時代舞台的期待。

新典範的總統。甘迺迪的迷人旋風為現代美國總統塑造了一
系列的新典範。甘迺迪集所有一切符合新時代下的期待條件：年
青、活力，配合動人的風采、口才，加上時尚的「飛機頭」髮型

與魅力不相上下的妻子賈桂林，成為國家象徵的總統甘迺迪，使政治不再是一群頑固老人總把國家弄得幕氣沈沈、緊張兮兮。

除「天命」的條件外，一九六〇年，電子媒體首度介入美國大選，也是外型、口才取勝的甘迺迪勝選加分因素，在首辦的大選電視辯論會（TV Debate）上，尼克森蒼白的面容與穿著和神采自若的甘迺迪呈現的強烈對比，經由電視畫面播送至美國家庭；加上甘迺迪在二次大戰，海軍服役時，被日軍擊沈炮艇後，英勇救出同袍的事蹟不斷塑以「勇者畫像」（Profiles in Courage）之英雄形象傳播，這使原先他負面的條件如年紀太輕及天主教徒的禁忌，更不足道取，鼓舞選民勇於突破。

甘迺迪也清楚美國人民祈求一個不同既往的年代，事實上，美國也的確需要一個嶄新的態度來面對極富刺激與不安的六〇年代，內政上有黑人民權運動、教育及貧窮問題；對外，美蘇無止境的武力競賽與地區衝突，讓世界隨時瀕臨大戰邊緣，在國內保守勢大氛圍下，甘迺迪首度正式向共產陣營伸出和解的雙手，也對黑人民權的爭取寄予同情，新思維（New Idea）、新領導（New Leadership）、改變（Change）、新疆界（New Frontier），也是自甘迺迪開始，成為日後美國大選候選人包括一九八四年民主黨的哈特、九二年柯林頓到現在的歐巴馬最愛效尤，也是最具動人效果的競選口號，因為它們幾乎立刻使選民感情連線到對甘迺迪的懷念，也為美國日後政黨政策的競爭，設定在保守與自由的觀點選擇，讓美國決策得反省思索、兼容並蓄，以中道治國。

甘迺迪也是自林肯以後，對文字運用最具敏銳與感性的美國總統，在每一次的危機中，總以四兩撥千斤，留下一語中的，讓人回味雋永、膾炙人口的佳句，取得人民諒解。甫就任，初試啼

聲,企圖推翻古巴的「豬灣事件」,結果是灰頭土臉,能力受到普遍質疑時,道出:「**成功時你會有一百個父親,失敗時你只能當孤兒。**」,贏得人民同情。由於初出毛蘆,被蘇聯領導人赫魯雪夫徹底看扁,一九六一年八月,逕自建起圍牆,隔離柏林人民分成自由與共產兩個世界時,甘迺迪親赴柏林,對柏林人民道出「**我也是柏林人。**」,表達同舟與共情感,也巧妙轉移了國內要求衝倒圍牆的壓力,免於美蘇交手衝突。隔年十月,食髓知味的赫魯雪夫更挑釁的將飛彈部署在離美國本土近在咫尺的古巴,是人類與核子毀滅惡夢最接近的時刻,在「驚爆十三天中」,甘迺迪與赫魯雪夫「**眼球對眼球,赫先眨眼**」,以極具耐心及不惜一戰的堅定態度迫使赫魯雪夫退縮,甚至因此下台,甘迺迪一掃以往青澀模樣,聲望達到巔峰。至於其他更膾炙人口的佳句莫過本篇出現之「**我們不懼怕談判;但決不在恐懼下談判。**」與「**別問國家能為你作什麼,而是你能為國家作什麼。**」

被咀咒的家族。賦予亞瑟王之「卡美羅特王朝」美譽,甘迺迪家族成為美國重要政治世家,全來自大家長約瑟夫甘迺迪的一手規劃安排,早期以私酒交易致富,二次大戰,任駐英大使,其教育子女方式就是一旦立定志向後,就要作到最好,永不屈服。所育四子,皆以總統為志,卻多數天不假年,長子駕機作戰失蹤,二子即約翰甘迺迪在一九六三年十一月被刺於達拉斯,一九六八年,三子羅伯甘迺迪亦刺於加州,約翰甘迺迪之子小約翰也難逃這一家族的命運詛咒,一九九九年,駕機墜海失事,有人謂是老約瑟作事不擇手段的天懲,但不論如何六〇年代,因為有甘迺迪,不只是給予了世人有如巨星般的吸引和魅力,也讓人在令人窒息,驚心動魄的世局中,感覺到活力、創意與希望的未來。

文獻介紹

總統就職演講詞　節錄

約翰·甘迺迪

　　一九六一年在野民主黨候選人甘迺迪，以歷史上最接近，僅0.5%總票數的差距，險勝了共和黨現任副總統尼克森，也許是這一「委任」（mandate）的不足，雖然大呼「求新、求變」自由主義的甘迺迪在就職演講詞中，仍維持「保守」的基調──盼望和平，但堅持這只有在強大武力保證上才有可能；雖然不懼怕談判，但決不在恐懼下談判，也敬告蘇聯謙卑不是懦弱，誠信需要證明──處處軟中帶硬，甘迺迪的新世界還是謹慎與有條件的。

　　甘迺迪大加羅列了「威爾遜道德式」的理想標的──追求世界和平、自由、民主，然亦坦言不可能「馬上好」，但卻可以自此開始希望、願景，進而道出最激發人民使命與責任感之「別問國家能為你作什麼，而是你能為國家作什麼」名言。最動人莫過民粹，永遠使人民感動陶醉，這是絕對永恆的政治語言法則。

Inaugural Address, 1961

John F. Kennedy

We observe today not a victory of party but a celebration of freedom- symbolizing an end as well as a beginning-signifying renewal as well as change.

The world is very different now. For man holds in his mortal hands the power to abolish all forms of human poverty and all forms of human life. And yet the same revolutionary beliefs for which our forefathers fought are still at issue around the globe-the belief that the rights of man come not from the generosity of the state but from the hand of God.

We dare not forget today that we are the heirs of that first revolution. Let the word go forth from this time and place, to friend and foe alike, that the torch has been passed to a new generation of Americans....

　　我們今天所看到的是自由的慶祝，而不是一黨的勝利；它象徵著結束，也是開始；意謂著重新，也是改變。

　　當今的世界已大為不同。因為人類手上所擁有的致命性力量已經既能去除所有形式的貧窮，也可以毀滅人類生命。雖然如此，我們祖先奮鬥而來的信仰——人類的權利非來自國家機器的施捨，而是上帝的授予——卻仍在世界各地爭議。

　　今天，我們自然不敢忘記我們是第一次人類權利革命的傳人。也讓我們在此時此地，向我們的朋友或敵人發出聲明：革命的火炬已經傳承到新一代的美國人之手了……

To those old allies whose cultural and spiritual origins we share, we pledge the loyalty of faithful friends....

To those new states whom we welcome to the ranks of the free, we pledge our word that one form of colonial control shall not have passed away merely to be replaced by a far more iron tyranny.

To those people in the huts and villages of half the globe struggling to break the bonds of mass misery, we pledge out best effort to help them help themselves.

Finally, to those nations who would make themselves our adversary, we offer not a pledge but a request: that both side begin anew the quest for peace ....

We dare not tempt them with weakness. For only when our arms are sufficient beyond doubt can we be certain beyond doubt that they will never be employed.... So let us begin anew-remembering on both sides that civility is not a sign of weakness and sincerity is always

對與我們有共同信仰與精神源流的盟友，我們向你承諾朋友的忠實……。

對那些願意加入自由陣營的新興國家，我們向你承諾舊日的殖民統治將永遠消失，而不是轉換另一種鐵腕的暴政方式。

對那些仍輾轉於茅草、陋舍，掙扎脫離生活悲慘壓迫的另一半世人，我們向你承諾會盡最大的努力扶持你們自立。

最後，對那些堅持與我們相左對抗的國家，我們不會向你承諾而是要求讓我們重新開始尋求和平……。

我們自不示以軟弱，誘其合作。我們也當然要追求武力的強大，因為力量到毫無疑問時，才能保證他們永遠不會被使用。所

subject to proof. Let us never negotiate out of fear. But let us never feat to negotiate.

Let both sides explore what problems unite us instead of …divide us.

Let both sides, for the first time, formulate serious and precise proposals for the inspection and control of arms.

Let both sides seek to invoke the wonders of science instead of its terror.

All this will not be finished in the first one hundred days. Nor will it be finished in the first one thousand days, nor in the life of this Administration, nor even perhaps in our lifetime on this planet. But let us begin.

In the long history of the world, only a few generations have been granted the role of defending freedom in its hour of maximum of danger. I do not shrink from this responsibility- I welcome it.

以讓我們重新開始,謹記謙卑不是懦弱,誠信需要證明。我們不懼怕談判;但決不在恐懼下談判。

讓我們去探索甚麼是團結我們的問題而非分裂雙方。

讓我們開始制訂認真與確實監督及限制我們武力發展的計畫。

讓我們尋求祈望科學的神奇奧妙而不是駭人恐怖的部分。

凡此一切當然不會在一百天完成,也不會在一千日結束,終其我政府任內,甚至在我們有生之年都無法達成,但是可由我們開始做起。

在漫長的歷史中,少有世代何其有幸能在時代最危險關鍵的這一刻被賦予扮演保衛自由的角色。我決不畏縮此重責大任,甚

And so, my fellow Americans : ask not what your country can do for you, ask what you can do for your country….My fellow citizens of the world: ask not what America will do for you, but what together we can do for the freedom of man.

至樂於接受。

　　因此，我親愛的同胞，別問國家能為你作什麼，而是你能為國家作什麼。對世界的公民同胞，別問美國能為你作什麼，而是我們能共同為全人類的自由作什麼。

第十四篇 我有一個夢

～黑人的美國夢

馬丁‧路德‧金恩

▶▶▶ 最動人的佳句！**The most touching words**！

In spite of the difficulties and frustrations of the moment I still have a dream. It is a dream deeply rooted in American dream.

~ Martin Luther King

儘管在困難與挫折的時刻，我永遠有著一個夢，這個夢深根於我們的美國夢。

～馬丁‧路德‧金恩

前言

在二十世紀的六〇年代，美國人逐漸認識到，南北內戰所致力的解放黑奴運動，並沒有讓美國黑人成為正常公民的理想，他們仍處在美國平等承諾與社會正義忽略的角落。在日常生活中美國黑人常被各州的歧視立法（Jim Crow）隔離，甚至遭三K黨的私刑。黑人無法與白人上同間學校，乘坐同一公車，同一餐廳共食，同一社區為鄰，投票、工作權利被剝奪，黑人仍不能平等參與美國社會生活。如何剷除種族歧視的隔離政策，爭取平等的民權，成為黑人必須再度承受的苦難，不同是，這次是黑人必須自己挺身而出。

從一八六三年，由內戰獲取自由再到真正平等之路，黑人又承受了一百年的磨難，彷彿聖經出埃及記中被上帝懲罰信仰不堅之以色列人，必須再流浪沙漠四十年之後，方得重返迦南一般；直到一九六三年八月二十八日，由黑人牧師馬丁路德金恩在華盛頓林肯紀念堂一場激勵人心的演講——「我有一個夢」（I have a Dream），帶領美國六〇年代的黑人民權運動走到最高潮，他義正嚴詞，充滿「林肯與甘地的精神和聖經的韻律」，公開「非暴力」（Non-Violence）的運動路線，以集體靜坐的方式癱瘓了南方所有隔離公共設施，終於為黑人的自由平等去除法律的歧視，也為他贏得一九六四年諾貝爾和平獎，一九六八年與林肯同，在曼菲斯遇刺身亡。

歷史背景

換湯不換藥的南方。一八六三年美國通過憲法第十三條修正案，廢止奴隸制度，黑人終於解放成為自由人；一八六四年內戰結束，北方為報復南方的叛亂，以「重建」的名義，將南方置於軍事管理下直至一八七七年，一旦軍管結束，南方拿回政權後，各州轉而進行黑人的隔離立法，將所有公共設施包括學校、社區、、教堂、交通工具、餐廳、電影院、圖書館、沙灘、公園、廁所到飲水檯都黑白分開使用，公權上，也以識字測驗或人頭稅剝奪黑人投票與服公職權利；對黑人日常生活行動，地方政府放任由白人種族主義者所組成之三K黨，任意對黑人施加私刑虐殺。更糟的是南方各州的黑人歧視立法，竟被最高法院全部合法化，一八九六年在「普萊西控告佛格遜」案，判下「隔離只要平等」（Separate but Equal）原則，就是只要公共設施的設備條件

一樣，黑白隔離就沒有歧視差別；至於以識字測驗阻止黑人參政權，一八九八年在「威廉斯控告密西西比州」案，高院也認同合法，南方黑人差不多又回到戰前處境，雖脫離了奴隸卻有如二等公民，導致黑人追求完整的民權，得再奮鬥一百年才能完成。

自小岩城開始鬆動的種族巨石。在南方州政府立法運作與最高法院的合理化下，美國黑人民權運動直到二次大戰後才開始逐漸發難，一來美國是以反法西斯主義參戰，反對德國以種族優越藉口，滅絕猶太人；加上黑人在大戰的英勇貢獻，美國民心自然會反省檢討南方對黑人的私刑及歧視之不義，戰後，退伍黑人大兵開始上大學，黑人大量進入都市工作居住，而黑人教會亦興起，有著如簧之舌的黑人牧師，用心靈的感動，凝固黑人力量，這也是日後美國黑人政治工作者多來自牧師。組織上，有識黑人之士成立之「全國有色人種促進協會」（NCCAP），不斷派員「以身試法」，計畫自最高法院下手，希望最高法院以違憲判例瓦解南方的歧視黑人立法。一九五四年，高院「布朗案」終於推翻一八九六年在「普萊西」案之「隔離只要平等」原則，認為黑白分校剝奪黑白小孩相互學習及人格發展的機會。對高院的判決，憤怒的南方卻以「南方宣言」發動大規模抵制，一九五七年，聯邦為貫徹司法，展現執法的決心，在阿肯色州的小岩城，以聯邦軍隊護送黑人學生進入學校，開始鬆動了堅如磐石的南方隔離政策，開始亂石崩雲的民權高峰。

小岩城事件不只鬆動了南方種族隔離的根本，可貴是也讓黑人認識到：儘管有高院、聯邦軍隊的介入幫助，但推倒南方固執人心的城牆，黑人最終還是必須親身投入，承受犧牲，贏得尊重，才能永久享有平等權利的果實。黑人民權運動的鳴槍，其

實在「布朗案」後一年，一九五五年，阿拉巴馬州一名黑人婦女蘿莎・帕克斯（據信也是NCCAP人士）在公車上，大膽回應要她往後坐的白人說：「不」，揭開序幕。小岩城事件後如火如荼，但最重要的還是黑人牧師馬丁路德金恩，所採用的「非暴力與不合作」策略下，黑人以「靜坐」方式，抗議於所有實施隔離的公共場所，成功的癱瘓了南方城市的生活機能；南方警察以水柱噴灑、警棍毆打、狼狗驅趕「靜坐」黑人的畫面，經由電視傳播至全美家庭，益激起全美人民對隔離政策的義憤，與手無寸鐵黑人的同情，一九六三年八月二十八日，由黑人牧師馬丁路德金恩所領導二十五萬人大遊行，齊聚頗具象徵性的林肯紀念堂，一場激勵人心的演講——「我有一個夢」，將民權運動達到巔峰。一九六四年六月，美國國會終於通過「民權法案」規定：任何選舉、教育及公共場合的歧視措施皆非法，聯邦政府得凍結該州補助款以懲處，同年，金恩博士也因此榮獲諾貝爾和平獎。美國黑人公民權之爭取終於勝利。

　　無奈命運捉弄人，美國人似乎有殺害能激勵民心領導人物之傳統，與林肯一樣，一九六八年，金恩博士繼甘迺迪總統，在曼菲斯旅館遇刺身殉。感慨六〇年代，這群有著最動人口才與時代前衛思想人物，捲起千堆雪後，一一遇刺殞落，直讓人有「廣陵散從此絕矣！」之嘆。

我有一個夢

馬丁・路德・金恩

　　美國黑人追求自由的歷程，第一階段的解奴抗爭自一六一九年至一八六三年，以最沉痛的內戰方式結束了非人的奴隸生活；第二階段的民權運動，則自一八六三年至一九六四年，通過民權法案止，達一百年。而其中成功的關鍵就是來自金恩博士的領導，他不只有著令人如癡如醉的話語，其所設定的抗爭手段「非暴力」運動，不但將社會動盪的成本降到最低，更以喚醒社會道德良知而非流血衝突的方式，促使美國人民反省認識到種族主義的謬誤。

　　金恩博士在「我有一個夢」中，將民權運動比擬成不過是兌現一張美國先賢自立國當時，就開出人生而平等的支票，但也警告一九六三年不是結束，而是開始，黑人不得公民權利，美國永無寧日。全文節奏明快，有如史詩般的激情，尤其念到不斷重覆「我有一個夢」的動人期望時，其中「我有一個夢，希望有一天，昔日奴隸與奴隸主的後代能同桌共坐，情同手足。」，這般卑微卻又高亢之作，輕易穿透所有人心，黑人也有能擁抱美國夢的權利及希望。

I have a Dream

Martin Luther King

Five score years ago, a great American, in whose symbolic shadow we stand, signed the Emancipation Proclamation. This momentous decree came as a great beacon light of hope to millions of Negro slaves who had been seared in the flames of withering injustice.

But one hundred years later, we must face the tragic fact that the Negro is still not free. One hundred years later, the life of the Negro is still sadly crippled by the manacles of segregation and the chains of discrimination. One hundred later, the Negro lives on the lonely island of poverty…. One hundred later, the Negro is still languished in the corners of American society….

In a sense we have come to our nation's Capital to cash a check. The Constitution and the Declaration of Independence were signing

一百年前，一位偉大的美國人簽署解奴宣言。這份時代性的文告有如燈塔照亮了正煎熬於不義火燄下數以百萬黑奴的希望。

但一百年後，我們必須面對黑人仍然沒有自由的悲劇事實。一百年後，黑人仍受隔離的束縛與歧視的生活鎖鏈而匍匐於地。一百年後，黑人仍孤獨地活在貧窮之島。一百年後黑人仍然在美國的角落腐蝕衰敗。

某種意義而言，我們今天來到首都不過是為了兌現一張支票。這是一張由憲法與獨立宣言承諾的支票。它承諾了人擁有與生俱來，不可剝奪的生命、財產與追求快樂的權利。

a promissory note. This note was a promise that all men would be guaranteed the unalienable rights of life, liberty, and the pursuit of happiness.

It is obvious that America today has defaulted on this promissory note….,America has given the Negro people a bad check…So we have come to cash this check-a check that will give us upon demand the riches of freedom and the security of justice.

It would be fatal for the nation to overlook the urgency of the moment and to underestimate the determination of the Negro. Nineteen sixty-three is not an end, but a beginning. There will be neither rest nor tranquility in America until the Negro is granted his citizenship rights.

And as we walk.., we cannot turn back. There are those who are asking the devotees of civil rights, "When will you be satisfied?"

We can nerve be satisfied as long as the Negro is the victim of the unspeakable horror of police brutality.

很顯然地，今天美國沒有兌現這張承諾支票。美國給了黑人一張空頭支票。所以我們是來兌現這張支票——承諾會給我們自由與司法安全的支票。

任何忽略這緊急的時刻與低估黑人的決心，必會貽害國家。一九六三年不是結束，而是開始。黑人不得公民權利，美國永無寧日。

我們既然踏出腳步，我們就不能再回頭。有人會問：什麼時候我們才會滿意？

我們不會滿意，只要黑人還要承受無以言喻的警察暴力。

We can nerve be satisfied as long as the Negro's basic mobility is from a smaller ghetto to larger one.

We can nerve be satisfied as long as a Negro in Mississippi cannot vote and a Negro in New York believes he has nothing for which to vote.

No, no, we are not satisfied, and we will not be satisfied until justice roll down like waters and righteousness like a mighty stream.

I say to you today, my friends, that in spite of the difficulties and frustrations of the moment I still have a dream. It is a dream deeply rooted in American dream.

I have a dream that one day this nation will rise up and live out the true meaning of its creed : " We hold these truths to be self-evident ; that men are created equal."

I have a dream that one day on the red hills of Georgia the sons of former slaves and the sons of former slaveowners will be able to sit down together at the table of brotherhood.

我們不會滿意，只要黑人的前途不過是從一個小貧民窟換到另外一個較大的貧民窟。

我們不會滿意，只要任何一個在密西西比州的黑人無法投票，一個在紐約的黑人投了票也沒用。

不會，不會，我們不會滿意，直到司法與正義如澎湃江水，洶湧奔騰之前，我們不會滿意。

我的朋友們，我要對你們說儘管在困難與挫折的時刻，我永遠有著一個夢，這個夢根深於我們的美國夢。

我有一個夢：總有一天，這個國家會奮起、活出一項教條的真理：我們視以下之事實為不變之真理——人生而平等。

I have a dream that one day even the state of Mississippi, a desert state sweltering with the heat of injustice and oppression, will be transformed into an oasis of freedom and justice.

I have a dream that my four little children will one day live in a nation where they will not be judged by the color of their skin but by the content of their character.

This is our hope. This is the faith with which I return to the South. With this faith we will be able to work together, to pray together, to go to jail together, to stand up together, to stand up for freedom together, knowing that will be free one day.

And if America is to be a great nation, this must become true. So let freedom ring…., when we let it ring from every village, from every state and every city, we will be able to speed up that day when all of God's children, black and white men, Jews and Gentiles, Catholics and Protestants will be able to join hands and sing in the words of the old

　　我有一個夢：總有一天，在喬治亞的紅土台地上，昔日奴隸之子孫與昔日奴隸主的後代，能同桌共坐，情同手足。

　　我有一個夢：總有一天，即使充滿不義與壓迫，有如酷熱沙漠之州的密西西比，也能變成自由與正義的綠洲

　　我有一個夢：終有一天，我的四個孩子所生活的國家，是以他們的內在品格來受評斷，而非以其皮膚之顏色。

　　這是我們的希望。我因信仰回到了南方。讓這一份信仰使我們工作在一起，禱告在一起，入獄在一起，挺立在一起，堅守自由在一起，我們知道：總有一天，自由會降臨。

　　美國要成就偉大，平等就要實現。所以讓自由響起，當我

Negro Spiritual, "Free at last! Free at last! Thank God Almighty, we are free at last!"

們讓自由之聲迴響在每一個村莊、每一個城鎮、每一個州，我們就可以加速那一天自由的到來，讓所有上帝子女──不論黑人與白人，猶太人與非猶太人，舊教徒與新教徒──手牽手在靈歌聲中，唱道：「終於自由了，終於自由了，感謝全能的上帝，我們終於自由了！」

第十五篇 沉默的大多數
～為脫手而脫手的越戰大計

理察‧尼克森

▶▶ 最動人的佳句！**The most touching words**！

So tonight, to you, the great silent majority of my fellow Americans, I ask for your support to end the war in a way thatwe could win the peace.

～Richard Nixon

因此，今晚，我親愛大多數沉默的美國人民，我需要你的支持，以和平的方式結束這場戰爭。

～理察‧尼克森

前言

戰爭，雖兵兇之事，然從歷史上看，美國國力之增長卻與每次重大戰爭有著不可磨滅之關係：獨立戰爭乃建國之戰；南北戰爭代價雖大，但推動族群融合；待十九世紀之美墨及美西戰爭，雖不脫帝國主義色彩，卻大幅增長美國領土及軍經的實力，賦予了美國與國際列強競爭的條件與自信；待一、二次世界大戰後，歐洲列強所受戰耗之巨，彼消我長下，美國輕易站上世界首強地位。

但美國也有灰頭土臉的時候，要數美國史上最心痛與挫折的戰爭，當屬越戰無疑。在跨歷四屆政府，二十二年的夢魘中，美

國事實是陷入國外的反共戰爭與國內的反戰運動兩個戰場，導致社會幾近分裂的慘境。一九六八年，尼克森東山再起，終於坐上美國總統大位，為實現選舉承諾，他寧可為退出而退出地結束這一場美國歷史最大錯誤的戰爭，但尼克森也深知承認美國失敗，所需承擔的壓力之大，因此，他需要一種「委命」。一九六九年十月三日，他創造「沉默的大多數」一詞，尼克森相信美國有一群廣大、保守的安靜民眾，但卻被敢喊敢秀的少數人士或只重腥羶的媒體所忽略；借這群「沉默多數」的保守民意作後盾，尼克森終於完成美國脫手越南的大計。

歷史背景

　　越戰：錯誤的戰爭。美國捲入越戰是在一九五四年法國在越南奠邊府一役戰敗後，決定放棄這個昔日的殖民地，美國艾森豪政府決定接棒，抵抗北越共產黨；一九六四年八月，北越在東京灣（Tonkin Bay）以魚雷攻擊美軍船艦，詹森總統決定以直接武力介入解決，越戰正式擴大，從此，久戰不下，國家陷入分裂的爭議，曾幾何時保衛自由的戰鬥竟成了不義之戰；一九六九年，尼克森為讓美國脫手，倡導越戰越南化，但已經倚賴成性的南越政府，怎堪大任；一九七五年，北越攻下西貢，美國大使館狼狽地作鳥獸散，結束長達二十二年，美國有史以來最長的海外干預。

　　美國之介入越戰，可說是兩難之下的妥協，同時也默示著圍堵政策，逢共必反的鐵律下，詹森總統慣性延續艾森豪與甘迺迪路線，奉行骨牌理論──美國放棄南越，那後果必定是由中南半島到印度甚或東南亞的全面赤化；再者，美國不能放棄其民主陣營老大哥的地位，美軍若不參戰，代表過去美軍投入的時間物力

全部拱手讓人，顯現美國只顧思考扶持親美政權，卻不求真實民主移植的現實。

美國於越戰最嚴重錯誤就是，自始至終沒有清楚地界定目的：到底是經由民主改革的談判？還是決定性的武力屈服北越？也沒有確定該用何種手段達到目的。美國自一九六四年直接以軍事人員與越共接火以來，截至尼克森上台時為止，不但未能得到決定性的勝利，反而花費了近一千億美元的軍費，及損失了五萬名子弟兵的生命，尤其每天美國媒體將不知為何而戰的美軍倒臥水稻田及士兵吸毒的報導、青年人反戰拒絕徵召入伍、城市示威、催淚彈瀰漫街頭的畫面，不斷在美國人民晚餐時間放送，加上經濟蕭條，人民厭戰，越共的頑抗，勝利既是遙遙無期，反戰聲浪越趨升高，而這種巨大的損耗又不知要拖到那一天，使美國人陷入國外怯戰，國內反戰，進退失據的困境中，事實上美國最大的敵人已不是戰場上的越共，而是分裂的自家人民。

尼克森的關島主義。尼克森入主白宮之時，正值美國國內陷入一片因越戰而引起的混亂與激辯之中，越戰的曠日持久造成美國國力的逐漸衰退，美國繼續越戰已是不符合其國家利益。一九六八大選年，當大部份的美國人都反對美國繼續介入越戰，詹森自知無法連任，宣佈退出該年的大選，尼克森便順從民意，以光榮結束越戰為諾言，一舉登上總統寶座，故其上任之後，積極尋求結束越戰之道。信仰現實外交，講求權力政治的尼克森是歷任總統以來，少數不那麼主張骨牌理論的總統，尼克森結束越戰的作法，有個專有名稱「越南化」便是脫身這場戰事的作法。一九六九年七月二十五日，尼克森出訪亞洲途經關島，宣佈對亞洲新政策：「美國仍將恪守既定的條約義務，但美鼓勵亞洲盟邦自己擔負國內安全和軍事

防衛責任，美國將避免捲入越南式的戰爭。」這一亞洲政策被稱為
「關島主義」。尼克森在一九七〇年國情咨文進而將此一政策延伸
為全球政策，提出「夥伴關係、實力、談判三大支柱之新和平戰
略。」其中心點是：美國不再承擔保衛自由世界的全部責任。而一
些高級官員直接把上述三大支柱稱為「尼克森主義」。尼克森會結
束越戰基本上是履行他的選舉政見，順著當時的反戰浪潮，是故他
在一九七二年將兵力由五十三萬人縮減到兩萬多人，而完全把國運
押注在美軍的南越政權，一旦失去美國的支持，沒多久即被赤化，
最終由北越統一了南越，越戰於一九七五年結束，結束了美國人長
達二十多年的惡夢。

　　越戰創傷症候群。越戰在美國整個歷史上有著不可磨滅的教
訓與心理的影響，美國人受越戰創痕太深痛苦太重，對這場有史
以來從未有過的失敗戰爭，感到茫然而不知所措，並在自尊上受
到嚴重挫折。而國際紛以背棄盟邦加諸在美國身上的指責，更使
美國人民感到惱怒，而國內分裂的意見爭辯徒使創痛加劇，再加
上美國傳播界對越戰訊息的負面傳播，他們對這麼一個不明不白
的戰爭，竟要付出如此龐大的代價內心自然無法平衡，越戰變成
了美國人一個永遠失落的慘痛記憶。當年反戰經典名片「越戰獵
鹿人」中，這種荒謬、憤怒與迷惑的情緒充分呈現在一對兄弟的
參戰遭遇與「越戰啟示錄」中一位上校（由馬龍白蘭度所飾）的
逃離背棄戰場，加以道德批判。直到八〇年雷根上任，越戰的歷
史形象才逐步得到平反，同樣投射在電影「藍波」片中，不斷凸
顯退伍軍人藍波忠心、愛國、服從的正面特質，卻一再受到人民
的歧視、壓迫，讓人感覺不平與同情。

　　越戰的慘敗教訓，反映在日後軍事上，美國從此再也不敢憑藉過往的自信與軍事的優越，草率承諾全面買單的方式，輕易走進盟邦的戰場糾紛；越戰式的泥淖已經為所有政治人物引以為誡，即使出兵一定是速戰速決，減少死傷，妥善控制媒體的負面報導，並宣導出兵對美重大利益之必要性，以教育人民為何而戰。

　　尼克森為脫身越南而創立的「沉默大多數」理論一詞，也成了政治新聞學中一個廣泛爭議的現象。有人認為沉默大多數是他「南方競選戰略」的一部分，作為吸取南方保守人士與共和黨團結選票的結合，催化美國保守主義大聯盟的形成。一九七二年的大選，尼克森囊括四十九州，沉默大多數的現象獲得全面的印證，從此保守政客喜以沉默大多數作為諷刺媒體只喜嘩眾取寵的政黨活動報導，這也的確解釋了相當多數保守共和黨人在不受媒體青睞地區的選舉勝利。

文獻介紹

沉默的大多數

理察‧尼克森

本文雖名為沉默的大多數，目的卻是尼克森精心設計，召告選民，決心將美國帶離越戰泥淖的文章，尼克森知道固然可以大喊「Bring Our Child Home！」，帶動煽情，但精於選舉的尼克森，更擅拿捏、掌握理性與感性的文字量，為這件撤退工程，賦與光榮與正當性，以正內外視聽，因此，他給了美國人民離開越南戰場的三項選擇方案並一一分析：一、不顧一切後果，立即撤兵。二、繼續無止無盡的和平談判。或三、尼克森本人偏重之上策「越戰越南化」，不疾不徐，金蟬脫殼。因此，他創造了「沉默的多數」的政治現象名詞，日後的選舉也證明，的確有一群保守而沉默的選民存在，非尼克森捏造的虛擬群眾，從此變成保守政治人物最有力的「委命」說詞，美國政治家也常將八〇年代雷根開創的保守王朝，引源至此，認為是尼克森首先將沉默的保守大眾吹起了集結號。

The Great Silent Majority

Richard M. Nixon

Tonight I want to talk to you on a subject of deep concern to all Americans and to many people in all parts of the world, the war in Vietnam.

I believe that one of the reasons for the deep division about Vietnam is that many Americans have lost confidence in what their Government has told them about our policy. The American people cannot and should not be asked to support a policy which involves the overriding issues of war and peace unless they know the truth about that policy.

Now let me begin by describing the situation I found when I was inaugurated on January 20: The war had been going on for four years. Thirty-one thousand Americans had been killed in action. The training program for the South Vietnamese was beyond [behind] schedule. Five

今晚，我要談的是所有美國人與世界相當多數人所最關切之話題——越戰。

我以為美國人所以被越戰深深割裂，其中一個理由，就是他們對政府所告訴他們的國家政策已失去信心。如果要求美國人民支持一項有牽涉到戰爭或和平的政策議題，我們就應該讓人民知道有關政策的真相是什麼。

現在就讓我報告自一月二十日上任後，我所發現的情況：越戰已經進行四年，三萬一千名士兵已捐軀，越南軍隊的訓練計畫也落後進度；駐紮越南的五十四萬美軍，目前尚無降低人數的計畫。巴黎和平談判毫無進展，美國也提不出任何廣泛的和平提案。

hundred and forty-thousand Americans were in Vietnam with no plans to reduce the number. No progress had been made at the negotiations in Paris and the United States had not put forth a comprehensive peace proposal.

The war was causing deep division at home and criticism from many of our friends, as well as our enemies, abroad. Let us all understand that the question before us is not whether some Americans are for peace and some Americans are against peace. The question at issue is not whether Johnson's war becomes Nixon's war. The great question is: How can we win America's peace?

Now many believe that President Johnson's decision to send American combat forces to South Vietnam was wrong. And many others, I among them, have been strongly critical of the way the war has been conducted. But the question facing us today is: Now that we are in the war, what is the best way to end it?

越戰正使我們產生國內嚴重裂痕並招致許多盟邦與敵人的批評。我們必須清楚我們現在的問題不是某些美國人支持這場戰爭,那些美國人反對這場戰爭;問題也不是原本詹森總統的戰爭現在變成是我的戰爭。爭議重點是:我們到底要如何才能為美國贏得和平?

現在很多人相信詹森總統決定派兵進入越南是錯誤的;很多其他人——我也是其一,也嚴厲批判這場戰爭的進行方式。但今天我們所面對的問題是:既然我們已深陷其中,怎樣才是最好解決戰爭之道?

In January I could only conclude that the precipitate withdrawal of all American forces from Vietnam would be a disaster not only for South Vietnam but for the United States and for the cause of peace. For the United States this first defeat in our nation's history would result in a collapse of confidence in American leadership not only in Asia but throughout the world.

For these reasons I rejected the recommendation that I should end the war by immediately withdrawing all of our forces. ...... I initiated a pursuit for peace on many fronts. ...... We have offered the complete withdrawal of all outside forces within one year. We have proposed a cease fire under international supervision. We have offered free elections under international supervision with the Communists participating in the organization and conduct of the elections as an organized political force. And the Saigon government has pledged to accept the result of the election.

一月時，我大可決議將美軍全體撤出越南，這可能不只是越南的災難，也會是美國與整個和平運動的災難。就美國而言，這史上第一次的戰敗不只將導致亞洲國家對美國領導信心的崩盤，也將連動到世界的對美信心。

因此，我拒絕了以立刻撤兵作為結束這場戰爭的建議。我已倡導各種追求和平的運動，我們提出一年內撤出所有的駐防軍隊；我們提出國際監督下的停火協定；我們提出由國際監督所舉辦的自由選舉，而且共產人士可以有組織性的政治力量參與一切選舉的舉辦與工作；且西貢政府也承諾接受選舉一切結果。

At the Paris peace conference Ambassador Lodge has demonstrated our flexibility and good faith in 40 public meetings. Hanoi has refused even to discuss our proposals. They demand our unconditional acceptance of their terms which are that we withdraw all American forces immediately and unconditionally and that we overthrow the government of South Vietnam as we leave.

We have not limited our peace initiatives to public forums and public statements. ...... I have explored every possible private avenue that might lead to a settlement.....But the effect of all the public, private, and secret negotiations which have been undertaken since the bombing halt a year ago, and since this Administration came into office on January 20th, can be summed up in one sentence: No progress whatever has been made......

Well, now, who's at fault? It's become clear that the obstacle in negotiating an end to the war is not the President of the United

在巴黎和會的四十次公開會面期間,洛奇大使已經展現了我們的彈性與善意。但河內政權不但拒絕我們所有提議,甚至要求我們接受立刻與無條件的撤出所有駐越美軍提議,然而,我們一旦如此離開越南,等同於推翻越南政府。

我們並不限制和平的倡導只在公開的會議或聲明上。我已經盡一切可能去開發私人的管道去尋求解決之道。但自停止轟炸以來,一切已經進行一年,加上我自一月二十日上任以來,不論是公開、私下與秘密的談判只能以一句話總結:毫無進展。

所以,現在,這是誰的責任?事情已經愈加清楚結束戰爭談判的阻礙不是美國總統一方;也不是越南政府一方。障礙是北越

States. It is not the South Vietnamese Government. The obstacle is the other side's absolute refusal to show the least willingness to join us in seeking a just peace.

Now let me turn, however, to a more encouraging report on another front. At the time we launched our search for peace, I recognized we might not succeed in bringing an end to the war through negotiations. I therefore put into effect another plan to bring peace -- a plan which will bring the war to an end regardless of what happens on the negotiating front. It is in line with the major shift in U. S. foreign policy which I described in my press conference at Guam on July 25. Let me briefly explain what has been described as the Nixon Doctrine -- a policy which not only will help end the war in Vietnam but which is an essential element of our program to prevent future Vietnams.

We Americans are a do-it-yourself people -- we're an impatient people. Instead of teaching someone else to do a job, we like to do it

連展示與我們追求和平的最低意願，都斷然的拒絕。

現在讓我們換個讓人較為鼓舞的報告。當我開始進行和平的探索時，我已認識到經由談判，我們不一定能成功地結束戰爭。因此，不論談判戰線上的發展如何，我已經進行另外一項的和平計畫。這項計畫我在七月二十五日於關島已經描述是完全配合美國外交政策的重大轉向。現在讓我簡短的說明什麼是所謂的尼克森主義——它不但是結束越戰的政策；更是讓未來不再有類似「越戰」的政策。

美國民族性就是自立自助，不愛假手他人——我們是不夠耐性的民族。相較於教人如何工作，我們寧可自己搞定，這種特性

ourselves. And this trait has been carried over into our foreign policy. ……. Before any American troops were committed to Vietnam, a leader of another Asian country expressed this opinion to me when I was traveling in Asia as a private citizen. He said: "When you are trying to assist another nation defend its freedom, U.S. policy should be to help them fight the war, but not to fight the war for them."

Well in accordance with this wise counsel, I laid down in Guam three principles as guidelines for future American policy toward Asia. First, the United States will keep all of its treaty commitments. Second, we shall provide a shield if a nuclear power threatens the freedom of a nation allied with us, or of a nation whose survival we consider vital to our security. Third, in cases involving other types of aggression we shall furnish military and economic assistance when requested in accordance with our treaty commitments.

The defense of freedom is everybody's business -- not just

也帶入了我們外交政策執行。美國軍事正式承諾於越戰之前,我正以私人身份在亞洲的巡迴之旅時,一位亞洲國家領導人向我表示意見:當美國努力協助盟國保衛其自由時,美國應該是輔助盟國作戰,而非親身代勞。

配合此一明智的忠告,我在關島立下三項未來亞洲政策的方針。第一,美國會維持所有條約的承諾。第二,對受核子威脅或我們認定某盟國生存對美國安全有重大關係時,我們將提供一切的防衛。第三,如果其他形式的侵略發生,美國將依條約的承諾,提供要求的軍、經協助。

自由的維護是每一個人的工作,不只是美國的。它尤其是自

America's business. And it is particularly the responsibility of the people whose freedom is threatened. In the previous Administration, we Americanized the war in Vietnam. In this Administration, we are Vietnamizing the search for peace. ….. And now we have begun to see the results of this long-overdue change in American policy in Vietnam. After five years of Americans going into Vietnam we are finally bringing American men home.

Let me now turn to our program for the future. We have adopted a plan which we have worked out in cooperation with the South Vietnamese for the complete withdrawal of all U.S. combat ground forces and their replacement by South Vietnamese forces on an orderly scheduled timetable. This withdrawal will be made from strength and not from weakness. As South Vietnamese forces become stronger, the rate of American withdrawal can become greater.

My fellow Americans, I am sure you can recognize from what I

由受到威脅當事國的工作。前任的美國政府，將越南的戰爭予美國化了，本屆政府現正追求的是越南化以換取和平。….現在我們已看到這早該改變的越戰政策的成果，終於在進入越戰的五年後，我們把美國士兵帶回加家鄉。

現在讓我指向我們未來的計畫。我們和越南政府已經合作按照順序步驟的時間表，推出一項可以讓美國地面戰鬥部隊全面撤出，並由越南部隊取代的計畫。這項撤兵計畫將以力量而非軟弱完成。因為只有當越南的兵力越強化，美國撤兵的比率才越大。

我親愛的美國人民，我確信你們能從我的報告察覺，我們有兩個開放的選擇，讓我們去結束這場戰爭。我可以立刻下令不顧

have said that we really only have two choices open to us if we want to end this war. I can order an immediate precipitate withdrawal of all Americans from Vietnam without regard to the effects of that action. Or we can persist in our search for a just peace through a negotiated settlement, if possible, or through continued implementation of our plan for Vietnamization,….

I recognize that some of my fellow citizens disagree with the plan for peace I have chosen. Honest and patriotic Americans have reached different conclusions as to how peace should be achieved. In San Francisco a few weeks ago, I saw demonstrators carrying signs reading, "Lose in Vietnam, bring the boys home." Well, one of the strengths of our free society is that any American has a right to reach that conclusion and to advocate that point of view.

But as President of the United States, I would be untrue to my oath of office if I allowed the policy of this nation to be dictated by the

一切的後果馬上將美軍撤出越南；或是我們堅持尋求一個經由談判解決的方式達成和平；或是，如果可能，繼續執行我們「越南化」的計畫……。

我也察覺部分美國人民並不贊同我所選擇的和平計畫。誠實且愛國的美國人民對和平有著各種不同的見解與決定。幾週前，我在舊金山看到遊行標語寫著：越戰失敗，讓孩子回家！不錯，自由社會偉大力量之一就是每一個美國人都有決定意見與維護他們觀點的自由。

但身為美國總統，我如果讓少數人的觀點，只是藉著升高街頭抗議手段，強加其意志於國人，就可以主宰國家大政，這是違背我對總統職務的宣誓。兩百年來，這一國家的大政方針乃依據

minority who hold that point of view and who try to impose it on the nation by mounting demonstrations in the street. For almost 200 years, the policy of this nation has been made under our Constitution by those leaders in the Congress and the White House elected by all the people. If a vocal minority, however fervent its cause, prevails over reason and the will of the majority, this nation has no future as a free society.

And now, I would like to address a word, if I may, to the young people of this nation …I respect your idealism. I share your concern for peace. I want peace as much as you do. This week I will have to sign 83 letters to mothers, fathers, wives, and loved ones of men who have given their lives for America in Vietnam. It's very little satisfaction to me that this is only one-third as many letters as I signed the first week in office. There is nothing I want more than to see the day come when I do not have to write any of those letters.

I want to end the war to save the lives of those brave young

憲法是由國會的議員與全民選出之總統制定。如果只是聲音大的少數，靠著它的活動頻繁，就能壓過多數人的理性與意志，那這個國家就無法具有自由社會的前途。

現在我想對年青人說一些話。我尊重你們的理想熱情，我也感同於你們關切之事。我期望和平程度，也與你們一樣。這週，我需簽署八十三封信函予在越南捐軀士兵的父母、妻子與他們所愛；儘管數量上只達我上任第一週所簽署信的三分之一，我無絲毫欣慰之意；因為我所期盼的是有一天，我再也不必簽下任何一封這種信。

我要結束這場戰爭，才能解救這群還在越南的勇敢年輕人。但我要結束這場戰爭的方法是還要能讓他們的子子孫孫將來免於

men in Vietnam. But I want to end it in a way which will increase the chance that their younger brothers and their sons will not have to fight in some future Vietnam some place in the world.

I have chosen a plan for peace. I believe it will succeed…… Let historians not record that, when America was the most powerful nation in the world, we passed on the other side of the road and allowed the last hopes for peace and freedom of millions of people to be suffocated by the forces of totalitarianism.

So tonight, to you, the great silent majority of my fellow Americans, I ask for your support. I pledged in my campaign for the Presidency to end the war in a way that we could win the peace. I have initiated a plan of action which will enable me to keep that pledge. The more support I can have from the American people, the sooner that pledge can be redeemed. For the more divided we are at home, the less likely the enemy is to negotiate at Paris.

再去任何世界中類似越南的地方作戰。

我已經選擇了一個和平計畫，我相信它能成功，我們一定要避免讓歷史家紀錄下：當美國是世界最強大國家之時，我們卻選擇另一條道路，讓數以百萬計人民最後和平之希望窒息於極體主義的暴力之下。

因此，今晚，對你們——我親愛大多數沉默的美國人民，我需要你的支持。在大選時，我向你們保證會以和平的方式結束這場戰爭。我已經倡導和平的行動，保證實踐我的承諾。我能得自越多美國人民的支持，這項保證就能越快實現，因為我們在國內越分裂，我們的敵人就越不可能在巴黎和談上就範。

Let us be united for peace. Let us also be united against defeat. Because let us understand -- North Vietnam cannot defeat or humiliate the United States. Only Americans can do that.

　　讓我們為和平而團結；也讓我們團結戰勝失敗。因為我們瞭解北越是無法打敗或羞辱美國，除非我們美國人願意。

第十六篇　美國控告尼克森判決文

～主權在民的董狐之筆

柏格　大法官

▶▶ 最動人的佳句！**The most touching words**！

　　Presidential privilege of immunity from judicial process must be considered in light of historical commitment to the rule of law. The very integrity of the judicial system and public confidence in the system depend on full disclosure of all the facts...

～Chief Justice Burger

　　總統豁免於司法程序之特權必需自歷史對法治的承諾來思考。司法系統的完整與人民對司法的信心完全依賴事實能充分的揭露……

～柏格　大法官

前言

　　二〇〇二年，聯合國公佈反貪腐公約，警示了二十一世紀民主最大之敵就是執政者之權力腐化，凌駕司法。

　　民主的成熟建立在法治的貫徹，而法治之精神就是「天子犯法與庶民同罪」，司法一旦服務於權力，屈服於誘惑，權勢者得悠遊於司法之外，使「法律之前，人人平等」變成空談，其民主只是門面裝飾罷了！

　　一九七四年八月八日美國總統尼克森因「水門事件」，涉及說謊、妨礙司法調查，終於在國會彈劾壓力下，自動辭職，而其中關鍵力量就是：美國司法之不畏權勢，尤其是特別檢察官，在尼克森一再以免職恐嚇辦案下，扮演了有如「在齊太史簡」角色，堅持尼克森必須交出犯罪錄音帶證據，配合司法調查，以昭人民對司法之公信，最終取得最高法院判決支持，尼見大勢已去，乃黯然下台。可見即便是世界最大權勢者如美國總統，違法亂紀一樣也要在法律之前低頭。民主政治真正展現了人民力量，寫下驚歎一頁，這也是世人並不以美國有尼克森為恥，卻景仰美國檢調、司法人員之超然獨立與勇氣，捍衛了民主生機。

歷史背景

　　狡猾的狄克（*Tricky Dick*）。美國史上目前惟二的國會彈劾總統投票，第一位是第十七任總統安德魯強森，因南北戰後，主張溫和的南方政策，在一八六八年，受國會報復反對，結果僅以一票之差身免；再來就是一九九八年十二月，第四十二任總統柯林頓因緋聞案的彈劾投票，但亦未達所需的參議院三分之二票數要求。因此，一般人以尼克森作美國史上第一個被彈劾成功的總統，嚴格說是不成立，但尼克森提前下台的原因，也的確是因為彈劾案在國會將篤定通過，他為避開這歷史臭名，只好決定不再戀棧。綜觀尼克森一生，這位出身雜貨店之子，在沒有任何政治背景與奧援下，養成了刻苦自立卻精明多疑的政治人格，如果說「性格決定命運」的話，「狡猾狄克」的性格綽號，絕對是尼克森一生政治事業載舟與覆舟的最好寫照。

尼克森畢業於北卡羅萊納杜克大學法學院，一九四六年，年僅三十三歲、默默無聞的尼克森決心參選眾議員；雖無背景的奧援，尼克森了解反共是當時選舉最低廉的成本，卻有最高投資報酬，如果候選人一旦被貼上共產黨標籤，不管是真是假，很快就會面臨失敗命運，因此，在沒有充分證據支持下，尼克森指責現任的民主黨渥里斯在國會中投票記錄都是站在「莫斯科陣線」上，渥里斯在共產黨「莫須有」紅色大帽子下難以招架，使尼克森贏取他政治首役。

一九五〇年，尼克森競選參議員，仍前事不忘後事之師，統計民主黨現任道格拉斯女士與親社會主義國會議員麥肯多尼歐有354次同樣投票記錄，而斷定道格拉斯亦是共產同路人士，並貫以「pink lady」之名，暗示性抹黑道格拉斯是共產黨人。尼克森雖然因此順利當選，但道格拉斯也為尼克森取了「Tricky Dick」綽號，此一綽號就此永遠伴隨著尼克森的整個政治生涯。之後，尼克森把握機會高舉反共大旗，成為反共報人亨利魯斯栽培下的「反共巨星」，得意於政壇，一九五六年，貴為艾森豪副總統。一九六〇年大選，尼克森代表共和黨，以極低票數與總統失之交臂；六二年捲土重來，再飲恨加州州長之役，六四年親睹以反共出名的共和黨總統候選人高華德歷史性的大選慘敗，這使尼克森大受警示：反共的招牌看來已利空出盡。經四年的沉潛，重悟「政治正確」議題──「低盪」政策，立場從反共變成容共，六八年大選，尼克森終於榮登大位。

水門事件。七二年大選到來，民主黨總統候選人推出麥高文，選前種種民調預測顯示：尼克森以在位者優勢及外交內政的穩健表現，加上麥高文太過激進的自由主義路線，連民主黨的主流都不太

支持下，尼克森是穩操勝券。開票結果，一如眾人意料尼克森取得
一場壓倒性的勝利：尼克森贏得全國選票的61%，選舉人票除麻薩
諸塞與哥倫比亞特區，其餘四十九州，尼克森也全部囊括。在這場
並非勢均力敵，其實勝負早已判定的選舉，照理，尼克森實在無需
行雞鳴狗盜之法，在當年六月十七日半夜，派人潛入麥高文位於華
府水門大廈內的競選總部，裝置竊聽器，弄得東窗事發，遺臭萬
年。深入尼克森內心世界，這實與他他一生赤手空拳，得取權力不
易歷程，所造就多疑過慮、心機太深的性格心理所致。

　　水門事件初始，尼克森以高民意及美國與中共正常化，尤其
希望以脫身越戰的光榮撤退加以淡化，加上白宮的不合作，直接證
物的缺乏，調查陷入膠著，如果不是在媒體華盛頓郵報記者伍華德
與聯邦調查局副局長費爾特（Mark Felt）——代號「深喉嚨」的爆
料指引，還有司法特別檢察官鍥而不捨的追查下，極有可能在總統
權力搓揉下，無疾而終。水門事件關鍵的突破直到七三年七月才出
現，一名白宮助理透露整個白宮裝有錄音設備，也就是說尼克森在
白宮一切的談話或電話都有錄音紀錄，這使案件急轉直下，因此，
特別檢察官命令尼克森交出關鍵期間的錄音帶內容，成為突破案情
焦點。色屬內荏的尼克森，一面以免職特別檢察官恐嚇，一面又掩
飾心虛，交出變造錄音帶拖延。七四年三月，美國大陪審團對水門
的七名涉案人員正式起訴，該大陪審團雖未起訴卻點名尼克森也是
共同正犯。四月，特檢對尼克森發出傳票，限期交出一切錄音帶。
五月，尼克森以總統行政之機密特權抵抗，進行困獸之鬥，七月上
訴最高法院，大法官以八：○判尼克森敗訴，尼克森見大勢已去，
八月八日，狡猾狄克只好辭職下台，以最不光彩的方式結束政治生
命。「天子犯法與庶民同罪」，民主因法治彰顯。

文獻介紹

美國控告尼克森判決詞節錄

柏格　大法官

　　美國在民主試煉過程中，歷經政黨惡鬥、族群對立、經濟不景氣、兩次反法西斯的戰爭與共產主義的冷戰考驗後，證明民主的確是人類現今最好的生活選擇。然而，民主生活的挑戰並不因此而終止，從不斷的國家發展經驗證實，當權者之貪腐將是二十一世紀民主最大之敵。權力使人腐化是不讓人意外的，但政治力介入司法，司法不能秉春秋之筆，竟讓權勢凌駕是非正義之上，才是讓人憂慮。在上個世紀的「水門事件」中，美國特別檢察官不受政治恐嚇辦案，堅持尼克森必須交出錄音帶證據，配合司法調查，最後在高院「總統特權效力必需依照對法治的承諾，而司法審判中相關證據的呈現乃公平執法之的最基本要求。」判定，確保司法獨立與法治精神，即使總統亦不得例外，為民主打了最漂亮一場勝仗。

United States v. Nixon

Chief Justice Burger delivered the opinion of the Court :

On March 1, 1974, a grand jury of the United States District for the District Court for the District of Colombia return an indictment charging seven named individuals with various offenses, including conspiracy to defraud the United States and to obstruct justice. Although he was not designated as such in the indictment, the grand jury named the President, as an unindicted coconspirator. On April 18,1974, upon motion of the Special Prosecutor, a subpoena was issued to the President by the district court….and required the production, in advance of September 9 trial date, of certain tapes, memorandum, papers , transcripts, or other writings relating to certain meetings between the President and others. On May 1, the President counsel filed a motion to quash the subpoena…. This motion was accompanied by a formal claim of privilege… Here at issue is the production or

美國最高法院伯格大法官發佈的判決書：

一九七四年，三月一日，美國哥倫比亞特區之地方法院的大陪審團提出對七名人員的起訴，罪名包括陰謀對美國詐欺與阻撓司法各項罪名；該大陪審團儘管沒有正式起訴，卻點名了美國現任總統為共同正犯。四月十八日，在特別檢察官的動議下，地院正式向總統發出傳票，命令在九月九日法院審理之前，交出任何有關總統與其他人物之特定證據錄音帶、紀錄、文件手稿。五月一日，總統經由律師提出廢止此一傳票動議，該動議附帶一份特權的聲明……因此，本案爭議所在是：該不該交出被特別檢察官認定某些正在審理中犯罪案件的特定相關證物；但最高行政首長

nonproduction of specified evidence deemed by the Special Prosecutor to be relevant and admissible in a pending criminal case. It is resisted by the Chief Executive on the ground of his duty to preserve the confidentiality of the communications of the President.

In support of his claim of absolute privilege, the President's counsel urge two grounds... The first ground is the valid need for protection of communications between Government officials and those who advise and assist them in the performance of their duties ; the importance of confidentiality is too plain to require further discussion. The second ground the President's claim of absolute privilege rest on the doctrine of separation of powers. Here is argued that the independence of the Executive Branch within its own sphere insulates subpoena in an ongoing criminal prosecution and thereby protects confidential Presidential communications.

However, neither the doctrine of separation of powers, nor the need for confidentiality of high-level communications can sustain an

卻以總統有保全資訊機密責任之根據抵抗。

　　總統委任律師以兩大論點，極力支持總統絕對特權的聲明……第一點是總統與咨詢、輔助他執行公務之公務人員間的資訊有確實保護性的需要；此保密重要性之明確，自不在話下。第二點總統絕對特權之聲明則是基於分權主義，基於行政部門的獨立，自然得免於進行中刑案審判之傳票命令效力，俾保障總統資訊的機密性。

　　然而，本院認為不論是分權主義或是高層資訊的保密皆不足以支持總統擁有絕對豁免於所有情況的司法程序……此一特權效力必需依照我們歷史對法治的承諾來決定，司法系統的完善與人

absolute Presidential privilege of immunity from judicial process under all circumstances…(Moreover,) this privilege must be considered in light of historical commitment to the rule of law. The very integrity of the judicial system and public confidence in the system depend on full disclosure of all the facts…. In this case, the President challenges a subpoena served on him…, he does so on the claim that he has a privilege against disclosure of confidential communications. He does not place his claim of privilege on the ground that they are military or diplomatic secrets.

The right to the production of all evidence at a criminal trial has constitutional dimensions. The Sixth Amendment confers upon every defendant in a criminal trial the right "to be confronted with the witness against him" and "to have compulsory process for obtaining witness in favor." Moreover, the Fifth Amendment also guarantees that no person shall be deprived of liberty without due process of law. It is the manifest duty of the courts to vindicate those guarantees, and to

民對司法的信心完全依賴事實能充分的揭露…在本案中,總統挑戰此一傳票對他的適用效力,所依據者,是他有反對揭曉一切機密資訊的特權;而並非將他的依據置於這些資料是屬於軍事或外交上的機密。

在刑事審判中,要求證據全面呈現的權利是有憲法層面的依據。憲法第六條修正案即賦予每一名被告與對他不利人證對質之權利、法院亦有義務召喚一切對被告有利人證出庭。憲法第五條修正案更進一步保證不得在非正當的法律程序下,剝奪任何人的自由。法院明白的義務就是確認這些憲法的保證並完成所有相關可得的證據呈供於審案。

accomplish that it is essential that all relevant and admissible evidence be produced.

In this case we must weigh the importance of the general privilege of confidentiality of Presidential communications in performance of the President's responsibilities against... the fair administration of criminal justice...On the other hand, the allowance of the privilege to withhold evidence that is demonstrably relevant in a criminal trial would cut deeply into the guarantee of due process of law and gravely impair the basic function of the court.... the constitutional need for production of relevant evidence in a criminal proceeding is specific and central to the fair adjudication of justice. Without access to specific facts a criminal prosecution may be totally frustrated. We conclude that when the ground asserting privilege as subpoenaed materials sought for in a trial...., it cannot prevail over the fundamental demands of due process of law in the fair administration of criminal justice.

　　本案我們所要衡量者乃總統在執行公務時普遍的資訊機密特權與刑事司法公平執法的執重。另一方面言，允許特權而不呈交司法案件中顯然有關證據，不但將深深割裂正當法律程序之保障，更嚴重破壞法院執行公務之基本能力……憲法對司法審判中相關證據的呈現，認定是法律公平執行之中心；在犯罪控訴中，失去取得特定事實證據之管道，是令人感到無比的挫折。我們最後的意見是法院因審判所需資料而發出的傳票是正當法律程序中，公平執法之的最基本要求，對此所主張之特權，自不得凌駕。

第十七篇　特赦尼克森
～民主的歷史交易

吉拉德‧福特

▶▶ 最動人的佳句！**The most touching words**！

My conscience tells me it is my duty, not merely to proclaim domestic tranquility but to use every means that I have to insure it.

～ Gerald R. Ford

我的良心告訴我，我的責任不只是宣示國內的寧謐，而是用盡一切我必須的手段，確保這份平靜。

～吉拉德‧福特

前言

美國總統一職可謂是世界政壇之權力極品，有志此大位之政治工作者，通常必需在黨內，經過長期能力歷練與品德挑別，取得一定聲勢，再歷初選提名，也只取得大選門票；大選期間，除需花費無限精力與金錢外，還得有運氣加持，才能攀上頂峰；因此，非有過人意志者，絕對望而怯步。

然而美國現今四十四位總統之中，卻有不必經過選舉的洗禮，卻幸運的先後榮登副總統、總統寶座者，就是第三十八任總統吉拉德福特。福特在位兩年半時期，作為平淡，最受人矚目就屬特赦尼克森。福特因尼克森水門事件辭職，而得繼承大位，

179

然而辭職後，成為平民的尼克森，是否仍令其接受司法的審判，成了福特上任的燙手山芋，最終，福特決定在「長痛不如短痛，避免美國陷入激情、對立與內外受辱」的考慮下，特赦尼克森，反對者以為這腐敗的交易大傷了司法之威信。一般咸信一九七六年，福特尋求連任時敗給民主黨候選人卡特，其特赦尼克森是一大主因。

但無論如何，福特總統穩健平實的作風、坦誠溫厚的人格，的確帶領當時美國走出水門案的陰影。而福特生前所期望日後史家能為他下的註腳：「福特總統在國家艱困時期上台，面對水門案醜聞、越戰挫敗、經濟問題叢生，白宮威信淪喪殆盡，是福特恢復了公眾對政府的信心。」二○○二年，水門案卅周年時，一項民調顯示60%民眾認為特赦尼克森是正確之舉，歷史終於還給福特公道。

歷史背景

意外的總統。福特是美國史上至今，唯一從未經過選舉，卻先後當上美國副總統與總統者。一九七三年十月，因副手安格紐收賄而辭職，尼克森總統提名福特繼任副總統，順利獲得參眾兩院同意，成為歷來第一位依據美國憲法增修條文第廿五條第二款上任的副總統。一九七四年八月九日，尼克森因水門事件纏身，同樣命運下台辭職，福特又以副總統身分更上層樓，成為美國第卅八位總統。

水門醜聞發生於一九七二年大選，尼克森在完全知情的情況下，由他的競選組織「尼克森連任總統委員會」派出五名人員深夜潛入民主黨全國委員會所在之水門大廈被補，經司法調查而

越演越大，發現白宮助理以至尼克森本人竟都牽涉其中，尼本人更說謊、偽證且阻撓司法調查。經過兩年與媒體、政府特別檢察官與國會兩院的頑抗，尼克森最終在避免彈劾的難堪下，辭去總統一職，問題是：成為一介平民的尼克森，是否就足以免去一切刑責的繼續追究呢？一個月後，繼位的福特以「在這段長期拖延的訴訟下，醜陋的激情勢必挑起，人民將陷入兩極的對立，我們政府自由體制的可信度，在國內外又要受到挑戰。」，決定特赦尼克森任內所有的違法犯罪，致全美為之震駭、譁然，他的民意急速下滑。福特並非沒有預料到民意的嚴屬反彈，也因此他特別選在星期日早上宣佈以避開炮火兇猛的華府政客、傳媒群起的政治風暴，福特堅稱此舉絕非事先安排的政治交易，而是為了讓國家徹底擺脫政治陰影，迎向未來。一九七六年，這位「意外的總統」投入連任選戰。但是美國經濟成長停滯，通貨膨脹、能源價格與失業率居高不下，讓福特先是在黨內遭遇加州州長雷根的強力挑戰，面對民主黨的喬治亞州長卡特，更是從一開始就陷入苦戰，最後以2.1%的普選票差距敗北，許多政論家認為一九七六年大選福特敗給卡特的最大原因之一是他特赦尼克森。

　　歷史的民主交易。常言：民主建立在法治的獨立運作，福特在就職演說中昭告全國同胞：「我親愛的美國同胞們，長久以來的夢魘已經結束。大家可以相信我們的憲法的確絲毫不偏袒。我們的聯邦是建立在法律之上，而不是個人的隻手遮天。在這個國家，人民才是統治者。」，但法治又不外乎人情，儘管福特沒什麼大才，但相較詭計多端、撒謊成性、踐踏憲法，把美國搞得烏煙瘴氣，變成無視法律與道德的帝國總統之尼克森，他的廉潔、誠實、正直卻是美國在後尼克森時代最需要的人格特質，他只憑

著常識與不忍人之心認定如果大審尼克森美國未來幾年勢必圍繞在對立與司法官司上的糾纏不清,福特在特赦文告中說:「**我的良心也告訴我,我的責任不只是宣示民主的寧謐,而是用盡一切我必須的手段,保護民主的平靜。**」,最後只有特赦的行使是他認定惟一達成保護民主安定的交易。

除水門事件重挫美國聲望外,福特於總統任期內,還經歷一九七五年四月,越南的全面淪陷,美國在越二十餘年的心血、承諾,付之灰燼,信心二度重傷害,為此福特發表演說:「今日,就美國而言,美國可以重回越戰前所擁有的驕傲,來建立我們的自信,不是以要求重回已經失守的戰場。」受到林肯的啟發,福特繼續鼓舞美國民眾「將眼光放在未來的時候,我們要團結,讓這個國家所受的創傷復原。」

福特是個任重道遠的人,至少他是當時環境下,美國最最需要的人選。而福特本人在卸任後受媒體訪問時說:「我希望五十年後的歷史學家會說:福特總統在國家艱困時期上台,面對水門案醜聞、越戰挫敗、經濟問題叢生。當時白宮威信淪喪殆盡,但是福特恢復了公眾對政府的信心。」二○○二年水門案卅周年時,一項民調顯示60%民眾認為特赦尼克森是正確之舉,歷史終於還給福特公道。

特赦尼克森

吉拉德‧福特

　　一九七四年八月八日，美國總統尼克森為避免因水門醜聞，彈劾留史的紀錄，宣佈辭職下台。九月八日，繼任總統福特下令特赦尼克森在任內所犯一切違背法律的犯行。一般相信就是因為這個動作，讓福特只當了一屆總統，同樣這件事卻也讓他在多年以後仍被傳頌。因為他的勇敢與果斷，才能讓這個國家步回軌道。

　　福特常愛自嘲他是「福特」（FORD）而不是「林肯」（LINCOLN）。他的意思是說他是一部大眾化的平民車子而不是大型豪華林肯轎車，只是一介平民，與所有的美國人都有一樣的同理心。在這篇文選中，也充分流露福特性格上的寬厚善良與體察國情的大局視野。美國經過六十年代的反戰動亂與七十年代的水門醜聞，國家已成分崩離析狀態；在歷史性關頭，福特穩定了人心，平息了紛爭，使美國的對立、紛擾到此為止，特赦尼克森或許當時不得諒解，多年後再看，歷史除給予他某種程度的平反，也很厚待福特，二○○六年十一月十二日，福特再度寫下一項紀錄：他超越兩年前過世的雷根，享年九十三歲成為美國歷來最高壽的總統。

Pardoning Richard Nixon

Gerald R. Ford

Ladies and gentlemen:

I have come to a decision which I felt I should tell you and all of my fellow American citizens, as soon as I was certain in my own mind and in my own conscience that it is the right thing to do.

I have learned already in this office that the difficult decisions always come to this desk. I must admit that many of them do not look at all the same as the hypothetical questions that I have answered freely and perhaps too fast on previous occasions.

My customary policy is to try and get all the facts and to consider the opinions of my countrymen and to take counsel with my most valued friends. But these seldom agree, and in the end, the decision is mine. To procrastinate, to agonize, and to wait for a more favorable turn of events that may never come, is itself a decision of sorts and a

我感覺我現在有一個要向所有美國人民報告的決定，而此一決定是我確定依我意識與良知下，所認定對的作為。

我早已知悉總統這個工作就是會有一大堆難解的問題不時湧入面前。我必須承認其中很多問題，決不似從前我面對假設性問題時，可以自由隨意甚至匆忙應答一般。

我習慣性的策略是盡力收集所有事實，考量國人的輿情並向益友徵詢良策。但這些意見往往不同，最終，還是得由我來拍板定案。拖延、苦悶地等待一個永遠也不可能降臨的有利轉機，其本身就是決策一種，就總統言，也是一個脆弱與潛在的危險歷程。

weak and potentially dangerous course for a President to follow.

I have promised to uphold the Constitution, to do what is right as God gives me to see the right, and to do the very best that I can for America.

I have asked your help and your prayers, not only when I became President but many times since. The Constitution is the supreme law of our land and it governs our actions as citizens. Only the laws of God, which govern our consciences, are superior to it.

As we are a nation under God, so I am sworn to uphold our laws with the help of God. And I have sought such guidance and searched my own conscience with special diligence to determine the right thing for me to do with respect to my predecessor in this place, Richard Nixon, and his loyal wife and family.

Theirs is an American tragedy in which we all have played a part. It could go on and on and on, or someone must write the end to it. I have concluded that only I can do that, and if I can, I must.

我已承諾堅守憲法，按上帝所示之正道，為所應為，並為美國行最有利之事。

我祈求你們的幫助與禱告，不只是我成為總統之當下，而是時時刻刻。憲法是這塊土地的最高法律，也是指導我們身為公民之行為；可以超越它者，惟有統治我們良心的上帝法律。

因為我們的國家是在上帝之下，所以，在上帝扶持之下，我宣誓堅守法律。並且，我努力地尋求上帝的指引與個人良知，希望在有關前任總統尼克森與他忠實的夫人與家庭上的事情，作出對的決定。

尼克森水門案是一個美國的悲劇，我們在其中都扮演了一份角色，除非有人為它寫下劇終，否則它將無止無盡的進行。我最終

There are no historic or legal precedents to which I can turn in this matter, none that precisely fit the circumstances of a private citizen who has resigned the Presidency of the United States. But it is common knowledge that serious allegations and accusations hang like a sword over our former President's head, threatening his health as he tries to reshape his life, a great part of which was spent in the service of this country and by the mandate of its people.

After years of bitter controversy and divisive national debate, I have been advised, and I am compelled to conclude that many months and perhaps more years will have to pass before Richard Nixon could obtain a fair trial by jury in any jurisdiction of the United States under governing decisions of the Supreme Court.

發現也只有我能為它劃下句點,如果我能,我也必需這麼作。

在歷史與法律上,由於史無前例對一位已辭去美國總統的現任公民該如何處理上,因此,我毫無參考的依據。但我們也清楚法律的涉嫌與控告已經向劍一樣,高懸在這位用盡大半生,受民委託,獻身服務這個國家的前總統頭顱之上,嚴重威脅到他身體的健康與他生活的重建。

經過這幾年的痛苦爭論與全國分裂的辯論,我不斷受到忠告,因此,我必須這樣確認在未來的幾個月,甚至幾年,我們在尼克森取得美國司法陪審團公平的審判與最高法院的判決前,是否都要這樣渡過。

The facts, as I see them, are that a former President of the United States, instead of enjoying equal treatment with any other citizen accused of violating the law, would be cruelly and excessively penalized either in preserving the presumption of his innocence or in obtaining a speedy determination of his guilt in order to repay a legal debt to society.

During this long period of delay and potential litigation, ugly passions would again be aroused. And our people would again be polarized in their opinions. And the credibility of our free institutions of government would again be challenged at home and abroad.

In the end, the courts might well hold that Richard Nixon had been denied due process, and the verdict of history would even be more inconclusive with respect to those charges arising out of the period of his Presidency, of which I am presently aware.

就我所見的事實將是：這位前任的美國總統不會如同任何其他違反法律的公民，受到平等的待遇；為了對社會法律的虧欠彌補，不論是在他無罪假設的保護或是他罪嫌快速決定的取得，他將被殘酷與極度的懲治。

在這段可能長期拖延與訴訟下，醜陋的激情勢必挑起，人民又要陷入兩極的對立，我們政府自由體制的可信度，在國內外也要受到挑戰。

最後，法院也可能判決尼克森沒有受到合法之審理程序，因此，就我所知有關在他總統期間被指控犯行的歷史性定罪，可能更將模糊不定。

But it is not the ultimate fate of Richard Nixon that most concerns me, though surely it deeply troubles every decent and every compassionate person. My concern is the immediate future of this great country.

In this, I dare not depend upon my personal sympathy as a longtime friend of the former President, nor my professional judgment as a lawyer, and I do not.

As President, my primary concern must always be the greatest good of all the people of the United States whose servant I am. As a man, my first consideration is to be true to my own convictions and my own conscience.

My conscience tells me clearly and certainly that I cannot prolong the bad dreams that continue to reopen a chapter that is closed. My conscience tells me that only I, as President, have the constitutional power to firmly shut and seal this book. My conscience tells me it is my duty, not merely to proclaim domestic tranquility but to use every

然而，我們最終所最關切不是尼克森本人的命運，儘管這的確困擾了每一位正直與悲憫之人。我所掛慮者乃是其所影響者乃是這偉大國家的近期未來。

鑑於此，我斷不敢依恃作為前任總統長期老友的個人同情，或是律師的專業判斷來看待。

身為總統，作為美國公僕，美國人民的最大利益是我首要關切者。身為個人，我第一考量則是必須忠實於我的自信與良知。

我的良心清楚確定的告訴我不能再延長惡夢，讓他重新翻開新頁。我的良心也告訴我，只有身為總統的我，擁有憲法上的權利，闔上這部書。我的良心也告訴我，我的責任不只是宣示國內

means that I have to insure it. I do believe that the buck stops here, that I cannot rely upon public opinion polls to tell me what is right. I do believe that right makes might and that if I am wrong, ten angels swearing I was right would make no difference. I do believe, with all my heart and mind and spirit, that I, not as President but as a humble servant of God, will receive justice without mercy if I fail to show mercy.

Finally, I feel that Richard Nixon and his loved ones have suffered enough and will continue to suffer, no matter what I do, ……

Now, therefore, I, Gerald R. Ford, President of the United States, pursuant to the pardon power conferred upon me by Article II, Section 2, of the Constitution, have granted and by these presents do grant a full, free, and absolute pardon unto Richard Nixon for all offenses against the United States which he, Richard Nixon, has committed or may have committed or taken part in during the period from July 20, 1969, through August 9, 1974.

的寧謐，而是用盡一切我必須的手段，保護這個平靜。我堅信所有責任由我承擔，我無法靠公共民調來告訴我什麼才是對的。我堅信正義就是力量，如果我錯了，即使十位天使為我立誓也沒差別。我全心全意堅信：作為上帝卑微的僕人，如果我不能展現憐憫，我將不受憐憫的接受正義審判。

最後，我覺得無論我作什麼，尼克森與支持愛護他的人都已承受了足夠苦難，未來也將繼續承受。

因此，現在，本人吉拉德福特──美國總統，根據憲法第二條第二款賦予之赦免權，全面、自由且絕對的赦免理察尼克森在他一九六九年七月二十日至一九七四年八月九日所犯或可能所涉

In witness whereof, I have hereunto set my hand this eighth day of September, in the year of our Lord nineteen hundred and seventy-four, and of the Independence of the United States of America the one hundred and ninety-ninth.

Gerald R. Ford - September 8, 1974.

或參與之一切侵害美國之行為。

一九七四年九月八日，美國獨立第一百九十九年，在見證下，我謹誓簽署。吉拉德　福特，一九七四年九月八日。

第十八篇　雷根大選電視辯論文
～美國保守主義王朝再現

隆納德・雷根

> ▶▶▶ 最動人的佳句！**The most touching words**！
>
> Are you better off than you were four years ago?
>
> ～ Ronald Reagan
>
> 你生活過得比四年前好嗎？
>
> ～隆納德・雷根

前言

　　狂飆的六〇年代，美國自由派政客開始當道，至七〇年代，尼克森、卡特的反共意志是不以實力為後盾，一廂強打「和解」與「人權」外交，結果是越戰失利、中東石油禁運、背棄台灣、蘇聯入侵阿富汗、伊朗人質事件，使美國威信盡失，盟邦陷入信心危機，美國進入歷史最挫折感的時刻。

　　因此，八〇年代雷根的當選，篤信保守主義的雷根，矢言恢復美國強大國力與自信，開始大幅度擴張軍備，對蘇聯的擴張由原本的低盪改為直接的對抗；面對國內經濟衰退，他的解決方式是減少政府的支出、減稅和撤銷管制，充分以自由市場機制自動修正所面臨的問題。他在就職典禮那天說出日後共和黨的治國名言：「政府並不是解決問題的方法，政府本身才是問題所在。」

美國自由放任的資本主義體制再度復活，展現了私人經濟的活力與勁道。

雷根的當選代表著美國八〇年代保守主義的捲土重來，他振奮了美國人低昂的士氣和尊嚴，成為美國政治上一個重要的分水嶺，並延續至下一世紀，在雷根兩屆任期結束後，同黨的老布希於一九八八年的選戰中，挾著雷根的高昂人氣而大獲全勝，為共和黨六十年來首次成功接任的總統，巧合是二〇〇〇～二〇〇八年，其子小布希更以新保守主義延續的保守主義香火，創建了長達二十年美國政治的保守王朝。

歷史背景

雷根革命。七〇年代，美國與共產蘇聯的一連串自中南半島到非洲軍事外交的競爭失利，尤其是卡特總統後期任內，蘇聯揮兵阿富汗與伊朗回教份子挾持境內美國大使館人質，卡特卻無力解救，讓美國人民對六〇年代以來自由主義「和解共生」的思維是徹底失望，開始鐘擺傾向至呼籲恢復美國強大國力與尊嚴的保守主義訴求。一九八〇年的選戰中，雷根擊敗了現任的卡特，同時共和黨在那年選舉中也贏得了二十六年來首次在參議院過半數的席次。雷根在一九八〇年的勝選，成為未來美國政治板塊的主要分水嶺。

一九八〇年，雷根的旋風造成政黨重組，開始結合民主、共和兩黨保守選民創建了一跨世紀的保守王朝。雷根能獲得如此龐大的支持度，乃民主黨長期在自由激進思想的浸泡，相對之下，南方民主黨人右派宗教（Right Religion）與家庭價值（family value）濃厚的保守理念，反更對味雷根共和黨傳統價值的主張。

此外，雷根在墮胎、黑人與社會福利等議題上的保守主張以及強硬的外交政策也頗吸引這批所謂的「雷根民主黨人」。這群雷根的民主黨人加上共和黨，使得雷根組成的保守聯盟控制了整個一九八〇年代——在一九八〇年、一九八四年，以及一九八八年他們都選擇投給共和黨，獲得壓倒性的勝利——此一整合的威效尤其顯現在一九八四年，雷根在普選中贏得了將近60%的選票，並且囊括四十九個州的選舉人團票，民主黨提名的孟岱爾只獲得他的老家明尼蘇達州和哥倫比亞特區，使雷根創下了獲得525張選舉人票（全部538張）的紀錄，即使是在明尼蘇達州，孟岱爾也只超過了雷根3,761票，意味著雷根差點就要創下贏得全部五十個州的歷史紀錄。雷根在一九八〇年代發起的「雷根革命」對保守主義運動的影響依然持續至今。除柯林頓政府的兩任八年外，二〇〇〇～〇八年，又再度回流結合，由小布希延續保守同盟。

雷根主義。與中國「無為」思想頗似的雷根始終強調他對於政府在處理問題上的能力抱持著懷疑態度，認為政府功用不該是限制人民的發揮，而是致力解除限制人民的服務，這也是他最早從信仰傑佛遜民主黨之降低政府權力管制，尤其是在經濟問題方面，轉而加入共和黨的原因。

雷根推行的經濟政策——「小政府，大市場」是他扭轉八十年代經濟的重要觀念，被人稱為雷根經濟學，而關鍵行動就是減稅，這也是近來台灣政、商人士期待解決國內景氣不斷低迷的特效藥。雷根任內致力大幅減稅25%、降低利率，還富於民，使國民有更開放、自由，創意活力的經濟環境。在兩黨的支持下，雷根排除了稅賦規則的漏洞，繼續對商業行為撤銷管制，解決了自一九七〇年代以來一直蔓延的經濟停滯，遏止了嚴重的通貨膨脹

以及經濟衰退，失業率由10.8%降至5.4%，而減稅也並未使高收入人士少繳納稅，七年間，年薪20萬美元的人多繳了5倍稅，政府稅收不減反增，由5,000億美元增加至10,000億美元；得以擴大軍費開支，同時增加政府舉債，以暫時支應社會福利的花費。雷根稱這些政策是使美國經濟在歷經一九八一～二年的急遽衰退後，開始茁壯的經濟成長復甦的主因。

在外交政策上，面對蘇聯的擴張，雷根則是採取強硬、積極性的圍堵與對抗，一九八三年以保僑名義入侵加勒比海島國格瑞那達，推翻親蘇政權；提供軍火支援予阿富汗及尼加拉瓜反抗軍，使蘇聯陷入如越戰般的泥淖，雷根成功的增加軍事預算，發起被人稱為「星際大戰」的戰略防禦倡導（SDI），與蘇聯展開無限上綱的軍備競賽，迫使改革派的蘇聯領導人戈巴契夫終於感到國力過度消耗與不支，一九八九年結束對於東歐地區的控制，柏林圍牆應聲而倒，蘇聯的共產主義最後也在一九九一年徹底垮台，許多的觀察家，尤其是美國的保守派，稱讚雷根是使蘇聯於一九九一年垮臺的主要推手。如同對雷根最激烈的批評者也承認的：「他最偉大的成就便是恢復了美國人對他們自己和他們政府的自尊，尤其是在經過了不堪回首的越戰、水門案、伊朗人質危機的挫敗、以及其他幾個無能的總統之後。」

雷根的任內也經歷了數次嚴重的政治醜聞，其中「伊朗尼游事件」的秘密軍事外交，規避國會監督管道，導致不少官員和幕僚被定罪，使他領導能力及風格備受質疑，但憑藉他誠懇與親民的形象，加上下屬扛過，他總是得以安然度過這些危機，媒體愛以政壇的鐵芙蓉（Teflon；不沾鍋）稱之。

文獻介紹

雷根大選電視辯論文

隆納德‧雷根

　　八〇年代常被稱為「雷根時代」。雷根可說是近代自甘迺迪以來，最具政治語言魅力的總統，原本出身好萊塢「B咖」演員，卻以豐富的表情與幽默的言詞，在政壇充分致用，走出一片天地；他以常識治國，一派治大國宛如烹小鮮，舉重若輕，總能抓住原則，一語中的，而有「偉大的溝通者」之稱，是近年來少數卸任後，仍大受美國人民懷念愛戴之總統。

　　因此，本文所特別選錄者是一九八〇年激烈選戰中，雷根與當時現任總統卡特最關鍵的一場電視辯論會。相對電視上卡特的緊繃、窘促，他機智風趣的談吐令選民絕倒，尤其他在答辯結論時，告知選民投票時只要自問「你有比四年前過得好嗎？」就夠判斷了，充分呈現他簡單明快的常識治國風格，咸認是雷根選戰致勝的關鍵語言。

The Carter-Reagan Presidential Debate
October 28, 1980

Ronald Reagan

Next Tuesday is Election Day. Next Tuesday all of you will go to the polls, will stand there in the polling place and make a decision. I think when you make that decision, it might be well if you would ask yourself, are you better off than you were four years ago? Is it easier for you to go and buy things in the stores than it was four years ago? Is there more or less unemployment in the country than there was four years ago? Is America as respected throughout the world as it was? Do you feel that our security is as safe, that we're as strong as we were four years ago? And if you answer all of those questions yes, why then, I think your choice is very obvious as to whom you will vote for. If you don't agree, if you don't think that this course that we've been on for the last four years is what you would like to see us follow for the next four,

下週二就是投票日，你將前往投票所，並在投票檯前，作出決定。我認為當你要作出投票決定前，你只要問一下自己，你生活有過得比四年前好嗎？當你在商店購物，你覺得有比四年前輕鬆嗎？相較四年前，有更多還是更少美國人民失業？美國還一如以往，受世界尊敬嗎？你覺得我們的國家的安全，仍有如四年前一樣強大嗎？如果你的答案是肯定的話，我認為你該選擇的人選是非常清楚了。但如果你不以為然，如果你認為過去四年的歷程，不是你未來四年還想要再要因循的生活的話，那我可以向你建議另外的選擇。

then I could suggest another choice that you have.

This country doesn't have to be in the shape that it is in. We do not have to go on sharing in scarcity with the country getting worse off, with unemployment growing. We talk about the unemployment lines. If all of the unemployed today were in a single line allowing two feet for each of them, that line would reach from New York City to Los Angeles, California. All of this can be cured and all of it can be solved. I have not had the experience the President has had in holding that office, but I think in being Governor of California, the most populous state in the Union - if it were a nation, it would be the seventh-ranking economic power in the world.

I know that the economic program that I have proposed for this nation in the next few years can resolve many of the problems that trouble us today. I know because we did it there. We cut the cost - the increased cost of government - in half over the eight years. We returned

這個國家真的可以不必過得像現在一般。我們可以不必繼續在貧乏中分享,將國家陷入持續貧窮與失業上揚。我們談一談失業的隊伍吧!如果今天我們讓所有失業人口,兩英尺間隔,排一直線,它可以從紐約排到洛杉磯。但所有的這一切是可以救治與解決的。我雖沒有總統職務的經驗,但我在擔任美國最大人口州的加州州長任內——如果加州是以國家身份的話,將是世界第七大經濟體。

我自信我所提出的國家經濟計畫,未來幾年內就能解決許多正困擾著我們的問題。我有把握是因為我們完成作到過。在八年任內,我們削減政府支出達到一半;我們以退稅、信貸或降除的

$5.7 billion in tax rebates, credits and cuts to our people. We, as I have said earlier, fell below the national average in inflation when we did that. And I know that we did give back authority and autonomy to the people.

I would like to have a crusade today, and I would like to lead that crusade with your help. And it would be one to take Government off the backs of the great people of this country, and turn you loose again to do those things that I know you can do so well, because you did them and made this country great. Thank you!

方法，退還人民五十七億美元。如我先前所述，當我們這樣執行後，加州人民是生活在全國通貨膨脹平均率之下，而且我知道我們確實將自主與自治還給百姓。

今天我需要一支救世軍，我也需要你們的協助去領導這支救世軍。它的目的就是要將政府對人民背負的管制卸除，讓你們能毫無負擔的去作我相信你們可以作的很好的工作，因為過去你們就是這樣，而使這個國家偉大。謝謝你們！

第十九篇 民主黨副總統提名演說

～女性的美國夢

吉拉汀‧費拉洛

▶▶ 最動人的佳句！**The most touching words**！

America is the land where dreams can come true for all of us. Our faith that we can shape a better future is what the American dream is all about.

～Geraldine Anne Ferraro

美國是一塊可以讓美夢成真之土地。我們能夠打造一個更美好未來之信念即是一切有關美國夢者。

～吉拉汀‧費拉洛

前言

一九八〇年，雷根開建美國近代史上最強的保守王朝，雷根對內，主張降低政府角色的重商措施，活絡市場；對外，進行積極干預政策，某種程度恢復了美國的國力與自信。但另一方面，由於放任工商資本家的營利與減少政府在社會福利的支出，美國也確實出現劫貧濟富，貧富不均與弱勢團體如黑人、婦女、兒童照顧不足下的虛榮假象。一九八四年，適逢大選，當美國沉醉在一連串的經濟景氣的數據與國外格瑞那達及阿富汗的干預成功，加上雷根個人魅力不減，保守氣勢達於頂峰時，民主黨為凸顯自

由進步的黨性，針對弱勢團體的不滿與雷根海外的窮兵黷武，大膽提名了美國史上首位女性副總統候選人吉拉汀費拉洛。

女性、義大利裔、天主教徒的費拉洛，完全是與美國的政治（正字）標記WASP背道而馳，象徵性的為美國女性的美國夢跨出了一大步，二十四年後，二〇〇八年大選，當民主黨希拉蕊可能完成更大夢想——總統候選人時，共和黨總統候選人麥肯歷史二度提名阿拉斯加州州長莎拉裴林作副總統競選搭檔，以示這個保守的老大黨也有進步思想的時候，我們絕對相信美國第一位女性的總統必然在本世紀出現。

歷史背景

費拉洛。一九三五年，出生於紐約，身為義大利移民後裔，從政前，作過老師，靠著上夜校進修法律，當上紐約地方檢察官，專事打擊女性侵害與兒童家暴犯罪；一九六八年進入國會，致力女性工作機會平等、同工同酬與退休制的立法工作，一九八四年大選，成為美國兩黨有史以來第一位最高公職——副總統之提名候選人，費拉洛七月十二日被告知這項邀請時，也難以置信說出：我真是嚇到了！（I am absolutely thrilled.），成為美國夢成真的第一位美國女性典型立說。

在全國女性組織（NOW）的促成與民主黨大老眾議院院長歐尼爾的背書下，孟岱爾最終挑選了費拉洛出任搭檔，希望能取得最大族群票源——女性的支持，尤其希望喚回一九八〇年，歸降雷根的民主黨選民。孟岱爾挑選費拉洛本身就是一項奇招，希望為他低迷的選情，製造性別的話題與美國夢的激情，帶動選情活力，費拉洛自信與銳利的口才也確實在開始階段造成奇襲的效

果，強力抨擊雷根劫貧濟富，崇尚武力的失政作為，曾在一段時間，將落後十六個百分點的民調拉平。

然成也費拉洛，敗也費拉洛，耀眼的光芒與話題性，媒體很快就盯上了費拉洛從事房地產業丈夫的逃稅問題，一開始費拉洛還信誓旦旦說，一個月內交待清楚，但也承認她在國會財產申報上，確實沒有納入丈夫財產收入的部分。之後，費拉洛發現事實較想像複雜，又改口因為公佈丈夫財務狀況，對其事業經營有不公平的影響又加拒絕。自此，整個孟岱爾競選陣營，就纏繞在電視報紙的費家逃稅報導。由於費拉洛處理的是「此地無銀三百兩」，再也難杜悠悠之口，其也承認「是我自己創造了一個怪獸。」（I created a monster），終於決定召開記者會，將逃稅以會計師的結算失誤帶過，希望就此打住，然巨大傷害已經造成，費拉洛在黨全國大會提名後所捲起的明星魅力大加失色，加上費拉洛身為天主教徒卻支持墮胎合法化與經驗上的不足及失言，更在選戰中成為攻擊與質疑的話柄。

一九八四年大選結果，孟岱爾——費拉洛得到41%的選民票，但選舉人票竟只在孟岱爾家鄉明尼蘇達州與哥倫比亞特區獲得勝利，餘皆盡墨，是美國大選史上勝負差距最大之一。至於費拉洛，別說紐約，連自己的國會選區都淪陷共和黨，55%的女性選民也把票投給了雷根，似乎費拉洛並沒有產生女性候選人的吸票效果。

民主黨的無力回天，自不能盡推大膽提名費拉洛所致，只能說雷根當時如日中天的聲望與吸引力，全美一片繁榮景象，雷根所喊的口號：「又是美國新的一天」（It's morning again in America.），舉重若輕的將選舉淡化處理，兩黨對決的選情氣

勢，始終無法凝聚發酵，美國分析家當時早已預料：民主黨出線的任何一組，皆非對手。持平而論，費拉洛的出現，反而是使這場原本預期乏味的選舉，有了歷史的意義與短暫激情，而不致淪為一場令人平凡以致遺忘的故事。

文獻介紹

民主黨副總統提名演說

吉拉汀・費拉洛

　　一九八四年民主黨全國黨代表大會上，最高潮動人的時刻，莫過於美國史上首位女性副總統候選人吉拉汀費拉洛宣佈被提名當時。自然，費拉洛的接受提名演說也成為美國女性美國夢的重要歷史文獻。全文，費拉洛以簡潔的文字，清楚道出美國夢的意涵：「你如果努力工作，規矩行事，你就可以贏取你應得的祝福。……選擇一位女性競選美國政府第二高之公職，正送出了一個訊號予全美人民：我們沒有打不開的大門，我們的成就是無限的。」，矢言恢復美國夢公平正義的傳統價值，改善雷根保守重商主義主政，照顧弱勢族群，重建家庭價值、改革稅制和「只知價格不知道價值」的教育、促進女性機會平等、與海外和平，重現為民所享、為民所治的政府。

Speech Accepting Democratic Vice-President Nomination

Geraldine Ferraro

Ladies and gentlemen of the convention:

My name is Geraldine Ferraro. I stand before you to proclaim tonight: America is the land where dreams can come true for all of us. As I stand before the American people and think of the honor this great convention has bestowed upon me, I recall the words of Dr. Martin Luther King Jr., who made America stronger by making America more free. He said, "Occasionally in life there are moments which cannot be completely explained by words. Their meaning can only be articulated by the inaudible language of the heart." Tonight is such a moment for me.

My heart is filled with pride. My fellow citizens, I proudly accept your nomination for Vice President of the United States.

大會上的女士與先生：

我是吉拉汀費拉洛。今晚，我站在你們面前宣告：美國是一塊可以讓美夢成真之土地。當我面對你們與思考著全國黨代表大會所授予我的榮耀時，我想起了使美國更強勁與自由的馬丁路德金恩的一些話。他說：「有時，生命中某些時刻，是無法完全以言語形容的。他們的意義只有來自內心靜默的語言足以道出。」對我而言，這一刻正是今晚。

我內心充滿驕傲。我親愛的同胞，我驕傲的接受你們美國副總統的提名。

And I am proud to run with a man who will be one of the great Presidents of this century, Walter F. Mondale. Tonight, the daughter of a woman whose highest goal was a future for her children talks to our nation's oldest party about a future for us all. Tonight, the daughter of working Americans tells all Americans that the future is within our reach, if we're willing to reach for it. Tonight, the daughter of an immigrant from Italy has been chosen to run for [Vice] President in the new land my father came to love.

Our faith that we can shape a better future is what the American dream is all about. The promise of our country is that the rules are fair. If you work hard and play by the rules, you can earn your share of America's blessings. Those are the beliefs I learned from my parents. And those are the values I taught my students as a teacher in the public schools of New York City.

我也很驕傲與將成為美國本世紀最偉大總統之一的華特孟岱爾搭擋競選。今晚,來自一位母親——她最高的目標是她子女的未來——的女兒將告訴這個國家最資深的政黨有關我們全體的未來。今晚,來自一位美國勞工家庭的女兒,將告訴美國人民未來已近在咫尺,只要我們願意迎接向前。今晚,來自一位義大利移民後代的女兒,已經被提名參選這塊我父親所熱愛土地的副總統。

我們的信仰是我們可以依照美國夢,打造一個更好的未來。我們國家的承諾就是規則都一定要公平。你如果努力工作,規矩行事,你就可以贏取你應得的祝福。這是我自我父母學習而來的信仰。這也是我在紐約公立學校當老師的時候,所教育我學生的價值。

At night, I went to law school. I became an assistant district attorney, and I put my share of criminals behind bars. I believe if you obey the law, you should be protected. But if you break the law, you must pay for your crime.

When I first ran for Congress, all the political experts said a Democrat could not win my home district in Queens. I put my faith in the people and the values that we shared. Together, we proved the political experts wrong. In this campaign, Fritz Mondale and I have put our faith in the people. And we are going to prove the experts wrong again. We are going to win. We are going to win because Americans across this country believe in the same basic dream.

Last week, I visited Elmore, Minnesota, the small town where Fritz Mondale was raised. And soon Fritz and Joan will visit our family in Queens. Nine hundred people live in Elmore. In Queens, there are 2,000 people on one block. You would think we'd be different, but

我利用晚上時間，上學進修法律。擔任地區助理檢察官時，我將罪犯繩之以法。我相信如果你守法，你應該得到保護。但如果你違背法律，你就必須為你的罪行，付出代價。

當我第一次參選國會議員時，所有美國政治專家都說：一位民主黨人，是不可能在我的家鄉皇后區勝選。但我把信任放在人民與我們共享的價值之上，結果我們共同讓這些政治專業跌破眼鏡。在這屆大選，我與孟岱爾再次寄信仰於人民，我們將證明這些專家再度錯誤。我們一定會贏。我們會贏，因為全國的美國人民相信共同基本的美國夢。

上週我拜訪孟岱爾長大的明尼蘇達州，Elmore小鎮。很快，孟岱爾與瓊安也會造訪我在皇后區的家庭。Elmore是個九百人的

we're not. Children walk to school in Elmore past grain elevators; in Queens, they pass by subway stops. But, no matter where they live, their future depends on education, and their parents are willing to do their part to make those schools as good as they can be. In Elmore, there are family farms; in Queens, small businesses. But the men and women who run them all take pride in supporting their families through hard work and initiative. On the 4th of July in Elmore, they hang flags out on Main Street; in Queens, they fly them over Grand Avenue. But all of us love our country, and stand ready to defend the freedom that it represents. Americans want to live by the same set of rules.

But under this administration, the rules are rigged against too many of our people. It isn't right that every year the share of taxes paid by individual citizens is going up, while the share paid by large corporations is getting smaller and smaller. The rules say: Everyone in our society should contribute their fair share. It isn't right that this year Ronald Reagan will hand the American people a bill for interest on

小鎮,而在皇后區單一條街就有兩千住民,人們一定會想我們兩人一定截然不同,但事實不是這樣。在Elmore的孩童總是走路穿過穀倉,而皇后區的兒童是地鐵站,但不論身處何地,他們的未來都是依賴教育,而他們的父母都願盡其所能的將社區的學校辦好。在Elmore,家家務農,皇后區,則是小型商業,但不論經營的男女都經由認真的工作與開創,驕傲地養家活口。七月四日,不論在Elmore或是皇后區,居民都在大街上掛出國旗,旗海飛揚。所有居民都熱愛國家,隨時準備保護她所代表的自由。這也是所有美國人生活上,堅守的同樣規律。

但在當今政府下,這些原本的規範都被舞弄違背了大多數人民。絕對錯誤的是:每年由個人公民支付的稅是越來越高,但大

the national debt larger than the entire cost of the federal government under John F. Kennedy. Our parents left us a growing economy. The rules say: We must not leave our kids a mountain of debt.

It isn't right that a woman should get paid 59 cents on the dollar for the same work as a man.

If you play by the rules, you deserve a fair day's pay for a fair day's work. It isn't right that, if trends continue, by the year 2000 nearly all of the poor people in America will be women and children. It isn't right that young people today fear they won't get the Social Security they paid for, and that older Americans fear that they will lose what they have already learned [earned]. Social Security is a contract between the last generation and the next, and the rules say: You don't break contracts.

公司的繳稅卻越來越低。規則是：社會每一份子貢獻的部分，當是公平的。但在今年，雷根將給美國人民一張國債的利息帳單，竟大於甘迺迪政府時期的全部支出。過去，我們的父母留給我們一個成長的經濟。規則告訴我們：我們決不能高築債台，留給子孫。

作同樣的工作，一位女性只能拿五毛九，男性是一塊錢，這是錯誤的。

如果你按照遊戲規則；每天，你就應得公平的報酬於公平的工作。照此趨勢，到了公元兩千年，美國的窮人都是婦人孺子，這是錯誤的。今天年輕人害怕將來享受不到由他們支付的社會安全保險金，老年人又恐怕會失去他們既得利益，這是錯誤的。社

It isn't right that young couples question whether to bring children into a world of 50,000 nuclear warheads. That isn't the vision for which Americans have struggled for more than two centuries. And our future doesn't have to be that way. Change is in the air, just as surely as when John Kennedy beckoned America to a new frontier; when Sally Ride rocketed into space; and when Reverend Jesse Jackson ran for the office of President of the United States.

By choosing a woman to run for our nation's second highest office, you send a powerful signal to all Americans: There are no doors we cannot unlock. We will place no limits on achievement. If we can do this, we can do anything.

Tonight, we reclaim our dream. We're going to make the rules of American life work fairly for all Americans again. To an Administration that would have us debate all over again whether the Voting Rights Act should be renewed and whether segregated schools should be tax exempt, we say, Mr. President: Those debates are over. On the issue

會安全保險是上下兩代的契約，規則是：你不可違反契約。

年青人質疑要不要生兒育女在一個充滿五千顆核子彈頭的世界，增產報國，這是錯誤的。這也決不是美國人兩百多年奮鬥的願景。而我們的未來也不必是被這樣安排。改變已在空氣中，就與甘迺迪時代比喻美國是新邊界一樣的確定；與莎莉賴德──第一位女太空人一樣的確定；與黑人牧師傑克遜競選美國總統一樣的確定。

選擇一位女性競選美國第二高之公職，正送出了一個訊號予全美人民：我們沒有打不開的大門，我們的成就無限。如果我作得到這點，我們可以作任何事。

今晚我們將重新取回夢想的權利。我們要恢復美國生活規

of civil rights, voting rights, and affirmative action for minorities, we must not go backwards. We must -- and we will -- move forward to open the doors of opportunity.

To those who understand that our country cannot prosper unless we draw on the talents of all Americans, we say: We will pass the Equal Rights Amendment. The issue is not what America can do for women, but what women can do for America.

To those concerned about the strength of American and family values, as I am, I say: We are going to restore those values -- love, caring, partnership -- by including, and not excluding, those whose beliefs differ from our own. Because our own faith is strong, we will fight to preserve the freedom of faith for others.

To those working Americans who fear that banks, utilities, and large special interests have a lock on the White House, we say: Join us; let's elect the people's President; and let's have government by and for the American people again.

範再度公平對待每位人民。對一個讓我們討論半天是否投票權利法要更改，實施隔離的學校是否應該免稅，我們應該說：總統先生，這些辯論該結束了。對公民權、投票權與少數民族的保障數額的行動法，我們都不該走回頭路。我們必須，我們也將，繼續向前打開機會大門。

除非我們誘發所有美國人民才華，否則不足以繁榮國家，我們會說：我們將支持通過平權法案。爭議不是美國能為女性作些什麼，而是女性能為美國作些什麼。

對關心美國國力與家庭價值者，我想說：我們要恢復愛、關懷與伙伴關係的價值，方法是包容而非排除與我們信仰相違背者。因為我有強大的信念，我們會為保護其他人的信仰自由而奮鬥。

To an Administration that would savage student loans and education at the dawn of a new technological age, we say: You fit the classic definition of a cynic; you know the price of everything, but the value of nothing.

To our students and their parents, we say: We will insist on the highest standards of excellence, because the jobs of the future require skilled minds. To young Americans who may be called to our country's service, we say: We know your generation will proudly answer our country's call, as each generation before you.

This past year, we remembered the bravery and sacrifice of Americans at Normandy. And we finally paid tribute to that Unknown Soldier who represents all the brave young Americans who died in Vietnam. Let no one doubt, we will defend America's security and the cause of freedom around the world. But we want a President who tells us what America's fighting for, not just what we are fighting against.

We want a President who will defend human rights, not just where it is convenient, but wherever freedom is at risk -- from Chile to

對害怕銀行、大企業與大型特殊利益團體控制白宮，辛勤工作的美國人民，我想說：加入我們；選出全民的總統；重現為民所享、為民所治的政府。

在新科技時代的黎明時期，對一個濫用學生貸款與教育的政府，我想說：你合適犬儒的典型定義，你知道所有東西的價格卻不知道價值。

對我們的學生與家長，我想說：我們會堅持卓越的標準，因為未來工作市場的要求是進步的心智。對可能會接受國家召喚服務的年輕美國人民，我想說：我知道你們這一代會驕傲的回應國家的召喚，就如同你們的前代一樣。

過去年間，我們緬懷在諾曼第勇敢犧牲的美國人。我們也要

Afghanistan, from Poland to South Africa. To those who have watched this administration's confusion in the Middle East, we wonder: "Will America stand by her friends and sister democracy?" we say: America knows who her friends are in the Middle East and around the world. America will stand with Israel always.

Finally, we want a President who will keep America strong, but use that strength to keep America and the world at peace. A nuclear freeze is not a slogan: It is a tool for survival in the nuclear age. If we leave our children nothing else, let us leave them this Earth as we found it: whole and green and full of life.

I know in my heart that Walter Mondale will be that President.

A wise man once said, "Every one of us is given the gift of life, and what a strange gift it is. If it is preserved jealously and selfishly, it impoverishes and saddens. But if it is spent for others, it enriches and beautifies." My fellow Americans: We can debate policies and programs, but in the end what separates the two parties in this election

向所有在越南犧牲生命的年青美國無名英雄致上敬意。不要讓人懷疑，我們將保衛美國的安全與世界的自由運動。但我們需要的總統是告訴我們為何而戰，而不是對什麼而戰。

我們要的總統是能在人類自由陷入危機的任何地方——從智利到阿富汗，從波蘭到南非，捍衛人權，不是見機行事。對看到這個政府在中東政策上混亂的人，我們不禁想知道：美國會站在她民主朋友的一邊嗎？

最後我們所要的總統不只能使美國保持強大，益能善用力量維護美國與世界的和平。凍結核武不只是個口號，他是在核子時代生存下去的工具。如果我們什麼也無法遺留子孫，至少我們可以給他們一個不多不少原來一樣的地球：充滿綠意與生命。

campaign is whether we use the gift of life for others or only ourselves.

To my daughters, Donna and Laura, and my son, John Junior, I say: My mother did not break faith with me, and I will not break faith with you.

To all the children of America, I say: The generation before ours kept faith with us, and like them, we will pass on to you a stronger, more just America.

在我內心，我知道孟岱爾正是我們所要的總統。

智者嘗言：每個人都擁有生命中的天賦，這是一份多麼奇異的厚禮。如果自戀、自私的加意以保留，它只帶來貧窮與悲傷。如果能善加於他人，則帶來富裕與美好。我親愛的美國同胞：固然我們不斷爭辯政策與計畫，但真正區隔這兩大政黨的是誰善用這生命的天份來利於他人或自私的利於自身。

向我的兒、女，我要說：我的母親沒有違背信仰於我，我也不會違背信仰於你們。

至於向所有的美國兒女們，我要說：上一代維持我們這一信仰，像他們一樣，我們將傳承給你們的會是一個更強大、更公平的美國。

第二十篇　我有罪

～緋聞──政治之致命吸引力？

比爾‧柯林頓

前言

古時，堯嘗以娥皇、女英兩女下嫁舜，作舜治國能耐之察測。但近代民主政治下，劈腿緋聞可是政治人物之致命吸引力，不論中、外，下場往往不是拋棄江山，就是退出政壇。但美國史上亦有例外者，就總統言，傑佛遜與女黑奴不但相戀，甚至結晶；如甘迺迪，自始花邊消息不斷，但皆無損他們在美國人民心中魅力地位，堪稱異數。最近者則數柯林頓與白宮實習生陸文斯基的不倫緋聞戀，不同他前輩是，柯林頓嚴重至被眾議院提出彈劾，雖然最後參議院表決未過，讓他驚險地躲過一劫。

雖然成為第一位因緋聞受國會彈劾的總統，事後，柯林頓卻仍能維持民間聲望不墜，卸任，更是四處遊走，大發演講財，這與尼克森一生銷聲匿跡，低調生活的下場，實在有如天壤之別，

我想這主歸功柯林頓的政績卓越，任內打平政府近乎天文的財政赤字，帶領美國享受了十年的景氣繁榮，贏得美國民眾的支持與肯定；另外，柯林頓個性上講求協調溝通，使他在內外都深具人緣；最後，畢竟緋聞屬私領域的過失，不似尼克森公領域的權力腐敗，無法取得諒解，加上柯林頓在緋聞上的危機控管，能誠實面對，宛若進入告解室，說出：I have sinned.，以宗教方式的懺悔，向全國人民道歉；的確有效打動了以基督教義——寬恕為基本價值的大部美國人民。

歷史背景

比爾・柯林頓，一九四六年八月十九日出生在阿肯色州，父親在他出生的三個月前因車禍喪生。四歲時，母親改嫁羅傑・柯林頓，但一直到中學時，他才改從繼父的姓氏：柯林頓。中學時代的柯林頓相當活躍，不僅是位優秀的學生，也是位出色的薩克斯風手，還一度想成為音樂家，直到代表阿肯色州到華府，接受甘乃迪總統表揚，柯林頓才立志選擇政治為事業。

一九七八年，柯林頓當選阿肯色州州長，但尋求連任失敗。一九八六年他捲土重來，再度當選；直到一九九二年，他打敗了當時的美國總統共和黨籍的老布希，順利地成為美國第四十二位總統。不但中斷美國自雷根八〇年代起建下的保守王朝，並創下白宮與國會多數皆由民主黨掌握的局勢，柯林頓與他的搭檔高爾也被視為是美國新一代的政治領袖。

九零年代的經濟繁榮：柯林頓執政期間最大的成就與引以為傲者就是美國的經濟榮景。柯林頓任內，將在尼克森經濟衰退與雷根過度信用擴張下，政府大量舉債所造成的巨大財政赤字逐年

減少，並在卸任時交出一份財政盈餘漂亮成績單，美國的失業率創下當代最低紀錄、通貨膨脹維持在三十年來最低水準，九○年代開始，一個嶄新的科技產業——網際網路革命，創造了一個帶有巨大產值的新產業，連帶創造了高薪的工作機會，帶動了經濟的運轉。股票市場的快速膨脹則讓股民享受了幾年的紙上富貴。同時，並擁有美國歷史上最高的自有住屋率、許多地方犯罪率下降。他讓教育升級，保障必須照顧生病孩童的父母工作權，限制手槍買賣並且強化環保法令。

在國際事務上，他擴大北大西洋公約組織，成功派出維和部隊協助飽受戰火摧殘的波士尼亞；對中國能彈性採取「交往」政策，將人權與經貿脫鉤，和平改變中國的民主，同時也能有為有守，堅定立場對中國一九九六年企圖以飛彈試射恫嚇台灣大選，派出航空母艦進行干預。他讓國際貿易在世界貿易組織架構下，更開放，並且發動世界性打擊毒品交易。當他訪問南美、歐洲、俄羅斯、非洲與中國等地方，推廣美國式的自由精神時，亦受到廣大民眾的歡迎。

「拉鏈門」案件。一九九八年，柯林頓同白宮女實習生莫妮卡・陸文斯基的性醜聞被曝光，受到司法部門調查。共和黨並在國會提出了彈劾議案，但定罪未獲通過。這就是著名的「拉鏈門」案件，由於事件太過煽情、八卦，陸文斯基事件成為柯林頓任內上最不光彩與最富記憶的一頁。

一九九六年大選結束後，柯林頓的白宮處於選後的放鬆狀態，碰巧當時共和黨的國會為了預算問題而與白宮抗爭，凍結了聯邦開支，許多政府僱員都被指示暫時不要來上班，造成了包括白宮在內的許多政府機關空空蕩蕩的沒有幾個人。就是在這樣

的一個大環境下，柯林頓和白宮實習生莫妮卡・陸文斯基邂逅、調情、並發展為情人關係。一九九七年四月，陸文斯基的上司擔心她與總統過從太密，於是把她調職到國防部。陸文斯基在國防部認識了琳達・崔普，陸文斯基開始向崔普透露與總統交往的內容。她不知道，關於這個滔天秘密的電話談話被崔普秘密錄音。

　　一九九八年一月，與柯林頓有染的寶拉・瓊斯性騷擾案的原告律師開始搜集總統拈花惹草的證據，大火燒到了陸文斯基，她雖呈交了書面證詞宣稱自己沒有和總統往來，但是崔普不願冒偽證罪的危險，於是將她的錄音帶拿給了特別檢察官肯尼斯・史達。於是，史達介入了這宗桃色事件的調查。柯林頓一開始否認跟陸文斯基有染。在公開的場合以及宣誓作證的情況下他都斬釘截鐵的宣稱自己和陸文斯基沒有性關係。柯林頓所賴以理直氣壯的撒謊的邏輯是，由於「自己只是接受服務的一方，因此不算有性關係」。但是錄音帶以及陸文斯基的詳細日記迫使她把事實合盤托出，而陸文斯基所提供的證據又證明總統說了謊。最關鍵的證據是一件沾有總統精液的藍色洋裝，陸文斯基原想把它留作紀念，沒想到卻留下了總統的DNA證據。當化驗結果出爐，總統不得不對全國發表講話，向人民道歉，承認自己和陸文斯基有不正當的交往。

　　史上第二次的總統彈劾。長久積弱不振的共和黨人抓住了這千載難逢的機會，想導入尼克森式的說謊及扣上刑事偽證罪的情境模式，對他提出了彈劾。很明顯，共和黨人起心於政黨權力的爭奪，而採取了偏激的立場，把小事化大，反使柯林頓更似一八六八年的強生總統因黨派利益，被國會報復式的濫起彈劾公器；他們的行為自然沒有被選民認同；一九九八年期中選舉，民主黨依然取得勝利。

　　但是柯林頓也承認是咎由自取，按照他自己的說法，是他「給了政敵們一把刀子，而他們把刀子刺進了他的心臟」。柯林頓成為美國歷史上第二位被彈劾的總統。按照美國憲法規定，對總統的控罪在參議院進行審判，最高法院首席大法官威廉・倫奎斯特擔任法官，全部參議員作為陪審團，眾議院則派出十五名眾議員擔任檢察官。必須有三分之二參議員投贊成票，控罪才能成立。結果，柯林頓於一九九八年十二月十九日被眾議院彈劾，指控其對大陪審團作偽證及妨礙司法公正。但決定性投贊成票的參議員沒有過半數；總統的控罪不成立。整個事件才終於落幕。

　　可見要看到總統彈劾案例已是難得，但要真正見到成功的彈劾總統，更幾近不可能，原因不外，如果彈劾案真的勢在必過，總統必定以辭職避免此一不光彩的紀錄，這也是為什麼尼克森雖然不受正式彈劾的歷史記載，但所有人也知道他確是受彈劾的壓迫，而不支下台。

我有罪

比爾・柯林頓

　　相較雷根在「伊朗、尼游案」以名言「我不知道。」（I had no idea.）規避，被人譏之「不是說謊就是昏庸」，當白宮女實習生陸文斯基的性醜聞曝光後，柯林頓面對檢察官史達的詰問偵察下，為避免類似的困境，卻以「我想不起來。」（I can't recall.）模糊地否認，深顯柯林頓的虛心與焦慮；待陸文斯基交出沾有總統精液的藍色洋裝，經化驗出染有柯林頓DNA證據，柯林頓又聲明與陸女僅限口交而無性交的牽強推諉，仍不得人民諒解後，柯林頓終於發表全國講話，向人民道歉，承認自己和陸文斯基的確有不正當的交往。

　　柯林頓以全國作一告解室（confession room），人民作傾聽告解之神父；全文拉高層次，以國家、人民、孩童教養以至家庭作致歉目標，關鍵女主角陸文斯基的名字僅出現一次；並引用告解話語「我有罪」，要求寬恕。在美國經典文獻上，柯林頓因桃色事件以致彈劾，這篇「緋聞懺悔錄」，自是希罕之作，全文充滿宗教包容大愛，也反映美國人民意識受宗教浸染之深，柯林頓除了訴求上帝的憐憫，以打動美國人心，取得原諒外，也別無他法了！

I have sinned

Bill Clinton

It is an unusual and, I think, unusually important day today. I may not be quite as easy with my words today as I have been in years past, and I was up rather late last night thinking about and praying about what I ought to say today. And rather unusual for me, I actually tried to write it down. So if you will forgive me, I will do my best to say what it is I want to say to you.

First, I want to say to all of you that, as you might imagine, I have been on quite a journey these last few weeks to get to the end of this, to the rock bottom truth of where I am and where we all are.

I agree with those who have said that in my first statement after I testified I was not contrite enough. I don't think there is a fancy way to say that I have sinned.

It is important to me that everybody who has been hurt know that the sorrow I feel is genuine: first and most important, my family; also

　　我想今天是不尋常且特殊重要的一日。今天，我也不能如同往年般輕鬆的暢所欲言。昨晚我徹夜禱告及思考今天我應該說些什麼。所以如果你們願意寬恕我，我將盡一切向你傾訴我的話語。

　　首先，如你所預計，我要向你們說的是過去幾個禮拜以來，我經歷了一段掙扎的長路才到盡頭，到那有如磐石般事實的深處。

　　我同意某些人所說的我出庭後的第一次說明，悔意實在不足。現在，我想我最坦白表達方式就是說出：我有罪。

　　現在對我最重要的是讓每一個受到傷害的人，能瞭解到我的歉意，其中之首要者就是我的家人，還有我的友人，幕僚，內閣，陸

my friends, my staff, my Cabinet, Monica Lewinsky and her family, and the American people. I have asked all for their forgiveness.

But I believe that to be forgiven, more than sorrow is required - at least two more things. First, genuine repentance - a determination to change and to repair breaches of my own making. I have repented. Second, what my bible calls a "broken spirit"; an understanding that I must have God's help to be the person that I want to be; a willingness to give the very forgiveness I seek; a renunciation of the pride and the anger which cloud judgment, lead people to excuse and compare and to blame and complain.

Now, what does all this mean for me and for us? First, I will instruct my lawyers to mount a vigorous defence, using all available appropriate arguments. But legal language must not obscure the fact that I have done wrong. Second, I will continue on the path of repentance, seeking pastoral support and that of other caring people so that they can hold me accountable for my own commitment.

文斯基及其家庭與全美人民，我在此祈求他們所有人的原諒。

但我相信要被原諒光是歉意是不夠的，至少還有兩件事情。第一，是真心的懺悔——決心改過並且修補我所造成的損傷。我已悔過。第二，是聖經所謂之「破損的靈魂」，我了解到必須有神的扶持我才能作我想要的自己，並願意給予我所追求的所有寬恕，拋棄驕傲與憤怒，因為它們會蒙蔽判斷，導致人們尋找藉口與計較及歸咎與抱怨。

現在所有的事件對我及我們的意義為何？首先，我會指示我的律師使用所有可得的適當理由，進行有力的辯護。但是法律語言不能遮蔽我犯過的事實。其次，我會繼續在懺悔的路程，尋求

Third, I will intensify my efforts to lead our country and the world toward peace and freedom, prosperity and harmony, in the hope that with a broken spirit and a still strong heart I can be used for greater good, for we have many blessings and many challenges and so much work to do.

In this, I ask for your prayers and for your help in healing our nation. And though I cannot move beyond or forget this - indeed, I must always keep it as a caution light in my life - it is very important that our nation move forward.

I am very grateful for the many, many people - clergy and ordinary citizens alike - who have written me with wise counsel. I am profoundly grateful for the support of so many Americans who somehow through it all seem to still know that I care about them a great deal, that I care about their problems and their dreams. I am grateful for those who have stood by me and who say that in this case and many others, the bounds of privacy have been excessively and unwisely invaded. Nevertheless, in this case, it may be a blessing, because I still

宗教與其他關心我朋友的支持，讓我對自己的承諾負責。

　　第三，我會加強努力領導國家與世界朝向和平與自由，繁榮與和諧；希望以一個受損的靈魂與強勁的心力，我還能為更大的公益而用，因為我們還有許多的祝福挑戰與工作等待我們去作。

　　在此，我祈求你們的禱告與支持來為國療傷。雖然我是不可能這從次事件得到解脫與忘卻———的確，我必須終身以此為戒，但讓我們的國家保持前進卻是最重要的。

　　我極為感謝許多人不論是宗教或一般平民寫信給我明智的建言。我對經歷過這一切卻能支持與知道我仍然關心他們的困難與夢想的眾多人士表達感激之意。我也要與我站在相同立場，與

sinned. And if my repentance is genuine and sustained, and if I can maintain both a broken spirit and a strong heart, then good can come of this for our country as well as for me and my family.

The children of this country can learn in a profound way that integrity is important and selfishness is wrong, but God can change us and make us strong at the broken places. I want to embody those lessons for the children of this country - for that little boy in Florida who came up to me and said that he wanted to grow up and be President and to be just like me. I want the parents of all the children in America to be able to say that to their children.

A couple of days ago when I was in Florida a Jewish friend of mine gave me this liturgy book called "Gates of Repentance." And there was this incredible passage from the Yom Kippur liturgy. I would like to read it to you:

在本案中直言個人私領域已受到過度、不明智侵犯的人士表示感謝。然而,在本案,它也許是個護佑 ,因為我仍然有罪。如果我能真正且持續懺悔,如果我能維持一個受傷的靈魂與強健的心靈,善反由此降臨到國家、個人甚至我的家庭。

這個國家的兒童也可以在一個最深刻的方式下,學到正直是對的,自私是錯的,上帝可以改變我們,讓我們在破碎的地方堅強。我要將這項教訓具體地教育這個國家的下一代——就像那位在佛州對我說將來長大要作總統且要與我一樣的小孩。我要所有全美小孩們的父母,以此告誡他們的子女。

幾天前,佛羅里達州的一位猶太朋友送給我一本名為《懺悔

"Now is the time for turning. The leaves are beginning to turn from green to red to orange. The birds are beginning to turn and are heading once more toward the south. The animals are beginning to turn to storing their food for the winter. For leaves, birds and animals, turning comes instinctively. But for us, turning does not come so easily. It takes an act of will for us to make a turn. It means breaking old habits. It means admitting that we have been wrong, and this is never easy. It means losing face. It means starting all over again. And this is always painful. It means saying I am sorry. These things are terribly hard to do. But unless we turn, we will be trapped forever in yesterday's ways. Lord help us to turn, from callousness to sensitivity, from hostility to love, from pettiness to purpose, from envy to contentment, from carelessness to discipline, from fear to faith. Turn us around, O Lord, and bring us back toward you. Revive our lives as at the beginning, and turn us toward each other, Lord, for in isolation there is no life."

之門》的祈禱文書，其中有關猶太贖罪日的祈禱文句，我想念給你們聽：

現在是改變的時候了！葉子正在由綠轉為紅，再變橘色。鳥兒也正轉向再度往南飛去。動物也忙著儲存食物，以備過冬。就葉子、鳥兒與動物，這些轉變出自本能，但對人類的我們，改變卻是何其難也。因為轉變意謂著羞辱；意謂著重頭來過；意謂著總是痛苦。這些都是極其難以作到的代價。但除非我們轉變，否則我們將永遠陷於過去的框架。上帝會扶助我們轉變，讓我們從空虛到敏慧，從敵視到愛惜，從遺憾到目標，從散漫到紀律，從恐懼到信仰。上帝！請你幫助轉變我們，帶我們回頭向你靠近。

I thank my friend for that. I thank you for being here. I ask you to share my prayer that God will search me and know my heart, try me and know my anxious thoughts, and lead me toward the life everlasting. I ask that God give me a clean heart, let me walk by faith and not sight.

I ask once again to be able to love my neighbour - all my neighbours - as my self, to be an instrument of God's peace; to let the words of my mouth and the meditations of my heart and, in the end, the work of my hands, be pleasing. This is what I wanted to say to you today.

Thank you. God bless you.

讓我們回到最初的生命，相互面對，因為生命不存在孤立之中。

我為此感激我的朋友。我感謝你們的陪伴，我祈求你們一起為我祈禱：上帝能發現我，明瞭我的心境，考驗我，且清楚我焦慮的心思，並引領我進入永恆的生命。我請求神給我一個乾淨的心靈，讓我以信仰而非所見行走人生。

我再次要求能夠愛護我的鄰居──所有的鄰居，如己；並成為上帝和平的工具，讓我口出的話語與心中的思索及最後手上的工作成為喜悅。這就是今天我想要向你所說的。

謝謝你們，願上帝保佑你

第二十一篇　二〇〇〇年敗選感言

～國家利益永遠在政黨利益之上

艾‧高爾

▶▶ 最動人的佳句！**The most touching words**！

There is a higher duty than the one we owe to political party. This
is America and we put country before party.

～ Al Gore

還有一個更高於我們對政黨的責任，就是美國，我們永遠把

國家置於政黨之前。

～艾‧高爾

前言

　　美國舉行總統大選，自首屆一七八八年至今二〇〇八年止，
已行之二二〇年，計五十六屆，共產生了四十四位總統，長久的歷
史，獨特的大選「選舉人團」制度，的確產生了多次的憲政危機，
譬如一八〇〇年傑佛遜的大選難產（見第三篇）或是像民選票少，
但卻拿到多數的選舉人票的「少數總統（minority president）」產
生，誇張者一八七六年大選，四個州發生計票糾紛，結果竟由兩黨
協議，弄出了美國歷史上首位的冒牌總統──共和黨海斯。最近一
次大選爭議，發生在二〇〇〇年總統大選，情況類似一八七六年的
計票糾紛，過程一路戲劇化，民主黨的高爾與共和黨的布希，自開

票後，選舉人票就一路僵持，最後勝負端看佛羅里達州，結果布希僅以極少數的選民票數差距險勝，但高爾按佛州法律，只要票數差距低於5%，可要求佛州重新驗票。在重新計、驗票過程中，出現了高爾極有翻盤可能時候，最高法院卻殺出認為佛州人工計票標準不一，有違法律平等保護原則，以五比四的裁決，判決布希贏得佛州選舉，布希失而復得，拿走所有二十五張選舉人票，而得以最低門檻的二七一張選舉人票，氣走高爾。

儘管美國大選不時險象環生，但令人佩服是歷年來這些大選憲政的爭議，只圍繞在制度的不清與複雜，候選人總能維持理性，不操弄民粹，可見民主之實力關乎素養而非制度。在二○○○年大選中，當最高法院一旦宣判勝負，即使高爾在全美選民票較布希多出三十萬，乃最具「民意」者，隔日，高爾毅然承認敗選，不但呈現他個人謂「國家利益永遠在政黨利益之上」的胸襟氣度，也看到了美國兩黨與選民高度成熟的政治互動。

歷史背景

二千年的美國大選，民主、共和兩黨可說是勢均力敵、勝負難分，十一月七日開票，選民票部分，高爾較布希高出三十多萬票。在選舉人票部分，高爾以二六七票比二四六票領先（當選門檻是二七○張），最後勝負端看佛羅里達州。結果，共和黨的小布希以極小多數，贏得該州，而獲得全部二十五張的總統選舉人票當選總統。八日早上民主黨候選人高爾以電話向布希道賀，然而沒多久，高爾的助理即告訴他由於佛州規定選票相差不到百分之五，可重新驗票，代表並未失敗。於是高爾又撤回認輸的前電，要求佛州重新計票。由於重新計票使得布希領先高爾的票

數，由一七八四票減為三二七票，共和黨見苗頭不對，隨即向法院請求制止人工計票，而民主黨則是請法院制止佛州州務卿哈莉士得依佛州法律，於大選後七日，即十一月十四日宣布結果，之後雙方陣營皆控告到聯邦最高法院。

由於佛州法律規定必須在十二月十二日報告總統選舉人名單，所以聯邦最高法院於十二月十二日以七票對二票，判定佛州未以統一標準驗票，有違憲法平等保障原則，故人工驗票應屬無效。又以五票對四票判決，由於佛州來不及做一個統一的標準重新驗票，因此只能依照原先機器統計結果，由小布希贏得佛羅里達州，而贏得佛州二十五張總統選舉人票，成為第一位由聯邦最高法院判決當選的美國總統，終告正式落幕。二千年的美國總統選舉，是相當特殊的，其歷史特別之處有四點：

一、選舉投票後過了三十五天，才決定誰當選總統：

　　在美國歷史上，這種狀況只有兩次：一八〇一年，眾議院投票三十六次，經過七天才確定傑佛遜當選總統；一八七六年，共和黨海斯與民主黨的泰登相爭，直到民主黨以犧牲泰登總統大位，換取了共和黨海斯當選後，承諾結束共和黨對南方的軍事統治與默許南方各州黑人歧視立法，結果計達兩個月才出籠。

二、其為唯一因聯邦最高法院判決大選驗票方式，贏得過半數總統選舉人票而當選的總統：類似一八七六年由國會與最高法院組成的十五人選舉委員會投票決定而當選的海斯。

三、其為美國歷史上以較少選民票，較多總統候選人票當選總統的第四個人：另有一八四二年的小亞當斯、一八七六的海斯、一八八八的哈里遜。

四、布希是繼亞當斯之後，第二對美國父子檔總統

以上種種的爭議，其實已臻國家憲政危機，也屢屢暴露了由來已久的爭議──美國大選選舉人團制度的適時與適法性。

贏者全拿的美國選舉人團制度。回顧到一七八七年的制憲會議上，如何選舉總統成為制憲會議爭議的焦點，最終出現了四種選舉方案：國會選舉，各州州長選舉，全國人民直選，選舉人團選舉。經過麥迪遜等人的反覆說明和辯論，大部分制憲代表認為：一是由人民直接選舉總統極其困難，因為國家幅員遼闊而當時的交通又不便，況且南北方的差別較大，人民不能全面了解情況，容易受少數陰謀家的操縱。二是立法、行政、司法三權應該相互獨立，相互制約，所以總統不應受到國會的控制，不應由國會選舉產生。最後，制憲代表們達成妥協，採納了選舉人團的方案，也就是總統不是由全國人民票選，用選舉人替代人民大眾選舉總統，才能最有效地繞過這些弊端。美國選舉人團制度的特別之處在於，除了緬因和內布拉斯加兩個州是按普選票得票比例分配選舉人票外，其餘48個州和華盛頓特區均實行「勝者全拿」制度（winner-take-all），即在該州獲得相對多數普選票的總統候選人，即可拿走本州的全部選舉人票。至於各州的總統選舉人在當選前一般都需向選民承諾支持某黨的總統候選人，最高法院曾裁定，憲法並未要求讓選舉人完全自由的去投票，因此政黨可以取得選舉人的保證，一定投票給該黨提名的候選人。有些州的法律規定，所謂的「不守信用選舉人」可處以罰鍰，或因投下無效票而遭取消資格，由替代選舉人加以取代。

至於每州有多少的選舉人票數額，則等同該州在國會的參、眾議員總人數，全國共計參議員100人，眾議員435人，共535人。

一九六一年批准的第二十三條憲法修正案，增加華盛頓特區3名選舉人，總統選舉人因此增到538人。目前，加利福尼亞州選舉人票最多，達55張，德克薩斯州34張，紐約州31張，而阿拉斯加、德拉瓦和懷俄明等每州只有3張。當選者必需得到超過半數選舉人票，即至少獲得270票的選舉人票。

選舉人團制度——民主的鍛鍊場？根據參考資料，過去兩百年來，國會內共提出過七百多個改革或取消選舉人團的提案。美國律師公會曾批評選舉人團為「古老」而「曖昧」，其一九八七年的調查顯示，69%的律師贊成廢除。其反對者的觀點有：第一、違背了選舉多數決的原則，讓得到普選票較少而選舉人票稍多的人當選為總統，違反了一人一票、每票等值的原則（one man, one vote）；第二、大小州選民的票值不等，不僅忽視了民意，也會產生幕後交易問題，如一八二四年的亞當斯犧牲了傑克遜和一八七六年的海斯當選；第三、第三黨在選舉人團制度中一向得票不多，實際上強化了兩黨制，限制了選民的選擇權；如一九六八年阿拉巴馬州州長喬治·華理士，在南方贏得不少選舉人票，雖可能影響選舉結果，但尚不足以真正挑戰到主要政黨的勝選者。羅斯·裴洛雖贏得一九九二年全國普選票的19%但未得到任何選舉人票，因為他並沒有在任何一州或幾個州得票特別多；選舉人團制度是針對十八世紀的問題，已經不適應二十一世紀的需要了，但美國選舉人團為什麼依然屹立不搖？選舉人團是美國憲法原始設計的一部分。必須通過憲法修正案才能改變這種制度。修憲的方法是：必須由參眾兩院三分之二的大多數通過提出修正案，再取得四分之三的州（三十七州）批准。諷刺是，「勝者全拿」的制度是有利人口少的小州，因為至少還有三張選

舉人票,使候選人不敢過於輕忽小州和偏遠地區的利益,所以亦有鞏固聯邦之效,這使小州與大州一樣都不願加入批准廢止選舉人團的修正案。這也是為何多年來許多建議由全國人民直接選舉總統的提議,均未獲得國會通過而交由各州批准。

　　因此,短期內,美國的大選制恐難有所變動,也許正如高爾所言美國民主的內涵,就在解決爭議,因為沒有一套制度是可以保障民主一百年的,只有人民的意見不斷在理性和平中考驗磨合,才是提昇民主的最好鍛鍊,而我們也確實看見美國民主的實力每經過一次選舉,就充實壯大一次,見及此,難道選舉人團的不完善,也是美國建國先賢刻意下的國家寶藏嗎?

文獻介紹

二○○○年敗選感言

艾‧高爾

今晚，為了全國人民的團結，與我們民主的力量，我願無異議的接受敗選事實。……．有關今晚結束的選戰，我堅信我父親曾說過：「不論失敗的有多慘，失敗與勝利一樣可以鍛造靈魂，綻放榮耀。」，美國歷史上很少有敗選者卻比當選者，更見吸引與氣度者，如高爾的敗選感言，完全掩蓋布希的勝選風采，呈現更高層次的大器、智慧與崇高風範，打動無數美國人民。到了二○○三年，當美國民主黨企圖擁戴高爾復出與小布希○四年，再一雌雄時，高爾竟以「如果我參選，大選勢將陷入二○○○年的爭議，美國應向前景瞻望。」回絕，完全放下個人的意氣與民粹的誘惑。

所謂「施比受更有福」，也的確，七年間，這兩位當初總統候選人的經歷遭遇，有著截然不同的發展與評價。當初的勝者，結局是身陷戰爭泥淖與金融風暴，成為自杜魯門以來卸任總統中，除尼克森外，民調最不受歡迎者，難堪下台；輸家卻跳脫政治成為保衛全球環境英雄，七年間，高爾拍攝「不願面對的真相」，持續倡議警覺地球暖化危機，被冠以和平之人榮耀。布希獲得伊拉克戰爭，高爾獲得諾貝爾和平獎。歷史造化善變，高爾也許會感謝當年最高法院的判決吧？

Concede the 2000 Election

Al Gore

Good evening

Just moments ago, I spoke with George W. Bush and congratulated him on becoming the 43rd President of the United States, and I promised him that I wouldn't call him back this time.

I offered to meet with him as soon as possible so that we can start to heal the divisions of the campaign and the contest through which we just passed.

Almost a century and a half ago, Senator Stephen Douglas told Abraham Lincoln, who had just defeated him for the presidency, "Partisan feeling must yield to patriotism. I'm with you, Mr. President, and God bless you."

Well, in that same spirit, I say to President-elect Bush that what remains of partisan rancor must now be put aside, and may God bless

就在幾分鐘前，我與布希通話並恭賀他當選美國第四十三屆總統，我也向他保證這次不會再打電話去否認。

我也請求儘快與布希見面，讓我們開始共同彌補因為這次剛結束大選所產生的分裂。

將近一個半世紀前，參議員道格拉斯在大選落敗後，告訴當選的林肯總統：政黨的利益現在必須退居於國家利益之後。總統先生，我與你同在，並願上帝保佑你。

因此，以同樣的精神，我也要向當選的布希總統說：現在一切政黨的恩怨必須拋棄，並願上帝保佑這位國家的公僕。

his stewardship of this country.

Neither he nor I anticipated this long and difficult road. Certainly neither of us wanted it to happen. Yet it came, and now it has ended, resolved, as it must be resolved, through the honored institutions of our democracy.

Over the library of one of our great law schools is inscribed the motto, "Not under man but under God and law." That's the ruling principle of American freedom, the source of our democratic liberties. I've tried to make it my guide throughout this contest as it has guided America's deliberations of all the complex issues of the past five weeks.

Now the U.S. Supreme Court has spoken. Let there be no doubt, while I strongly disagree with the court's decision, I accept it. And tonight, for the sake of our unity of the people and the strength of our democracy, I offer my concession.

　　不論是布希或我本人都沒意料到這條競選之路會如此艱辛與冗長，當然我們任何一人也決不願發生這樣的意外。然而它發生了，而現在也經由我們民主的光榮機制，以它應該被結束的方式而結束，解決。

　　在一所偉大的法學院圖書館之上，竣刻著一句名言：不是在人治之下，而是上帝與法律之下。這就是美國處理自由的原則與美國民主自由的根據。在過去幾個禮拜的紛擾爭議中，我盡力的以此訓誡作為我的導引，如同它導引美國的思考方式一樣。

　　現在最高法院已作出決議，就讓它毫無疑義，雖然，我強烈的無法贊同高院決議，我還是接受。今晚，為了全國人民的團

I also accept my responsibility, which I will discharge unconditionally, to honor the new president elect and do everything possible to help him bring Americans together in fulfillment of the great vision that our Declaration of Independence defines and that our Constitution affirms and defends.

This has been an extraordinary election. But in one of God's unforeseen paths, this belatedly broken impasse can point us all to a new common ground, for its very closeness can serve to remind us that we are one people with a shared history and a shared destiny.

Indeed, that history gives us many examples of contests as hotly debated, as fiercely fought, with their own challenges to the popular will.

結，與我們民主的力量，我願無異議的接受敗選事實。

我也願無條件的接受我的責任支持新任的總統並盡一切可能團結美國人民，輔助他實踐我們獨立宣言與憲法所明訂、規範及保障的人民願景。

這是一場極不平凡的大選。但又在一條上帝不可預見的道路上，這一段久耗不破的僵局卻為我們所有人指向了一個新的共識。因為這一次票數的接近，提醒了我們是一群分享著共同的歷史與命運的民族。

的確，歷史給予我們很多激烈爭議，與挑戰人民意志挑戰的大選案例。

Other disputes have dragged on for weeks before reaching resolution. And each time, both the victor and the vanquished have accepted the result peacefully and in the spirit of reconciliation.

So let it be with us.

I know that many of my supporters are disappointed. I am too. But our disappointment must be overcome by our love of country.

And I say to our fellow members of the world community, let no one see this contest as a sign of American weakness. The strength of American democracy is shown most clearly through the difficulties it can overcome.

Some have expressed concern that the unusual nature of this election might hamper the next president in the conduct of his office. I do not believe it need be so.

其他的爭議在達成解決前，也拖延了數週，但每一次，不論輸贏雙方都能以和解精神，平和的接受結果。

所以就讓一切如此若落幕吧。

我知道許多支持我的人會非常失望，我也感同身受。但我們的失望一定要被對這個國家的愛所克服。

我也要向世界的成員伙伴說出，不要讓任何人將這次的競選視為美國衰弱的訊號。美國民主的力量就在她能克服所有的困難。

有些人也表達了這次大選的不尋常，是否將造成總統當選人公務執行的阻礙。我對此不表認同。

President-elect Bush inherits a nation whose citizens will be ready to assist him in the conduct of his large responsibilities.

I personally will be at his disposal, and I call on all Americans -- I particularly urge all who stood with us to unite behind our next president. This is America. Just as we fight hard when the stakes are high, we close ranks and come together when the contest is done.

And while there will be time enough to debate our continuing differences, now is the time to recognize that that which unites us is greater than that which divides us.

While we yet hold and do not yield our opposing beliefs, there is a higher duty than the one we owe to political party. This is America and we put country before party. We will stand together behind our new president.

　　總統當選人布希所繼承國家的公民將隨時幫助他執行他的重責大任。

　　我個人將任其驅使，我要呼籲所有美國人，我尤其要催促與我站在一起的人，大家一起團結在總統當選人之下。這才是美國。就如同我們為最高利益，努力奮戰，但當競爭結束時，我們則不分階級，團結一起。

　　我們仍有足夠的時間去探討我們持續的差異，但現在應該是認識到團結大於分裂的時候。

　　雖然我們仍堅持且不屈從於我們反對的信仰，然而我們還有一個責任，且更高於我們對政黨的義務。這就是美國，我們永遠

Some have asked whether I have any regrets and I do have one regret: that I didn't get the chance to stay and fight for the American people over the next four years, especially for those who need burdens lifted and barriers removed, especially for those who feel their voices have not been heard. I heard you and I will not forget.

I've seen America in this campaign and I like what I see. It's worth fighting for and that's a fight I'll never stop.

As for the battle that ends tonight, I do believe as my father once said, that no matter how hard the loss, defeat might serve as well as victory to shape the soul and let the glory out.

Now the political struggle is over and we turn again to the unending struggle for the common good of all Americans and for those multitudes around the world who look to us for leadership in the cause of freedom.

把國家置於政黨之前。我們將團結在新當選總統人身後。

有些人問我是否我會有所遺憾，我的確是有一個遺憾：就是我無法有機會在未來四年，留下為美國同胞們奮鬥，尤其是那些急需解脫重擔與障礙之人，與弱勢無人聞問者，但我確實聽到了你們聲音，我決不會遺忘你們。

在這場大選中，我看到了美國而且我也愛我所見。這是一場值得的奮鬥，也是一場我永遠不會停止的奮鬥。

有關今晚結束的選戰，我堅信我父親曾說過：不論失敗的有多慘，失敗與勝利一樣可以鍛造靈魂，綻放榮耀。

現在政治爭鬥已經結束，我們又將回到為全美大眾的共同利

And now, my friends, in a phrase I once addressed to others, it's time for me to go.

Thank you and good night, and God bless America.

Al Gore - December 13, 2000

益與世界期待我們領導自由運動的無止盡奮鬥。

現在，朋友們，我僅以一句老話，向你們說：是我該離開的時候了。

晚安！謝謝你們，願天佑美國。

第二十二篇　九一一全國文告

～故遠人不服則修文德以來之

喬治W. 布希

▶▶▶ 最動人的佳句！**The most touching words**！

Terrorist attacks can shake the foundations of our biggest buildings, but they cannot touch the foundation of America. These acts shattered steel, but they cannot dent the steel of American resolve.

～ George W. Bush

　恐怖主義的攻擊可以動搖我們最巨大建築物的基礎，但無動於美國之根本。這些行動可以撼動鋼架，卻於美國鋼鐵般的決心無絲毫之傷。

～喬治W. 布希

前言

　　二〇〇一年九月十一日，回教蓋達組織在美國本土，發動聖戰或恐怖攻擊，史稱「九一一事件」，這種不對稱自殺式的攻擊，使美國人民從此宛若驚弓之鳥，再難以生活在免於恐懼的自由之內，一場無邊無盡的全球反恐戰爭也宣告開始，這場戰爭規模大者可到出兵阿富汗、伊拉克或強制伊朗、北韓放棄核武談判，瑣碎者也可以到圖書館借書監控或機場搜身，連國際洗錢也

在管制之內。布希向恐怖主義立即宣戰後，如今七年下來，美國人民有感覺到安全嗎？顯然，布希以暴制暴的強硬霸道作風，「死活不拘」的追殺奧薩馬・賓拉登，並沒增加美國人民太多的安全感。這般國力越強，安全卻越弱的弔詭，美國學者奈依指出美國一味仇視回教，不願去真正瞭解回教徒的文化、教義與想法，才是問題的癥結，民主貴在多元與包容，奈依提出了美國應以自省、寬容的「軟權力」（soft power）及多邊外交手段處理國際事務，才是正途。這與中國儒家講求「故遠人不服則修文德以來之」的王道精神頗似。最後，在美國史無前例的超強時刻，我們還是期望一位有力量卻講義理的亞瑟王，而非「烽火外交」亞歷山大式的征服者，帶領人類邁向長久的和平與安全。

歷史背景

　　九一一恐怖攻擊。一九八九年柏林圍牆倒塌，蘇聯集團瓦解，冷戰結束，美國成為獨霸世界的惟一超級強權後，不知是否基於「無敵國外患者，國恆亡」之心理，美國學者汲汲開始關切他們下一個敵人是誰？在預期經濟將是後冷戰之國際主題，最初假設是日本，又有人提出中國威脅論，但政治學大師杭廷頓卻精準的提出美國日後的大敵將衍自東西文明的衝突對立，美國尤需注意伊斯蘭教的影響力量。

　　二〇〇〇年，布希當選美國總統，這位以亞力山大自居，堅信美國冷戰的勝利是來自雷根保守主義的延續，而自行加冕是新保守主義者，布希政府主張「片面主義」（Unilateralism）的單邊霸權外交，是一種帶著濃厚十字軍的宗教使命感，散佈美國式的生活價值於世，不顧民族文化與社會發展的差異。終於二〇〇一

年九月十一日，回教組織蓋達在美國本土，發動恐怖攻擊，史稱「九一一事件」。

蓋達通過劫持四架美國國內航班，其中兩架撞擊位於紐約曼哈頓的摩天大樓世界貿易中心，一架襲擊了首都華盛頓五角大廈—美國國防部所在地。世貿的兩幢110層大樓在遭到攻擊後相繼倒塌，附近多座建築也受震而坍塌，而五角大廈的部分結構被大火吞噬。第四架被劫持飛機在賓西法尼亞州墜毀，失事前機上乘客試圖從劫機者手中重奪飛機控制權。這架被劫持飛機目標不明，但相信劫機者撞擊目標是美國國會山莊或白宮。在這次自殺式恐怖攻擊事件中，蓋達造成2,998人死亡，這次事件是自第二次世界大戰，繼珍珠港事件後，歷史上第二次外國勢力對美國本土造成重大傷亡的襲擊，事件中死亡的總人數已經超過珍珠港事件中的2,400人。

反恐戰爭。美國政府在事件發生後，很多美國人相信，回教徒應為此次事件負責。美國政府立即做出反應，公開表示會以軍事手段打擊事件的策劃者。九月底，前英國首相東尼‧布萊爾援引西方情報機構手上證據，指稱沙烏地阿拉伯富豪奧薩馬‧賓‧拉登為事件的幕後主使。該組織發言人在一卷寄給卡達半島電視台的錄影帶中說，「美國人應該知道，更多的飛機風暴將不會停止，在伊斯蘭世界，有成千上萬年輕人渴望犧牲，他們死的信念與美國人生的信念一樣強烈。」

賓‧拉登與阿富汗塔利班政權有密切關係，美國在塔利班政權拒絕引渡賓‧拉登或其他基地組織頭目後，美國領導的聯軍於十月七日對阿富汗發動軍事攻擊，雖擊潰塔利班政權，但賓‧拉登卻從此杳然；美國乃轉而針對早有傳聞也捲入襲擊事件之伊

拉克，二○○三年，布希以該國發展大規模毀滅性武器，即使至今依然沒有證據證實，通牒海珊總統四十八小時下台無效後，出兵伊拉克，將海珊逮捕後，也送上絞刑，但至今關鍵人物賓‧拉登，在美國「全民公敵」、天羅地網的追捕下，仍依然無所獲，看來美國政府之「反恐戰爭」實難善了。

反恐代價。部分人認為，美國在全球的政治以及經濟、文化的政策才是恐怖攻擊事件的主要根源。根據這派的觀點，美國對第三世界國家所進行的經濟、文化與政治政策，令一些國家的人民產生了普遍的反美情緒。這些理由包括了美國在中東地區的大量軍事干預，西方通俗文化的氾濫，主要是對性、酒精的開放觀念，這些觀念對於伊斯蘭基本教義派而言根本無法接受等。美國政府事後也的確承認，九一一當晚，白宮就已經決定要更換伊拉克政權，雖然沒有任何證據顯示海珊政權到底與信奉伊斯蘭原教旨主義的蓋達組織之間有任何聯繫。布希政府通過利用九一一事件，挑起民意支持攻打伊拉克，與事後證實伊拉克有發展大規模毀滅性武器完全是政府捏造下的作法，令美國人感到憤怒，認為這種行為導致了許多美國人生命的無謂喪失，侵犯了許多美國人的自由，而且違背了美國立國時的根本原則。美國政府在事件發生後立即秘密拘留、逮捕、盤問了至少1200人，大多數是非美國公民的阿拉伯或穆斯林男子。美國司法部也查問了5000名來自中東的男子，為政府監視民眾提供便利的法律也獲得通過。

除民主制度的犧牲外，九一一事件在經濟上產生了重大及即時的影響。大量設在世界貿易中心的大型投資公司喪失了大量財產、員工與數據資料。全球許多股票市場受到影響，一些例如倫敦證券交易所還不得不進行疏散。紐約證券交易所直到九一一後

的第一個星期一才重新開市。道瓊斯工業平均指數開盤第一天下跌14.26%。其中跌幅最嚴重的要數旅遊、保險與航空股。美國的汽油價格也大幅度上漲。當時美國經濟已經放緩，九一一事件則加深全球經濟的蕭條。

　　九一一事件將美國人民生活方式帶入一個史無前例的挑戰，然而美國應了解這場戰爭不是對美國軍經實力的挑戰，而是美國價值的考驗，我們發現美國民主生活制度之經得起人類歷史的試煉與成長，重在歷次危機時刻，有領導者如傑佛遜、林肯、老羅斯福乃至金恩博士等人，能以反省、包容與尊重的精神方針面對，才能治本的解除危機。美國勢必需要調整片面霸權的思維，反躬自省這種過度自我中心的政策才是恐怖攻擊的源由，也只有這樣才能根本的反駁回教以聖戰合理化下的恐怖攻擊。

文獻介紹

九一一全國文告

喬治 W. 布希

　　九一一攻擊足以為二次大戰以來，美國最沉痛之國殤，身為最高領導人布希總統在「九一一全國文告」文告中，以堅定、簡約的文字，展示出冷靜、信心與對美國人民失落與震驚的感同深受。布希全文柔硬交錯，一面引用耶穌聖經名句：「我雖穿越死亡的幽谷，但我絲毫無懼，因為你與我同在。」撫平人民傷痛，穩定情緒，宛如悲憫化身；另外又展示決心宣告對這場邪惡行動的幕後黑手，決不留情，追殺到底，有如復仇天使。不到一個月內，美國機能不但一切恢復正常，甚至兵臨阿富汗，美國民主機制復原的快速與人民信心之強勁，的確驚人！

Statement by the President in His Address to the Nation

George W. Bush

Good evening. Today, our fellow citizens, our way of life, our very freedom came under attack in a series of deliberate and deadly terrorist acts. The victims were in airplanes, or in their offices; secretaries, businessmen and women, military and federal workers; moms and dads, friends and neighbors. Thousands of lives were suddenly ended by evil, despicable acts of terror.

The pictures of airplanes flying into buildings, fires burning, huge structures collapsing, have filled us with disbelief, terrible sadness, and a quiet, unyielding anger. These acts of mass murder were intended to frighten our nation into chaos and retreat. But they have failed; our country is strong.

A great people has been moved to defend a great nation. Terrorist attacks can shake the foundations of our biggest buildings, but they

午安，我親愛的國人，就在今天，我們的生活方式，我們的自由受到一連串精心與致命的恐怖攻擊行動。受害者罹難在飛機或辦公內；他們可能是秘書、商人和女士，或軍方與聯邦的公務員，爸爸與媽媽；朋友或鄰居。數以千計的性命瞬間就被邪惡的恐怖行為所終結。

飛機衝撞建築物，起火燃燒，與巨大建物粉碎的畫面使我們滿懷失落、悲慟和一種沉默難以釋放的憤怒。這些大規模謀殺的行動目的就是要讓美國恐懼，進而陷入混亂與倒退。但我們的強韌足以讓他們失敗。

一個偉大的民族已經受到感動去保衛一個偉大的國家。恐怖

cannot touch the foundation of America. These acts shattered steel, but they cannot dent the steel of American resolve.

America was targeted for attack because we're the brightest beacon for freedom and opportunity in the world. And no one will keep that light from shining.

Today, our nation saw evil, the very worst of human nature. And we responded with the best of America -- with the daring of our rescue workers, with the caring for strangers and neighbors who came to give blood and help in any way they could.

Immediately following the first attack, I implemented our government's emergency response plans. Our military is powerful, and it's prepared. Our emergency teams are working in New York City and Washington, D.C. to help with local rescue efforts.

Our first priority is to get help to those who have been injured, and to take every precaution to protect our citizens at home and around the world from further attacks.

的攻擊可以動搖建築物的基礎，但動搖不了美國的根本。這些行動可以撼動鋼架，卻於美國鋼鐵般的決心無絲毫之傷。

美國所以成為攻擊的目標，因為我們是全球自由與機會的最亮燈塔。沒有人可阻止它繼續發亮發光。

今天我們看到人類中最劣質之邪惡，而我們卻回應了美國人最優質的性情：像是救難人員的大愛及對毫不相識者之照顧與盡其所能捐血或給予一切幫助的近鄰。

在第一波恐怖攻擊後，我立刻啟動政府緊急因應計畫。強大的軍事也準備完畢。緊急隊部也在紐約及華盛頓努力協助當地救助。

The functions of our government continue without interruption. Federal agencies in Washington which had to be evacuated today are reopening for essential personnel tonight, and will be open for business tomorrow. Our financial institutions remain strong, and the American economy will be open for business, as well.

The search is underway for those who are behind these evil acts. I've directed the full resources of our intelligence and law enforcement communities to find those responsible and to bring them to justice. We will make no distinction between the terrorists who committed these acts and those who harbor them.

America and our friends and allies join with all those who want peace and security in the world, and we stand together to win the war against terrorism. Tonight, I ask for your prayers for all those who grieve, for the children whose worlds have been shattered, for all whose sense of safety and security has been threatened. And I pray they will be comforted by a power greater than any of us, spoken through

我們的第一優先是讓受到傷害者得到妥善的協助並保護國內及全球的美國公民免於進一步的攻擊。

政府的功能將維繫不斷。今天必須遷移的華府機關,重要人員將在今晚準備重新作業,並於明天正常營運。我們的金融機構依然強勁,美國的經濟也將立即重新上路。

追捕這場邪惡行動的幕後黑手已經展開。我已下令將用盡一切我們情報力量及執法單位的資源將任何涉嫌行動者繩之以法。對這場行動不論是直接參與者或加以間接包庇的人,我們將一視同仁對待。

美國將與友邦盟國與所有渴求安全和平的人士聯合,一起打

the ages in Psalm 23: "Even though I walk through the valley of the shadow of death, I fear no evil, for You are with me."

This is a day when all Americans from every walk of life unite in our resolve for justice and peace. America has stood down enemies before, and we will do so this time. None of us will ever forget this day. Yet, we go forward to defend freedom and all that is good and just in our world.

Thank you. Good night, and God bless America.

贏這場反恐怖主義戰爭。今晚我要求你們為這場事件的悲痛者、內心世界已動搖的孩童與所有安全感已受威脅的人禱告。我禱告他們可藉由從超越一切人類力量的聖經中一句話感到平安:「我雖穿越死亡的幽谷,但我絲毫無懼,因為你與我同在。」

這是來自所有生活階層美國人決心團結在正義與和平的一天。美國過去擊倒敵人無數,未來我們也不手軟。我們永遠不會忘記這一天。我們將繼續向前保衛自由與一切正義與善良於世。

謝謝你們,晚安,願天佑美國。

第二十三篇　是！我們做得到

～歐巴馬的夢想之路

巴拉克・歐巴馬

▶ 最動人的佳句！**The most touching words**！

We are one people; and one nation.

～Barack Obama

我們是一個民族，一個國家。

～巴拉克・歐巴馬

前言

　　二○○八年，在民主黨初選期間，歐巴馬還只是一個地方政治人物，所面對的是早已名震內外的前第一夫人、紐約參議員希拉蕊，當時，希拉蕊所挾高支持度與雄厚資源，顧盼自雌，聲勢之壯，大有橫掃黨內群雄，成為美國第一位女性總統；歐巴馬所憑藉者只是他那掌握人心，抓住選民心中疑問與希望的口才，歐巴馬一生傾慕林肯的思想，是甘迺迪理想與金恩博士夢想的綜合魅力化身，而三者共同的特點就是具有超越美國一般人民的思維與視野，在國家陷入內戰、民權與種族泥沼之時，可以發人省思的話語，帶領群眾走出迷惑，邁向更高層次的境界。

　　強調「改變和希望」的歐巴馬，自身就是「美國夢」的最佳代言，多數美國選民克服膚色的差別認同歐巴馬，就是受到他無

畏的希望鼓舞，他那來自金恩博士再現的語言穿透力，令人如癡如醉之餘，也啟發了心靈的改變力。

歷史背景

「我有一個夢：終有一天，我所有四個孩子生活的國家，是以他們的內在品格來受評斷，而非以其皮膚之顏色。」。

這是金恩博士在他著名演講「我有一個夢」的一段句落，膚色從此是世人普遍看待所謂「美國夢」能否真正存在的最後考驗。

二〇〇八年，民主黨的初選最終只剩下希拉蕊與歐巴馬一決雌雄時，美國人就開始決定今秋美國到底是會有第一個女性總統抑或第一個黑人總統。但女性當總統在當今已是毫不希罕之事，世人焦點興趣者還是在美國人對種族——這道四百年的心理障礙能否跨越，這也是歐巴馬大聲疾呼改變與Yes! We Can的原因，藉此不斷鼓舞催眠美國求新、勇於嘗試的潛在性格，帶領美國人克服膚色的歧視，完成真實的美國夢。

一九六一年八月，歐巴馬在夏威夷州出生。他的父親老歐巴馬是肯亞人，稍早之前以國際學生的身分來到夏威夷大學就讀，母親是堪薩斯州的白人，也是夏大的學生，兩人相識相戀後結婚，生下了這個長子。不久老歐巴馬前往哈佛攻讀學位，父母分居並離婚。母親改嫁印尼籍的同學蘇托洛。歐巴馬六歲時隨母親從夏威夷遷居到繼父在印尼雅加達郊區的家中。那裡的生活環境堪比貧民窟，但歐巴馬適應得很快，一九七一年，歐巴馬獨自回到夏威夷，歐巴馬中學畢業，轉往紐約市的哥倫比亞大學就讀，主修政治及國際關係。九一年，自哈佛大學法學院以優異成績畢業，獲得法學士的學位。之後，歐巴馬到芝加哥，受雇於一家律

師事務所擔任民權律師，同時也在芝加哥大學法學院任教。二○○四年，七月，歐巴馬幫忙民主總統候選人凱瑞助選，在民主黨全國代表大會，以激勵人心「無畏的希望」為題的演說一舉站上全國舞台，開始嶄露頭角。十一月當選聯邦參議員，成為美國歷史上第三位普選產生的黑人參議員，得票高達百分之七十，創下州史紀錄。四年後，未滿一任，即雄圖進取大位。

　　我們翻閱歐巴馬的個人歷史，我們會訝異的發現：第一、他不是一個完全的黑人，他母親是白人；第二、他也不是完全的美國人，他父親是肯亞人；第三、他出生、幼年成長的背景，是在夏威夷、亞洲的印尼，都不是在美國的本土。這些跨越種族、地理、宗教及性別的成長元素，使他成為一個不是「樣板」美國黑人，一九九五年，歐巴馬出版「歐巴馬的夢想之路——以父之名」，在這本回憶錄中，歐巴馬敘述自己在母親的白種人中產家庭成長的經歷。他對於自小就不在身邊的父親的印象只能來自於家庭故事和照片。歐巴馬說，他從小就注意到父母膚色的對比。「爸爸的膚色像瀝青一樣黑，而媽媽則像牛奶一般白。我對此印象深刻。」，歐巴馬以自己多樣而複雜的血緣與出身背景暢談希望，不但具有親身見證的說服力，黑白混血的他，代表了族群融合，代表了美國的精神，立刻造成廣大基層民眾的共鳴。我們從選戰中看到，歐巴馬的策略就是決不訴求黑人悲情，與黑人保持等距的態度。此外，歐巴馬如此受到歡迎是他重視協調，願意聽取不同意見，達成共識的行事風格，也是符合全球化下需要合作與信任解決問題的領導品質。

是！我們做得到

巴拉克・歐巴馬

　　美國民主黨這次初選，在很多地方都寫了歷史：無論參與投票的人數之多，募得競選經費之多，選舉支出之多，還是纏鬥時間之長，都是破紀錄的。而歐巴馬本身，更代表了歷史的新頁，因為美國立國二三二年後，是否今秋將出現第一位黑人（或說是黑白混血）總統，自更引人矚目。這位來自肯亞的黑人後裔，成功融合甘迺迪的政治魅力與馬丁路德金恩極具煽動爆發力的口才。而這篇動人的演說，其實是歐巴馬在民主黨初選首戰──新罕布什夏州，失利於希拉蕊後的登台謝票感言，言中充滿激情、理想與永不放棄的美國人精神，歐巴馬這項演講霎時震撼全場，驚艷各方，這樣的演說結構令人想起民權運動領袖馬丁・路德・金恩的傳世名言「我有一個夢」之後，再現動人口號「Yes, we can」，成功將敗選的氣氛一掃而空，超越種族與膚色，大聲疾呼「we are one people; and one nation」，號召一個新的美國多數（new American majority）完成改變，成功凝聚更大的力量。

Yes, we can.

Barack Obama

Jan. 8th, 2008

A few weeks ago, no one imagined that we'd have accomplished what we did here tonight. For most of this campaign, we were far behind, and we always knew our climb would be steep.But in record numbers, you came out and spoke up for change. And with your voices and your votes, you made it clear that at this moment- in this election- there is something happened in America.

There is something happening when Americans who are young in age and in spirit – who have never before participated in politics – turn out in numbers we've never seen because they know in their hearts that this time must be different.

There is something happening when people vote not just for the party they belong to but the hopes they hold in common – that

幾週以前，沒有人能想像得到我們今晚達到的成就。在這場選戰的大部分時候，我們都處於落後，我們也知道我們的前景陡峭，不被看好。然而你們以創紀錄的人數挺身而出，呼喊改變。你們用心聲與選票，清楚的顯示出在這個時刻，在美國，有些事情發生了。

有些事情發生了，當已往從不參與政治的美國年輕人，這次卻前所未有的踴躍現身投票，因為他們發自內心清楚，這次一定要不同。

有些事情發生了，當人民不再以所屬政黨，而是以他們共同抱持的希望作投票的決定——不分貧、富，不分黑、白，不分拉

whether we are rich or poor; black or white; Latino or Asian we are ready to take this country in a fundamentally new direction. That is what's happening in America right now. Change is what's happening in America.

You can be the new majority who can lead this nation out of a long political darkness – Democrats, Independents and Republicans who are tired of the division and distraction that has clouded Washington; who know that we can disagree without being disagreeable; who understand that if we mobilize our voices to challenge and influence that's stood in our way and challenge ourselves to reach for something better, there's no problem we can't solve – no destiny we cannot fulfill.

Our new American majority can end the outrage of unaffordable, unavailable health care in our time. …. Our new majority can end the tax breaks for corporations that ship our jobs overseas and put a middle-class tax cut into the pockets of the working Americans who deserve it.

丁、亞洲後裔，我們已經準備好帶領這個國家走向一個基本新方向。這就是正在美國發生的事情。改變正在美國發生。

你們可以組成一個新的多數，一起把國家帶離長久以來的政治黑暗，不論民主黨、共和黨或獨立的選民，老早厭倦華府政客愛搞分裂與分化的翻雲覆雨；也清楚我們可以不必為反對而反對；更明白如果我們動員改變的力量，影響阻撓我們的障礙，挑戰更美好的事物，就沒有我們解決不了的問題，沒有我們完成不了的使命。

我們的新美國多數可以結束貴得付不起也享用不到的醫療保險，我們的新美國多數可以終結盡把工作機會移往海外的大企業

We can stop sending our children to schools with corridors of shame and start putting them on a pathway to success. We can stop talking about how great teachers are and start rewarding them for their greatness. We can do this with our new majority.

And when I am President, we will end this war in Iraq and bring our troops home; we will finish the job against al Qaeda in Afghanistan; we will care for our veterans; we will restore our moral standing in the world; and we will never use 9/11 as a way to scare up votes, because it is not a tactic to win an election, it is a challenge that should unite America and the world against the common threats of the twenty-first century: terrorism and nuclear weapons; climate change and poverty; genocide and disease.

逃稅行為，並為美國中產階級的工作人口，進行他們應得的減稅措施。

我們也可以結束只得把小孩送往簡陋的學校，開始為他們鋪設成功道路。我們也可以結束僅限口惠於老師的傑出，開始獎勵他們的偉大。我們的新美國多數都可以作到這些事情。

我當選總統，我們將結束在伊拉克的戰爭，讓我們的部隊返鄉；我們也會結束在阿富汗針對蓋達組織的任務；我們會照顧退伍軍人，而且我們決不會利用9/11作為驚嚇美國人投票的手段，它應該是如何團結美國人與世界，挑戰面對二十一世紀的共同威脅：恐怖主義、核子武器、氣候變遷、貧窮、族群滅絕與疾病。

All of the candidates in this race share these goals. All have good ideas. And all are patriots who serve this country honorably.

But the reason our campaign has always been different is because it's not just about what I will do as President, it's also about what you, the people who love this country, can do to change it.

That is why tonight belongs to you. …We know the battle ahead will be long, but always remember that no matter what obstacles stand in our way, nothing can withstand the power of millions of voices calling for change. We have been told we cannot do this by a chorus of cynics who will only grow louder and more dissonant in the weeks to come.

For when we have faced down impossible odds; when we've been told that we're not ready, or that we shouldn't try, or that we can't, generations of Americans have responded with a simple creed that sums up the spirit of a people.

所有這次選戰之候選人都贊成這些目標。他們都有很好的構想。他們也都深愛這個國家,並以服務這個國家為光榮。

但這次選舉,我們與眾不同的原因在於:這場選舉不光是我當上了總統之後會作什麼,而是你們這群深愛這個國家的人民,能為改變這個國家作些什麼。

這就是為何今晚是屬於你們的。我們知道這場選戰之路尚遠,但謹記不管前途有任何的阻礙,數百萬計要求改變的聲音是無法抵禦的。我們也被一再嘲訕的人士告誡我們做不到任何改變,而且這種聲音在未來的幾週會越加大聲與刺耳。

因為當我們逆勢中被看衰,當我們被告誡我們還準備不夠,或是

Yes we can.

It was a creed written into the founding documents that declared the destiny of a nation.

Yes we can.

It was whispered by slaves and abolitionists as they blazed a trail toward freedom through the darkest of nights.

Yes we can.

It was sung by immigrants as they struck out from distant shores and pioneers who pushed westward against an unforgiving wilderness.

Yes we can.

說我們能力不足，數以世代的美國人民只以一簡單的精神標語回覆：

是！我們做得到。

此一精神口語，老早寫在宣稱此一國家命運的建國文件之中。

是！我們做得到。

這句話不斷在最暗淡的黑夜中，被黑奴與廢奴人士在為自由先驅奮鬥時，輕聲傳誦。

是！我們做得到。

這句話不斷在祖先移民過海，乘風破浪；或西部拓荒者在披荊斬棘時，歌聲傳誦。

是！我們做得到。

It was the call of workers who organized; women who reached for ballot; a President who chose the moon as our new frontier; and a King who took us to the mountaintop and pointed the way to the Promised Land.

Yes we can to justice and equality. Yes we can to opportunity and prosperity. Yes we can heal this nation. Yes we can repair this world. Yes we can.

We will remember that there is something happening in America; that we are not as divided as our politics suggested; we are one people; and one nation; and together, we will begin the next great chapter in America's story with three words that will ring from coast to coast; to shine from sea to sea- Yes we can.

它呼喚勞工團結、婦女前往投票、一位總統（指甘迺迪）開闢月球為新疆域與金恩帶領我們登上高峰，走向許諾之地。

正義與平等，我們做得到。機會與富裕，我們做得到。復原國家，是！我們做得到。整治全世界，我們做得到。

我們將謹記美國有些事正在發生；我們並非如某些政治上的主張是分離的；我們是一個民族，一個國家。我們也將以這三個字——是！我們做得到——它將從西岸到東岸響亮，閃鑠在兩大洋——，開展美國歷史的下一偉大篇章。

第二十四篇　負責任的新時代

～美國夢的終極象徵

巴拉克・歐巴馬

▶▶ 最動人的佳句！**The most touching words**！

We are ready to lead once more.

　　　　　　　　　　　　～Barack Obama

我們準備好再次領導世界。

　　　　　　　　　　　　～巴拉克・歐巴馬

前言

　　二〇〇九年一月二十一日，歐巴馬宣誓就任美國第四十四任總統，歐巴馬的當選不但震撼於美國也同樣引起全世界的關心，首先，作為第一個黑人總統，歐巴馬的勝選，代表著一個魔咒時刻的結束，四百年來，黑人民權運動的艱辛路，從奴隸而自由，從自由而平等，從平等但隔離（separate but equal），到真正的族群融合，如今已達終點，金恩的美國夢終於實現。

　　走了一個舊的時代，新時代的日子卻一樣艱辛。甫走馬上任的歐巴馬，馬上面臨嚴厲的挑戰還是全球經濟景氣低迷，有人將歐巴馬的遭遇與三〇年代，羅斯福上任時的經濟大恐慌類比，同樣面臨了一千一百萬人的失業，股市與房地產的泡沫蒸發；但更

甚者，卻有三百萬人因次貸案房子法拍，無屋可住；以及兩個錢坑戰場──阿富汗與伊拉克。過去八年美國在小布希以硬權力追求單邊霸權體制與杭廷頓狹隘推崇白人、基督教文明與英美民族思想才是建構美國文化價值核心下，忘記了民主之多元、包容與平等的軟實力價值，才是其所憑藉領導世界的中心，導致美國國力快速衰頹、下滑。布希施政失敗幫助歐巴馬贏得選舉，演說能贏得選戰的勝利，如何使演說轉變成有效的治國政策，則是美國未來最大挑戰。這也是歐巴馬在就職演說中所要傳遞的最重要訊息，靈活運用美國的軟硬實力與「希望與美德」，歐巴馬相信美國終將再起，領導世界。

歷史背景

　　負責任的新時代。美國總統歐巴馬一月二十一日在華府宣誓就任，成為美國第四十四任總統，就職大典吸引了兩百多萬人冒著零下低溫，見證歷史的這一刻！歐巴馬在就職演說中，號召美國人「從今天起，振作精神，拍掉灰塵，重建美國」，同時向全世界宣告，他將帶領人民，再造美國，重新建立美國在全球的領導地位。當歐巴馬以動人的詞藻描述了美國對未來世界的願景。不但美國人民在聆聽，世界也在聆聽他所描繪的新美國世紀的藍圖。

　　歐巴馬在當年黑奴參與興建的國會山莊，手按林肯總統當年就職的聖經宣誓下，登上美國權力的頂峰。身為美國史上第一位黑人總統，歐巴馬昭示一段苦難歷史的終結，和一個新的國家團結的象徵，歐巴馬再度重申種族、宗教融合與美國熔爐、多元文化，「**我們是由基督徒和穆斯林，猶太教徒和印度教徒，以**

及非信徒組成的國家。我們由不同語言和文化所形塑。因為我們嘗過內戰和種族隔離的苦果，並且在走出那黑暗篇章之後，變得更堅強和團結，這讓我們不得不相信舊日的仇恨終究會過去，種族之間的界線很快就會泯滅。」。目前美國人口結構中，白人佔75.9%，黑人佔13.1，而今年一月中旬由華盛頓郵報與美國廣播公司所作民調顯示，73%民眾相信美國已經或很快就會達到種族的平等。這不但是美國非洲裔族群的勝利，也代表理性、寬容的價值回復。

　　其次，在就職演說中，歐巴馬毫不掩飾美國正深處全球經濟危機之中，有如華盛頓上任時面對建國考驗、林肯解放黑奴的內戰分裂，小羅斯福的經濟大恐慌與二次大戰，他點出全球金融海嘯的根源，正是華爾街某些商人貪婪且不負責任的後果，然而歐巴馬指出不論美國**生產力、創意**，產品和勞務的能力並未減損。因此，美國經濟需要大膽而快速的行動，不只創造新工作，更要打下成長的新基礎。更重要的是，他祈望美國人民繼承建國先賢的理念、傳統，回復「**我們賴以成功的價值觀——辛勤工作和誠實、勇氣和公平競爭、容忍和好奇心、忠實和愛國心——這些固有真實的價值，是美國歷史上進步的沈默力量。我們有必要找回這些真實價值。我們現在需要一個勇於負責的新時代。**」他誓言美國將在「**希望與美德**」上重建，但這個重建的責任在美國有責任感的公民身上，而非利益集團，但也明白表示美國的經濟絕非短期內所能解決，以降低美國人民的期望。

　　軟實力或聰明力（*Soft/Smart Power*）。演說中，就美國未來國際相處之道，歐巴馬完全採用奈依教授「軟權力」的主張，或希拉蕊聰明力，也就是理想、正義及自制的運用，以希望與諒

解，透過折衝協調取代過去布希政府營建在軍事力量，一味輸出仇恨與恐懼的單邊霸權外交。「今天，我們聚在這裡，因為我們選擇用希望超越恐懼，用團結超越衝突與不和……回想先前的世代力抗法西斯主義和共產主義，靠的除了飛彈和戰車之外。他們知道單單力量本身不足以讓我們自保，也不能讓我們為所欲為。相反地，他們知道我們的力量因為謹慎使用而增強，我們的安全源自我們理想的正當性，我們所樹立楷模的力量，以及謙遜和克制所具有的調和特質」。

歐巴馬指出：「對那些想要藉由恐怖與殺害無辜以遂其目的者，我們現在告訴你，我們的精神強過你們，無法摧折，你們不可能比我們長久，我們必定打敗你們」他誓言美國將如當年阻擋法西斯主義共產主義那樣，阻擋恐怖主義肆虐，但將使用世界接受的方法站在歷史正確的一邊。

歐巴馬最後表示，寒冷的冬天終將會過去，當什麼都沒有時，唯一有的就是希望，憑著這一線希望，美國將重拾過去的自由、民主、正義與繁榮。自由與信念會把幸福的成果傳給世世代代子孫。美國依然有著開創歷史的潛力，在這個時刻，改變已經開始，美國準備好再次領導世界。

負責任的新時代

巴拉克・歐巴馬

　　毫無疑問，歐巴馬的演說，是美國處於艱難時刻，宣布新時代開啟的宣誓，在長達二十五分鐘的就職演說中，歐巴馬坦言美國正深陷國內、外的經濟與戰爭危機，並指出未來自救之道。仔細閱讀我們會發現，歐巴馬該篇的演說架構，基本上是小羅斯福與甘迺迪總統就職演說的混合：國內部分，歐巴馬「希望與恐懼」文字運用；將這次金融海嘯歸因於「部分人的貪婪與不負責任」；要求「經濟情勢要求大膽、果決的行動，我們將有所行動」，但真正的勝利之路仍賴美國固有價值的「希望和美德」，完全取法小羅斯福首任就職文的主題安排鋪陳。國外部分，則效仿甘迺迪軟中帶硬口氣，對「那些努力散播衝突並把自己社會的問題怪罪於西方的領袖，須知你的國民藉以判斷你的，是你能建立什麼，而非你能毀壞什麼。須知你們站在歷史錯誤的一邊，但只要你願意放手，我們就會伸出友誼的手。」

　　整體言，歐巴馬這篇演講的文字是動人的，但論創意上仍遠落後於先賢之後，原本期待並最能紀念黑人民權終底勝利的感性文字或許是歐巴馬不想在國難之時，再挑動這敏感神經，反到是低調掠過。

A New Era of Responsibility

Barack Obama

My fellow citizens:

I stand here today humbled by the task before us, grateful for the trust you have bestowed, mindful of the sacrifices borne by our ancestors. I thank President Bush for his service to our nation, as well as the generosity and cooperation he has shown throughout this transition.

Forty-four Americans have now taken the presidential oath. The words have been spoken during rising tides of prosperity and the still waters of peace. Yet, every so often the oath is taken amidst gathering clouds and raging storms. At these moments, America has carried on not simply because of the skill or vision of those in high office, but because We the People have remained faithful to the ideals of our forbearers, and true to our founding documents.

各位同胞：

今天我站在這裡，為即將面對的重責大任感到謙卑，對各位的信任亦滿懷感激，對先賢的犧牲更念茲在茲。我要感謝布希總統為這個國家的服務，並感謝他在政權轉移期間的慷慨與配合。

四十四位美國人已就總統誓言宣誓，這些誓詞或是在繁榮時的高峰或是在和平時的風平浪靜時間進行。然而，它也常在烏雲密布，暴風雨來臨之時進行。在艱困的時候，美國總能堅韌維繫，不僅因位居高位者之能力或遠見，也因為我們人民信守先人的思想及忠實於建國的教義。

So it has been. So it must be with this generation of Americans.

That we are in the midst of crisis is now well understood. Our nation is at war, against a far-reaching network of violence and hatred. Our economy is badly weakened, a consequence of greed and irresponsibility on the part of some, but also our collective failure to make hard choices and prepare the nation for a new age. Homes have been lost; jobs shed; businesses shuttered. Our health care is too costly; our schools fail too many; and each day brings further evidence that the ways we use energy strengthen our adversaries and threaten our planet.

These are the indicators of crisis, subject to data and statistics. Less measurable but no less profound is a sapping of confidence across our land - a nagging fear that America's decline is inevitable, and that the next generation must lower its sights.

因此，美國才能成其偉大。所以，這一代美國人必須傳承維繫。

大家都知道我們現在正置身危機之中，國家正對抗無遠弗屆暴力和仇恨聯手的戰爭。部分人的貪婪與不負責任，使我們的經濟大受傷害，但這也是我們全體的選擇所致，與為國家進入新時代的準備。許多人失去房子，丟了工作，生意垮了。我們的醫療照護太昂貴，學校教育讓人失望。每天都有更多證據顯示，我們利用能源的是在加深我們的困境，危害我們的星球。

這些就資料和統計所得的危機指標雖然無法量化，沉重的是舉國信心的流失，美國將無可避免衰退的恐懼與子孫願景視野的必然退步。

Today I say to you that the challenges we face are real. They are serious and they are many. They will not be met easily or in a short span of time. But know this, America - they will be met. On this day, we gather because we have chosen hope over fear, unity of purpose over conflict and discord.

On this day, we come to proclaim an end to the petty grievances and false promises, the recriminations and worn out dogmas, that for far too long have strangled our politics.

We remain a young nation, but in the words of Scripture, the time has come to set aside childish things. The time has come to reaffirm our enduring spirit; to choose our better history; to carry forward that precious gift, that noble idea, passed on from generation to generation: the God-given promise that all are equal, all are free, and all deserve a chance to pursue their full measure of happiness.

今天我要告訴各位，我們面臨的挑戰是真的。這些挑戰既多且嚴重。它們也不易或馬上好。但是，美國要了解，這些挑戰會被解決。在這一天，我們聚在一起，因為我們選擇希望而非恐懼，我們的目的是團結而非對抗和不合。

在這一天，我們在此宣示與結束渺茫自憐和虛偽的承諾，及政治扭曲已久的相互指控和陳腐的教條。

我們仍是個年輕的國家，依照聖經的話，拋棄不成熟的時刻到來了，肯定堅忍精神的時刻到來了，我們可以選擇更好的歷史，實踐那種代代傳承的珍貴天賦，高貴理念：就是上帝的應許，我們每個人都是平等的，每個人都是自由的，每個人都應該

In reaffirming the greatness of our nation, we understand that greatness is never a given. It must be earned. Our journey has never been one of short-cuts or settling for less. It has not been the path for the faint-hearted - for those who prefer leisure over work, or seek only the pleasures of riches and fame. Rather, it has been the risk-takers, the doers, the makers of things - some celebrated but more often men and women obscure in their labor, who have carried us up the long, rugged path towards prosperity and freedom.

For us, they packed up their few worldly possessions and traveled across oceans in search of a new life.

For us, they toiled in sweatshops and settled the West; endured the lash of the whip and plowed the hard earth.

有機會追求充分的幸福。

再次肯定我們國家的偉大，我們了解偉大絕非毫無代價，必須靠努力贏取。我們的歷程從來沒有捷徑或輕易達成。這條路一直都不是給心智昏暗，好逸樂，疏懶工作，或者只想追求名利就滿足的人。相反的是，踏上這條路的是勇於冒險的人，劍及履及，實事求是的人，雖然有出名者，但更常見的是默默付出勞力的男女，在這條漫長崎嶇的道路上，支撐我們邁向繁榮與自由。

為了我們，他們身無恆產，遠渡重洋，追尋新生活。

為了我們，他們胼手胝足，在西部安頓下來；忍受風吹雨打，篳路藍縷。

For us, they fought and died, in places like Concord and Gettysburg; Normandy and Khe Sahn.

Time and again these men and women struggled and sacrificed and worked till their hands were raw so that we might live a better life. They saw America as bigger than the sum of our individual ambitions; greater than all the differences of birth or wealth or faction.

This is the journey we continue today. We remain the most prosperous, powerful nation on Earth. Our workers are no less productive than when this crisis began. Our minds are no less inventive, our goods and services no less needed than they were last week or last month or last year. Our capacity remains undiminished. But our time of standing pat, of protecting narrow interests and putting off unpleasant decisions - that time has surely passed. Starting today, we must pick ourselves up, dust ourselves off, and begin again the work of remaking America.

為了我們,他們奮鬥不懈,埋骨葬身在康科特和蓋茨堡,諾曼地和溪山等地。

先人的奮鬥與犧牲,直到雙手皮開肉綻,我們才能享有比較好的生活。他們將美國看重於所有個人野心之總和與出身、財富或派系的差異。

這是我們今天繼續前進的旅程。我們仍然是全球最繁榮強盛的國家。這場危機爆發時,我們的勞工生產力並未減弱。我們擁有同樣的創意,和上周或上個月或去年相比,我們的產品和勞務一樣大受需求。我們的能力並未減損。但是我們墨守成規、保護狹小利益、遲疑不決,這種時刻已經過去。從今天起,我們必須

For everywhere we look, there is work to be done. The state of the economy calls for action, bold and swift, and we will act - not only to create new jobs, but to lay a new foundation for growth. We will build the roads and bridges, the electric grids and digital lines that feed our commerce and bind us together. We will restore science to its rightful place, and wield technology's wonders to raise health care's quality and lower its cost. We will harness the sun and the winds and the soil to fuel our cars and run our factories. And we will transform our schools and colleges and universities to meet the demands of a new age. All this we can do. And all this we will do.

Now, there are some who question the scale of our ambitions - who suggest that our system cannot tolerate too many big plans. Their memories are short. For they have forgotten what this country has already done; what free men and women can achieve when imagination is joined to common purpose, and necessity to courage.

捲起衣袖、撣去灰塵，再次重建美國。

我們無論朝何處望去，都有工作有待完成。經濟情勢要求大膽、果決的行動，我們將有所行動，不只是創造新工作，更要鋪下成長的新基礎。我們將造橋鋪路，安裝電力網與數位線路以滿足企業，並將我們緊密聯繫。我們將讓科學回歸正途，運用科技的神奇來提高醫療品質並降低費用。我們將利用太陽能、風力和土壤作為汽車的燃料和工廠營運的能源。我們將改變讓中小學及大學趕上新時代的需要。這些我們可以作到。我們也將會作到。

現在，有人質疑我們的企圖規模，提示我們的體制無法承受太多的大計畫。這些人的記憶太淺。因為他們忘記了這個國家早

What the cynics fail to understand is that the ground has shifted beneath them - that the stale political arguments that have consumed us for so long no longer apply. The question we ask today is not whether our government is too big or too small, but whether it works - whether it helps families find jobs at a decent wage, care they can afford, a retirement that is dignified. Where the answer is yes, we intend to move forward. Where the answer is no, programs will end. And those of us who manage the public's dollars will be held to account - to spend wisely, reform bad habits, and do our business in the light of day - because only then can we restore the vital trust between a people and their government.

先的成就及當自由的男女讓想像力會同一個共同的目標與決心結合勇氣時，所可以完成的成就。

懷疑者無法理解的是他們的主張已經站不住腳，長期以來折磨我們的陳腐政治爭議已經行不通。我們今天的問題不是政府太大或太小，而是有無功效，是否能幫助家庭找到薪水不錯的工作，支付得起照顧費用，有尊嚴的退休。哪個方向能夠提供肯定的答案，我們就往那裡走。答案是否定的地方，計畫就會停止。所有我們這些管理大眾金錢的人都將負起責任，花錢要精明，改掉惡習，正大光明作事情，只有這樣我們才能重建政府與人民間最重要的信任。

Nor is the question before us whether the market is a force for good or ill. Its power to generate wealth and expand freedom is unmatched, but this crisis has reminded us that without a watchful eye, the market can spin out of control - and that a nation cannot prosper long when it favors only the prosperous. The success of our economy has always depended not just on the size of our Gross Domestic Product, but on the reach of our prosperity; on our ability to extend opportunity to every willing heart - not out of charity, but because it is the surest route to our common good.

As for our common defense, we reject as false the choice between our safety and our ideals. Our Founding Fathers, faced with perils we can scarcely imagine, drafted a charter to assure the rule of law and the rights of man, a charter expanded by the blood of generations. Those ideals still light the world, and we will not give them up for expedience's sake. And so to all other peoples and governments who are watching today, from the grandest capitals to the small village

我們當前的問題不在於市場的力量到底是善或惡。市場創造財富和擴大自由的力量無可匹敵，但是這場危機提醒我們沒有監督時，市場發展將失控，當市場只偏愛有錢人時，國家無法永續繁榮。我們經濟成功的依據，不只是國內生產毛額的規模，還有繁榮可及的範圍，以及我們將機會拓展給每個願意打拚的人，不是因為施捨，而是因為這就是達到我們共同利益最穩健的途徑。

至於我們的共同防衛，我們認為必須在我們的自由和理想之間作一抉擇是不確實的，我們拒絕接受。我們建國諸父在我們難以想像的危難之中。擬具了確保法治和人權的憲章，被一代代以鮮血擴大充實的憲章。這些理想依然照亮這個世界，我們不會為

where my father was born: know that America is a friend of each nation and every man, woman, and child who seeks a future of peace and dignity, and that we are ready to lead once more.

Recall that earlier generations faced down fascism and communism not just with missiles and tanks, but with sturdy alliances and enduring convictions. They understood that our power alone cannot protect us, nor does it entitle us to do as we please. Instead, they knew that our power grows through its prudent use; our security emanates from the justness of our cause, the force of our example, the tempering qualities of humility and restraint.

We are the keepers of this legacy. Guided by these principles once more, we can meet those new threats that demand even greater effort - even greater cooperation and understanding between nations. We will begin to responsibly leave Iraq to its people, and forge a hard-earned peace in Afghanistan. With old friends and former foes, we will work tirelessly to lessen the nuclear threat, and roll back the specter of a

了便宜行事而揚棄它。同樣地,今日在觀看此情此景的其他民族和政府,從最宏偉的都城到家父出生的小村莊,我要說:任何一個國家、男、女、和孩童,只要你在追求一個和平且有尊嚴的未來,美國就是你的朋友,我們準備再次帶領大家。

回想先前的世代力抗法西斯主義和共產主義,靠的除了飛彈和戰車之外,還有強固的聯盟和持久的信念。他們知道單單力量本身不足以讓我們自保,也不能讓我們為所欲為。相反地,他們知道我們的力量因為謹慎使用而增強,我們的安全源自我們理想的正當性,我們所樹立楷模的力量,以及謙遜和克制所具有的調和特質。

我們是這些遺產的保存者。在這些原則的再次指引下,我

warming planet. We will not apologize for our way of life, nor will we waver in its defense, and for those who seek to advance their aims by inducing terror and slaughtering innocents, we say to you now that our spirit is stronger and cannot be broken; you cannot outlast us, and we will defeat you.

For we know that our patchwork heritage is a strength, not a weakness. We are a nation of Christians and Muslims, Jews and Hindus - and non-believers. We are shaped by every language and culture, drawn from every end of this Earth; and because we have tasted the bitter swill of civil war and segregation, and emerged from that dark chapter stronger and more united, we cannot help but believe that the old hatreds shall someday pass; that the lines of tribe shall soon dissolve; that as the world grows smaller, our common humanity shall reveal itself; and that America must play its role in ushering in a new era of peace.

們可以面對那些新的威脅，這些威脅有賴國與國間更大的合作與諒解方能因應。我們將開始以負責任的方式把伊拉克還給它的人民，並在阿富汗建立贏來不易的和平。我們會努力不懈地與老朋友和昔日的對手合作，以減輕核子威脅，和地球的暖化。我們不會為我們的生活方式而道歉，也會毫不動搖地保護它，對那些想要藉由帶來恐怖與殺害無辜以遂其目的者，我們現在告訴你，我們的精神強過你們，無法摧折，你們不可能比我們長久，我們必定打敗你們。

因為我們知道，我們混合補綴而成的遺產是我們的強處，而非弱點。我們是由基督徒和穆斯林，猶太教徒和印度教徒，以

To the Muslim world, we seek a new way forward, based on mutual interest and mutual respect. To those leaders around the globe who seek to sow conflict, or blame their society's ills on the West - know that your people will judge you on what you can build, not what you destroy. To those who cling to power through corruption and deceit and the silencing of dissent, know that you are on the wrong side of history; but that we will extend a hand if you are willing to unclench your fist.

To the people of poor nations, we pledge to work alongside you to make your farms flourish and let clean waters flow; to nourish starved bodies and feed hungry minds. And to those nations like ours that enjoy relative plenty, we say we can no longer afford indifference to suffering outside our borders; nor can we consume the world's resources without regard to effect. For the world has changed, and we must change with it.

及非信徒組成的國家。我們任由各種語文和文化所形塑。而且由於我們曾嘗過內戰和種族隔離的苦果,並且在走出那黑暗篇章之後,變得更堅強和團結,這讓我們不得不相信舊日的仇恨終究會過去,部族之間的界線很快就會泯滅。隨著世界越來越小,我們共通的人性也會彰顯,而美國必須扮演引進新和平時代的角色。

對穆斯林世界,我們尋求一條新的前瞻道路,以共同的利益和尊重為基礎。那些努力散播衝突並把自己社會的問題怪罪於西方的領袖,須知你的國民藉以判斷你的,是你能建立什麼,而非你能毀壞什麼。那些靠著貪腐欺騙和箝制異己保住權勢的人,須知你們站在歷史錯誤的一邊,但只要你願意放手,我們就會伸出友誼的手。

As we consider the road that unfolds before us, we remember with humble gratitude those brave Americans who, at this very hour, patrol far-off deserts and distant mountains. They have something to tell us today, just as the fallen heroes who lie in Arlington whisper through the ages. We honor them not only because they are guardians of our liberty, but because they embody the spirit of service; a willingness to find meaning in something greater than themselves. And yet, at this moment - a moment that will define a generation - it is precisely this spirit that must inhabit us all.

For as much as government can do and must do, it is ultimately the faith and determination of the American people upon which this nation relies. It is the kindness to take in a stranger when the levees break, the selflessness of workers who would rather cut their hours than see a friend lose their job which sees us through our darkest hours. It is the firefighter's courage to storm a stairway filled with smoke, but also a parent's willingness to nurture a child, that finally decides our fate.

　　那些窮國的人民，我們承諾與你們並肩工作，使你們的農場豐收，讓清流湧入，滋養你們受餓的軀體及飢餓的心靈。而對那些和我們一樣比較富裕的國家，我要說，我們不能再對國界以外的苦痛視而不見，也不能再消耗世上的資源而不計後果。因為世界已經變了，我們也要跟著改變。

　　在我們思索眼前道路的此際，我們以謙虛感激的心想到，有些勇敢的美國同胞正在遙遠的沙漠和高山上巡弋。今天他們有話要對我們說，就和躺在阿靈頓公墓的英雄們世世代代輕聲訴說的一樣。我們尊榮他們，不只因為他們捍衛我們的自由，更因為他們代表著服務的精神；一個追求大我的願意。而在此刻，能夠界

Our challenges may be new. The instruments with which we meet them may be new. But those values upon which our success depends - hard work and honesty, courage and fair play, tolerance and curiosity, loyalty and patriotism - these things are old. These things are true. They have been the quiet force of progress throughout our history. What is demanded then is a return to these truths. What is required of us now is a new era of responsibility - a recognition, on the part of every American, that we have duties to ourselves, our nation, and the world, duties that we do not grudgingly accept but rather seize gladly, firm in the knowledge that there is nothing so satisfying to the spirit, so defining of our character, than giving our all to a difficult task.

定一個世代的此刻，必須常駐你我心中的，正是這種精神。

　　即使政府能做和必須做，美國人民的信念與決心才是這個國家之最終依靠。決堤時，是人們的善心讓他們救溺素昧平生者。是無私，讓工人寧可減工時，也不願看到朋友失業，陪伴我們度過最黑暗時期。是勇氣，讓消防員衝進滿是濃煙的樓梯間。是父母心甘情願培育孩子，最終決定我們的命運。

　　我們的挑戰也許是新的，我們迎接挑戰的受命也許也是新的，但我們賴以成功的價值觀──辛勤工作和誠實、勇氣和公平競爭、容忍和好奇心、忠實和愛國心──這些都是固有的。這些價值是真實的，是我們歷史上進步的沈默力量。我們有必要找回

This is the price and the promise of citizenship.

This is the source of our confidence - the knowledge that God calls on us to shape an uncertain destiny.

This is the meaning of our liberty and our creed - why men and women and children of every race and every faith can join in celebration across this magnificent mall, and why a man whose father less than sixty years ago might not have been served at a local restaurant can now stand before you to take a most sacred oath.

So let us mark this day with remembrance, of who we are and how far we have traveled. In the year of America's birth, in the coldest of months, a small band of patriots huddled by dying campfires on the shores of an icy river. The capital was abandoned. The enemy was advancing. The snow was stained with blood. At a moment when the outcome of our revolution was most in doubt, the father of our nation ordered these words be read to the people:

這些真實價值。我們現在需要一個勇於負責的新時代，每一個美國人都體認到我們對自己、對國家、對世界負有責任，我們不是不情願地接受這些責任，而是欣然接受，堅信沒有什麼比全力以赴完成艱難的工作，更能得到精神上的滿足，更能找到自我。

這是公民的代價和承諾。

這是我們信心的來源，體認上帝召喚我們創造不確定的命運。

這是我們的自由和信條的真諦，為什麼不同種族和信仰的男女老幼能在這個大草坪上共同慶祝，為什麼一個人的父親在不到六十年前也許還不能進當地的餐廳用餐，現在卻能站在你們面前做最神聖的宣誓。

"Let it be told to the future world...that in the depth of winter, when nothing but hope and virtue could survive...that the city and the country, alarmed at one common danger, came forth to meet [it]."

America. In the face of our common dangers, in this winter of our hardship, let us remember these timeless words. With hope and virtue, let us brave once more the icy currents, and endure what storms may come. Let it be said by our children's children that when we were tested we refused to let this journey end, that we did not turn back nor did we falter; and with eyes fixed on the horizon and God's grace upon us, we carried forth that great gift of freedom and delivered it safely to future generations.

　　讓我們記住這一天，記住我們是誰、我們走了多遠。在美國誕生這一年，在最寒冷的幾個月，在結冰的河岸，一群愛國人士抱著垂死的同志。首都棄守，敵人進逼，血染白雪。在那時，我們革命的成果受到質疑，我們的國父下令向人民宣讀這段話：「讓這段話流傳後世，在深冬，在只剩下希望和美德時候，這個城市和國家，警覺到一個共同危險，勇往直前面對它。」

　　美國，面對我們的共同危險與這個艱困的冬天，讓我們記得這些永恆的話語。懷著希望和美德，我們會再度勇渡寒流，克服即臨的暴風雪。讓我們子孫流傳：當我們受到考驗時，我們堅持旅程，不退縮，不猶豫；眼睛直視地平線，靠著上帝的恩典，我們帶著自由的偉大禮物向前，安全傳世未來的代代子孫。

國家圖書館出版品預行編目

「悅」讀美國史的二十四堂課 / 涂成吉著. --
一版. -- 臺北市 : 秀威資訊科技, 2009.06
　　面 ；　公分. -- (語言文學類 ; AG0111)
BOD版
ISBN 978-986-221-214-1 (平裝)

1.美國史

752.1　　　　　　　　　　　　98006055

語言文學類　　AG0111

「悅」讀美國史的二十四堂課

作　　　　者 / 涂成吉
發　行　　人 / 宋政坤
執 行 編 輯 / 賴敬暉
圖 文 排 版 / 黃莉珊
封 面 設 計 / 陳佩蓉
數 位 轉 譯 / 徐真玉　沈裕閔
圖 書 銷 售 / 林怡君
法 律 顧 問 / 毛國樑　律師
出 版 印 製 / 秀威資訊科技股份有限公司
　　　　　　台北市內湖區瑞光路583巷25號1樓
　　　　　　電話：02-2657-9211　傳真：02-2657-9106
　　　　　　E-mail：service@showwe.com.tw
經　　銷　　商 / 紅螞蟻圖書有限公司
　　　　　　台北市內湖區舊宗路二段121巷28、32號4樓
　　　　　　電話：02-2795-3656　傳真：02-2795-4100
　　　　　　http://www.e-redant.com

2009 年 6 月　BOD 一版
定價：330 元

讀 者 回 函 卡

感謝您購買本書，為提升服務品質，煩請填寫以下問卷，收到您的寶貴意見後，我們會仔細收藏記錄並回贈紀念品，謝謝！

1. 您購買的書名：_____

2. 您從何得知本書的消息？

　　□網路書店　□部落格　□資料庫搜尋　□書訊　□電子報　□書店

　　□平面媒體　□ 朋友推薦　□網站推薦　□其他_____

3. 您對本書的評價：(請填代號　1.非常滿意 2.滿意 3.尚可 4.再改進)

　　封面設計_____　版面編排_____　內容_____　文/譯筆_____　價格_____

4. 讀完書後您覺得：

　　□很有收獲　□有收獲　□收獲不多　□沒收獲

5. 您會推薦本書給朋友嗎？

　　□會　□不會，為什麼？_____

6. 其他寶貴的意見：_____

_____

_____

_____

讀者基本資料

姓名：_____　年齡：_____　性別：□女 □男

聯絡電話：_____　E-mail：_____

地址：_____

學歷：□高中(含)以下　　□高中　　□專科學校　　□大學

　　　□研究所(含)以上 □其他_____

職業：□製造業 □金融業 □資訊業 □軍警 □傳播業 □自由業

　　　□服務業 □公務員 □教職　□學生 □其他_____

To：114

台北市內湖區瑞光路 583 巷 25 號 1 樓

秀威資訊科技股份有限公司　　　收

寄件人姓名：

寄件人地址：□□□

(請沿線對摺寄回,謝謝!)

秀威與 BOD

BOD（Books On Demand）是數位出版的大趨勢，秀威資訊率先運用 POD 數位印刷設備來生產書籍，並提供作者全程數位出版服務，致使書籍產銷零庫存，知識傳承不絕版，目前已開闢以下書系：

一、BOD 學術著作—專業論述的閱讀延伸
二、BOD 個人著作—分享生命的心路歷程
三、BOD 旅遊著作—個人深度旅遊文學創作
四、BOD 大陸學者—大陸專業學者學術出版
五、POD 獨家經銷—數位產製的代發行書籍

BOD 秀威網路書店：www.showwe.com.tw
政府出版品網路書店：www.govbooks.com.tw

永不絕版的故事·自己寫·永不休止的音符·自己唱